Moods of the Sea

Moods of the Sea

MASTERWORKS OF SEA POETRY

Selected and Arranged by
George C. Solley and Eric Steinbaugh

NAVAL INSTITUTE PRESS
Annapolis, Maryland

Copyright © 1981
by the United States Naval Institute
Annapolis, Maryland

Second printing, 1988

Library of Congress Cataloging in Publication Data
Main entry under title:

Moods of the sea.
    Includes index.
    1. Sea poetry, English.   2. Sea poetry, American
I. Solley, George C., 1946—   II. Steinbaugh, Eric,
1943—
PR1195.S417M6   821'.008'032162   81-81667
ISBN 0-87021-606-6   AACR2

Printed in the United States of America

To all United States Marines,
past and present,
who have served at sea

Contents

Preface

THIS BOOK BEGAN as a search. We were looking for an anthology of sea poetry to use in the classroom here at the Naval Academy, and we compiled an impressive array of such works. None, however, was suitable for our purpose: many of the collections were British publications and understandably contained mostly English poems; others included logbook entries, letters, travel accounts, and other miscellaneous prose with only a smattering of sea poetry; still others concentrated on chanteys at the expense of other forms of sea poetry. The least suitable of the anthologies included only obscure poems by very minor poets, and the best were out of print and contained virtually no twentieth-century poetry. In short, the anthology we sought did not exist, so we decided to compile our own.

Before collecting poems for possible inclusion, we agreed to follow several guidelines: we would examine the collected poems of every major British and American poet and extract each poem written about the sea; we would examine the works of minor poets who wrote extensively about the sea; we would collect individual poems, perhaps unknown outside the sub-genre of sea poetry, that appeared in many sea anthologies or had particular merit; and we would comb twentieth-century poetry for poems worthy of possible inclusion. Using these guidelines, we collected over a period of time a considerable number of poems. We thus began a process of selection, the results of which appear in this volume.

Selection hinged on our goals for the book: we wanted to include those standard sea poems without which any anthology of sea poetry would be incomplete, to present the best sea poems of major literary figures, and to offer a wide range of poems from different periods, of many different types, and by many different poets. Other criteria emerged as we studied the poems. First, with the exception of *The Rime of the Ancient Mariner*, we have included in their entirety none of the many longer sea poems we collected, such as John Masefield's *Dauber* or Rudyard Kipling's *McAndrew's Hymn*. We have provided excerpts from some long poems; however, being opposed in principle to presenting fragments of a poet's work, we have avoided this practice save for passages of exceptional merit from the Bible and major works of William Shakespeare, Edmund Spenser, Homer, John Milton, Lord Byron, Lord Tennyson, and others. Second, we were of necessity particularly selective with the work of such poets as Herman Melville, Walt Whitman, Rudyard Kipling, and John Masefield, who have produced a large body of sea poetry. Third, we have excluded, reluctantly in some cases, poems in which the sea is mere background or in which it is treated only incidentally; thus the reader will not find in this volume such standards as Emily Dickinson's *There is no frigate like a book*, or Robert Louis Stevenson's *Requiem*. Fourth, the only translations we have selected are widely recognized as being admirable poetic works in their own right (Chapman's *Odyssey* and the King James version of the Bible) and those fine renditions by Charles W. Kennedy of our parent language—Old English. Finally, we measured each poem, regardless of its reputation, against our own test of quality before including it in this volume. Since it is we who were the judges of quality, this anthology necessarily reflects our personal tastes and judgments, which we hope the reader will in large part share.

The arrangement of the poems within the book, we decided, should be thematic, as it is in most anthologies of sea poetry. However, organizing the poetry into overly specific sections (storm, shipwreck, calm, morning, evening, and so forth) has certain drawbacks: the chronological pattern of development in the genre disappears, and many poems cannot be easily classified. The present arrangement, therefore, is based somewhat loosely on themes suggested by the poetry itself: poems describing the physical sea and its creatures, poems treating man's relation to the sea, narrative poems, humorous poems, poems portraying legends and the supernatural, and poems using the same as metaphor for other aspects of existence. Each section contains poetry arranged roughly in chronological sequence in order to show possible patterns of development; in order to facilitate comparison, we have grouped together poems of similar specific theme within that sequence.

Our final decisions concerned the texts of the individual poems. We have taken our selections from definitive editions whenever possible and have made no normalizations or other textual changes of our own, although we have allowed to stand those that have become widely accepted. All excerpts from longer works cite the parent work and identify the place in that work from which the passage was extracted. We have restricted our textual remarks to three: section introductions that briefly discuss the theme of the particular section, notes that are meant to be neither comprehensive nor explanatory but rather to offer only enough information to make the text comprehensible, and marginal notes that define archaic terms used in the text. Any further research we have left to the reader.

Finally, we owe a debt of gratitude to several people who have aided us in this venture: to Dr. Fred Fetrow, chairman, and our other colleagues in the Department of English at the U. S. Naval Academy for their support and advice, but especially to Dr. Wilson Heflin, longtime director of the Literature of the Sea program, whose infectious enthusiasm, humor, and good sense have made their mark not only on us but on an entire generation of Naval and Marine officers; to Mary Veronica Amoss, of the Naval Institute Press, for her skillful and diligent editing; to the Naval Institute Press for the selection of a title; and to our wives, Pat Solley and Jo Steinbaugh, for their forbearance and their many direct contributions to a project dreamed up by two Marines who have found themselves in, and learned to love, the world of literature.

Sounds of the Sea

MOST PEOPLE HOLD IN AWE that which they can least understand, and sometimes even worship natural forces that hold sway over their lives and fortunes. The sea, for example, has long commanded man's respect and, by virtue of its immensity, its seemingly limitless power, and its unfathomable mysteries, has elicited his wonder. In most cultures, things that lie beyond human comprehension are ascribed to the gods; so it was with the Greeks, whose sea god was Poseidon, and the Romans, who believed Neptune to be the ruler of the deep. This tradition was modified somewhat by the monotheistic Hebrews, but is still reflected in the excerpts from the Psalms at the beginning of this chapter. In *Paradise Lost,* John Milton sees the oceans as evidence of God's handiwork, as does William Cullen Bryant, whose reverence for nature is never more obvious than in *A Hymn of the Sea.* A sense of wonder and amazement at the size and power of the sea is evident in the poems of William Gilmore Simms and Lloyd Frankenberg. Edmund Spenser introduces a new aspect of this theme in *The Faerie Queene* when he speaks of the "abundant progeny" of the sea, and it is interesting to compare the poems about sea creatures by Herman Melville, Rupert Brooke, Marianne Moore, Elizabeth Bishop, and D. H. Lawrence. Also instructive is a comparison of Melville's *The Tuft of Kelp* with Lawrence's *Sea-Weed.*

The sea, then, is many things to many people. Ken Noyle explores this protean quality in *The Sea,* and Rudyard Kipling notes it in *The Sea and the Hills.* But just as the poet sings many different songs about the sea, so the sea sings many songs to the poet. And the poet in turn uses the musical devices of his medium to imitate the sounds of the sea, as evidenced by James Stephens's onomatopoeic *The Main-Deep.* Here then are the sounds of the sea.

From **Psalm** 104

25   So is this great and wide sea,
wherein are things creeping innumer-
able, both small and great beasts.
26   There go the ships: there is
that leviathan, whom thou hast made
to play therein.
27   These wait all upon thee; that
thou mayest give them their meat in
due season.
28   That thou givest them they gather:
thou openest thine hand, they are
filled with good.

From **Psalm** 77

16   The waters saw thee, O God, the
waters saw thee; they were afraid: the
depths also were troubled.
17   The clouds poured out water: the
skies sent out a sound: thine arrows
also went abroad.
18   The voice of thy thunder was in
the heaven: the lightnings lightened
the world: the earth trembled and shook.
19   Thy way is in the sea, and thy
path in the great waters, and thy
footsteps are not known.

A Hymne in Prayse of Neptune

Of Neptunes Empyre let vs sing,
At whose command the waues obay:
To whom the Riuers tribute pay,
Downe the high mountaines sliding.

To whom the skaly Nation yeelds
Homage for the Cristall fields
    Wherein they dwell;
And euery Sea-god paies a Iem,°   gem
Yeerely out of his watry Cell,

2

To decke great *Neptunes* Diadem.

The *Trytons*[1] dauncing in a ring,
Before his Pallace gates, doo make
The water with their Ecchoes quake,
Like the great Thunder sounding:
The Sea-Nymphes chaunt their Accents shrill,
And the *Syrens*[2] taught to kill
  With their sweet voyce;
Make eu'ry ecchoing Rocke reply,
Vnto their gentle murmuring noyse,
The prayse of *Neptunes* Empery.

THOMAS CAMPION

From *The Faerie Queene*
Book IV, Canto XII, I

O what an endlesse worke have I in hand,
To count the seas abundant progeny,
Whose fruitfull seede farre passeth those in land,
And also those which wonne° in th' azure sky!   dwell
For much more eath to tell° the starres on hy,   easy to count
Albe they endlesse seeme in estimation,
Then to recount the seas posterity:
So fertile be the flouds in generation,
So huge their numbers, and so numberlesse their nation.

EDMUND SPENSER

From *Paradise Lost*
Book VII
Lines 276–309

  The Earth was form'd, but in the Womb as yet
Of Waters, Embryon immature involv'd,
Appear'd not: over all the face of Earth
Main Ocean flow'd, not idle, but with warm
Prolific humor soft'ning all her Globe,   280
Fermented the great Mother to conceive,
Satiate with genial moisture, when God said,
Be gather'd now ye Waters under Heav'n
Into one place, and let dry Land appear.
Immediately the Mountains huge appear
Emergent, and thir broad bare backs upheave

Into the Clouds, thir tops ascend the Sky:
So high as heav'd the tumid Hills, so low
Down sunk a hollow bottom broad and deep,
Capacious bed of Waters: thither they   290
Hasted with glad precipitance, uproll'd
As drops on dust conglobing from the dry;
Part rise in crystal Wall, or ridge direct,
For haste; such flight the great command impress'd
On the swift floods: as Armies at the call
Of Trumpet (for of Armies thou hast heard)
Troop to thir Standard, so the wat'ry throng,
Wave rolling after Wave, where way they found,
If steep, with torrent rapture, if through Plain,
Soft-ebbing; nor withstood them Rock or Hill,   300
But they, or under ground, or circuit wide
With Serpent error wand'ring, found thir way,
And on the washy Ooze deep Channels wore;
Easy, ere God had bid the ground be dry,
All but within those banks, where Rivers now
Stream, and perpetual draw thir humid train.
The dry Land, Earth, and the great receptacle
Of congregated Waters he call'd Seas:
And saw that it was good.

Lines 391–416

And God created the great Whales, and each
Soul living, each that crept, which plenteously
The waters generated by thir kinds,
And every Bird of wing after his kind;
And saw that it was good, and bless'd them, saying,
Be fruitful, multiply, and in the Seas
And Lakes and running Streams the waters fill;
And let the Fowl be multipli'd on the Earth.
Forthwith the Sounds and Seas, each Creek and Bay
With Fry innumerable swarm, and Shoals   400
Of Fish that with thir Fins and shining Scales
Glide under the green Wave, in Sculls that oft
Bank the mid Sea: part single or with mate
Graze the Seaweed thir pasture, and through Groves
Of Coral stray, or sporting with quick glance
Show to the Sun thir wav'd coats dropt with Gold,
Or in thir Pearly shells at ease, attend
Moist nutriment, or under Rocks thir food

4

In jointed Armor watch: on smooth the Seal,
And bended Dolphins play: part huge of bulk
Wallowing unwieldly, enormous in thir Gait
Tempest the Ocean: there Leviathan
Hugest of living Creatures, on the Deep
Stretcht like a Promontory sleeps or swims,
And seems a moving Land, and at his Gills
Draws in, and at his Trunk spouts out a Sea.

410

JOHN MILTON

SONNET: On the Sea

It keeps eternal whisperings around
   Desolate shores, and with its mighty swell
   Gluts twice ten thousand Caverns, till the spell
Of Hecate leaves them their old shadowy sound.
Often 'tis in such gentle temper found,
   That scarcely will the very smallest shell
   Be mov'd for days from where it sometime fell,
When last the winds of Heaven were unbound.
Oh ye! who have your eye-balls vex'd and tir'd,
   Feast them upon the wideness of the Sea;
     Oh ye! whose ears are dinn'd with uproar rude,
Or fed too much with cloying melody—
     Sit ye near some old Cavern's Mouth, and brood
Until ye start, as if the sea-nymphs quir'd!

JOHN KEATS

SONNET: To Ailsa Rock[3]

Hearken, thou craggy ocean pyramid!
   Give answer from thy voice, the sea-fowls' screams!
   When were thy shoulders mantled in huge streams?
When, from the sun, was thy broad forehead hid?
How long is't since the mighty power bid
   Thee heave to airy sleep from fathom dreams?
   Sleep in the lap of thunder or sunbeams,
Or when grey clouds are thy cold coverlid.
Thou answer'st not; for thou art dead asleep;
   Thy life is but two dead eternities—

5

The last in air, the former in the deep;
   First with the whales, last with the eagle-skies—
Drown'd wast thou till an earthquake made thee steep,
   Another cannot wake thy giant size.

JOHN KEATS

A Hymn of the Sea

   The sea is mighty, but a Mightier sways
His restless billows. Thou, whose hands have scooped
His boundless gulfs and built his shore, Thy breath,
That moved in the beginning o'er his face,
Moves o'er it evermore. The obedient waves
To its strong motion roll and rise and fall.
Still from that realm of rain Thy cloud goes up,
As at the first, to water the great earth,
And keep her valleys green. A hundred realms
Watch its broad shadow warping on the wind,   10
And in the drooping shower, with gladness hear
Thy promise of the harvest. I look forth
Over the boundless blue, where joyously
The bright crests of innumerable waves
Glance to the sun at once, as when the hands
Of a great multitude are upward flung
In acclamation. I behold the ships
Gliding from cape to cape, from isle to isle,
Or stemming towards far lands, or hastening home
From the old world. It is Thy friendly breeze   20
That bears them, with the riches of the land,
And treasure of dear lives, till, in the port,
The shouting seamen climb and furl the sail.
   But who shall bide Thy tempest, who shall face
The blast that wakes the fury of the sea?
O God! Thy justice makes the world turn pale,
When on the armèd fleet, that royally
Bears down the surges, carrying war, to smite
Some city, or invade some thoughtless realm,
Descends the fierce tornado. The vast hulks   30
Are whirled like chaff upon the waves; the sails
Fly, rent like webs of gossamer: the masts
Are snapped asunder; downward from the decks,
Downward are slung, into the fathomless gulf,

Their cruel engines, and their hosts, arrayed
In trappings of the battlefield, are whelmed
By whirlpools, or dashed dead upon the rocks.
Then stand the nations still with awe, and pause
A moment from the bloody work of war.
    These restless surges eat away the shores 40
Of earth's old continents; the fertile plain
Welters in shallows, headlands crumble down,
And the tide drifts the sea-sand in the streets
Of the drowned city. Thou, meanwhile, afar
In the green chambers of the middle sea,
Where broadest spread the waters and the line
Sinks deepest, while no eye beholds Thy work,
Creator, Thou dost teach the coral-worm
To lay his mighty reefs. From age to age
He builds beneath the waters, till, at last, 50
His bulwarks overtop the brine, and check
The long wave rolling from the southern pole
To break upon Japan. Thou bidd'st the fires,
That smoulder under ocean, heave on high
The new-made mountains, and uplift their peaks,
A place of refuge for the storm-driven bird.
The birds and wafting billows plant the rifts
With herb and tree; sweet fountains gush; sweet airs
Ripple the living lakes that, fringed with flowers,
Are gathered in the hollows. Thou dost look 60
On Thy creation and pronounce it good.
Its valleys, glorious in their summer green,
Praise Thee in silent beauty; and its woods,
Swept by the murmuring winds of ocean, join
The murmuring shores in a perpetual hymn.

WILLIAM CULLEN BRYANT

Night Storm

This tempest sweeps the Atlantic!—Nevasink
    Is howling to the Capes! Grim Hatteras cries
Like thousand damnèd ghosts, that on the brink
    Lift their dark hands and threat the threatening skies;
Surging through foam and tempest, old Román
    Hangs o'er the gulf, and, with his cavernous throat,
    Pours out the torrent of his wolfish note,
And bids the billows bear it where they can!
Deep calleth unto deep, and, from the cloud,

Launches the bolt, that, bursting o'er the sea,
Rends for a moment the thick pitchy shroud,
　　And shows the ship the shore beneath her lee:
Start not, dear wife, no dangers here betide,-
And see, the boy still sleeping at your side!

WILLIAM GILMORE SIMMS

The Sound of the Sea

The sea awoke at midnight from its sleep,
　　And round the pebbly beaches far and wide
　　I heard the first wave of the rising tide
　　Rush onward with uninterrupted sweep;
A voice out of the silence of the deep,
　　A sound mysteriously multiplied
　　As of a cataract from the mountain's side,
　　Or roar of winds upon a wooded steep.
So comes to us at times, from the unknown
　　And inaccessible solitudes of being,
　　The rushing of the sea-tides of the soul;
And inspirations, that we deem our own,
　　Are some divine foreshadowing and foreseeing
　　Of things beyond our reason or control.

HENRY WADSWORTH LONGFELLOW

By the Sea

Why does the sea moan evermore?
　　Shut out from heaven it makes its moan,
It frets against the boundary shore:
　　All earth's full rivers cannot fill
　　The sea, that drinking thirsteth still.

Sheer miracles of loveliness
　　Lie hid in its unlooked-on bed:
Anemones, salt, passionless,
　　Blow flower-like—just enough alive
　　To blow and multiply and thrive.

Shells quaint with curve or spot or spike,
　　Encrusted live things argus-eyed,
All fair alike yet all unlike,
　　Are born without a pang, and die
　　Without a pang, and so pass by.

CHRISTINA ROSSETTI

A Visit from the Sea

Far from the loud sea beaches
  Where he goes fishing and crying,
Here in the inland garden
  Why is the sea-gull flying?

Here are no fish to dive for;
  Here is the corn and lea;
Here are the green trees rustling.
  Hie away home to sea!

Fresh is the river water
  And quiet among the rushes;
This is no home for the sea-gull
  But for the rooks and thrushes.

Pity the bird that has wandered!
  Pity the sailor ashore!
Hurry him home to the ocean,
  Let him come here no more!

High on the sea-cliff ledges
  The white gulls are trooping and crying,
Here among rooks and roses,
  Why is the sea-gull flying?

                    ROBERT LOUIS STEVENSON

The Sea and the Hills

Who hath desired the Sea?—the sight of salt water unbounded—
The heave and the halt and the hurl and the crash of the comber wind-
        hounded?
The sleek-barrelled swell before storm, grey, foamless, enormous, and
        growing—
Stark calm on the lap of the Line[4] or the crazy-eyed hurricane
        blowing—
His Sea in no showing the same—his Sea and the same 'neath each
        showing:
                His Sea as she slackens or thrills?
So and no otherwise—so and no otherwise—hillmen desire their Hills!

Who hath desired the Sea?—the immense and contemptuous surges
The shudder, the stumble, the swerve, as the star-stabbing bowsprit
        emerges?

9

The orderly clouds of the Trades,[5] the ridged, roaring sapphire
   thereunder—   10
Unheralded cliff-haunting flaws and the headsail's low-volleying
   thunder—
His Sea in no wonder the same—his Sea and the same through each
   wonder:
              His Sea as she rages or stills?
So and no otherwise—so and no otherwise—hillmen desire their Hills.

Who hath desired the Sea? Her menaces swift as her mercies?
The in-rolling walls of the fog and the silver-winged breeze that
   disperses?
The unstable mined berg going South and the calvings and groans that
   declare it—
White water half-guessed overside and the moon breaking timely to
   bare it—
His Sea as his fathers have dared—his Sea as his children shall dare it:
              His Sea as she serves him or kills?   20
So and no otherwise—so and no otherwise—hillmen desire their Hills.
Who hath desired the Sea? Her excellent loneliness rather
Than forecourts of kings, and her outermost pits than the streets where
   men gather
Inland, among dust, under trees—inland where the slayer may slay
   him—
Inland, out of reach of her arms, and the bosom whereon he must lay
   him—
His Sea from the first that betrayed—at the last that shall never betray
   him:
              His Sea that his being fulfils?
So and no otherwise—so and no otherwise—hillmen desire their Hills.

                                                          RUDYARD KIPLING

The Tuft of Kelp

All dripping in tangles green,
   Cast up by a lonely sea,
If purer for that, O Weed,
   Bitterer, too, are ye?

HERMAN MELVILLE

The Maldive⁶ Shark

About the Shark, phlegmatical one,
Pale sot of the Maldive sea,
The sleek little pilot-fish, azure and slim,
How alert in attendance be.
From his saw-pit of mouth, from his charnel of maw,
They have nothing of harm to dread,
But liquidly glide on his ghastly flank
Or before his Gorgonian⁷ head;
Or lurk in the port of serrated teeth
In white triple tiers of glittering gates,
And there find a haven when peril's abroad,
An asylum in jaws of the Fates!⁸
They are friends; and friendly they guide him to prey,
Yet never partake of the treat—
Eyes and brains to the dotard lethargic and dull,
Pale ravener of horrible meat.

                                    HERMAN MELVILLE

The Fish

In a cool curving world he lies
And ripples with dark ecstasies.
The kind luxurious lapse and steal
Shapes all his universe to feel
And know and be; the clinging stream
Closes his memory, glooms his dream,
Who lips the roots o' the shore, and glides
Superb on unreturning tides.
Those silent waters weave for him
A fluctuant mutable world and dim,   10
Where wavering masses bulge and gape
Mysterious, and shape to shape
Dies momently through whorl and hollow,
And form and line and solid follow
Solid and line and form to dream
Fantastic down the eternal stream;
An obscure world, a shifting world,
Bulbous, or pulled to thin, or curled,
Or serpentine, or driving arrows,
Or serene slidings, or March narrows.   20

11

There slipping wave and shore are one,
And weed and mud. No ray of sun,
But glow to glow fades down the deep
(As dream to unknown dream in sleep);
Shaken translucency illumes
The hyaline of drifting glooms;
The strange soft-handed depth subdues
Drowned colour there, but black to hues,
As death to living, decomposes—
Red darkness of the heart of roses,   30
Blue brilliant from dead starless skies,
And gold that lies behind the eyes,
The unknown unnameable sightless white
That is the essential flame of night,
Lustreless purple, hooded green,
The myriad hues that lie between
Darkness and darkness! ...

                                And all's one.
Gentle, embracing, quiet, dun,
The world he rests in, world he knows,   40
Perpetual curving. Only—grows
An eddy in that ordered falling,
A knowledge from the gloom, a calling
Weed in the wave, gleam in the mud—
The dark fire leaps along his blood;
Dateless and deathless, blind and still,
The intricate impulse works its will;
His woven world drops back; and he,
Sans providence, sans memory,
Unconscious and directly driven,   50
Fades to some dank sufficient heaven.

O world of lips, O world of laughter,
Where hope is fleet and thought flies after,
Of lights in the clear night, of cries
That drift along the wave and rise
Thin to the glittering stars above,
You know the hands, the eyes of love!
The strife of limbs, the sightless clinging,
The infinite distance, and the singing
Blown by the wind, a flame of sound,   60
The gleam, the flowers, and vast around
The horizon, and the heights above—
You know the sigh, the song of love!

But there the night is close, and there
Darkness is cold and strange and bare;
And the secret deeps are whisperless;
And rhythm is all deliciousness;
And joy is in the throbbing tide,
Whose intricate fingers beat and glide
In felt bewildering harmonies   70
Of trembling touch; and music is
The exquisite knocking of the blood.
Space is no more, under the mud;
His bliss is older than the sun.
Silent and straight the waters run.
The lights, the cries, the willows dim,
And the dark tide are one with him.

RUPERT BROOKE

The Fish

wade
through black jade.
   Of the crow-blue mussel shells, one keeps
   adjusting the ash heaps;
      opening and shutting itself like

an
injured fan.
   The barnacles which encrust the side
   of the wave, cannot hide
      there for the submerged shafts of the   10

sun,
split like spun
   glass, move themselves with spotlight swiftness
   into the crevices—
      in and out, illuminating

the
turquoise sea
   of bodies. The water drives a wedge
   of iron through the iron edge
      of the cliff; whereupon the stars,   20

pink
rice-grains, ink-
   bespattered jellyfish, crabs like green
   lilies, and submarine
      toadstools, slide each on the other.

All
external
    marks of abuse are present on this
    defiant edifice—
        all the physical features of   30

ac-
cident—lack
    of cornice, dynamite grooves, burns, and
    hatchet strokes, these things stand
        out on it; the chasm side is

dead.
Repeated
    evidence has proved that it can live
    on what can not revive
        its youth. The sea grows old in it.   40

MARIANNE MOORE

The Fish

I caught a tremendous fish
and held him beside the boat
half out of water, with my hook
fast in a corner of his mouth.
He didn't fight.
He hadn't fought at all.
He hung a grunting weight,
battered and venerable
and homely. Here and there
his brown skin hung in strips   10
like ancient wallpaper,
and its pattern of darker brown
was like wallpaper:
shapes like full-blown roses
stained and lost through age.
He was speckled with barnacles,
fine rosettes of lime,
and infested
with tiny white sea-lice,
and underneath two or three   20
rags of green weed hung down.
While his gills were breathing in
the terrible oxygen

—the frightening gills,
fresh and crisp with blood,
that can cut so badly—
I thought of the coarse white flesh
packed in like feathers,
the big bones and the little bones,
the dramatic reds and blacks   30
of his shiny entrails,
and the pink swim-bladder
like a big peony.
I looked into his eyes
which were far larger than mine
but shallower, and yellowed,
the irises backed and packed
with tarnished tinfoil
seen through the lenses
of old scratched isinglass.   40
They shifted a little, but not
to return my stare.
—It was more like the tipping
of an object toward the light.
I admired his sullen face,
the mechanism of his jaw,
and then I saw
that from his lower lip
—if you could call it a lip—
grim, wet, and weaponlike,   50
hung five old pieces of fish-line,
or four and a wire leader
with the swivel still attached,
with all their five big hooks
grown firmly in his mouth.
A green line, frayed at the end
where he broke it, two heavier lines,
and a fine black thread
still crimped from the strain and snap
when it broke and he got away.   60
Like medals with their ribbons
frayed and wavering,
a five-haired beard of wisdom
trailing from his aching jaw.
I stared and stared
and victory filled up
the little rented boat,

from the pool of bilge
where oil had spread a rainbow
around the rusted engine
to the bailer rusted orange,
the sun-cracked thwarts,
the oarlocks on their strings,
the gunnels—until everything
was rainbow, rainbow, rainbow!
And I let the fish go.

ELIZABETH BISHOP

Whales Weep Not!

They say the sea is cold, but the sea contains
the hottest blood of all, and the wildest, the most urgent.

All the whales in the wider deeps, hot are they, as they urge
on and on, and dive beneath the icebergs.
The right whales, the sperm-whales, the hammer-heads, the killers
there they blow, there they blow, hot wild white breath out of the sea!

And they rock, and they rock, through the sensual ageless ages
on the depths of the seven seas,
and through the salt they reel with drunk delight
and in the tropics tremble they with love   10
and roll with massive, strong desire, like gods.
Then the great bull lies up against his bride
in the blue deep bed of the sea.
as mountain pressing on mountain, in the zest of life:
and out of the inward roaring of the inner red ocean of whale blood
the long tip reaches strong, intense, like the maelstrom-tip, and comes to
        rest
in the clasp and the soft, wild clutch of a she-whale's fathomless body.

And over the bridge of the whale's strong phallus, linking the wonder
        of whales
the burning archangels under the sea keep passing, back and forth,
keep passing archangels of bliss
from him to her, from her to him, great Cherubim[9]
that wait on whales in mid-ocean, suspended in the waves of the sea   20
great heaven of whales in the waters, old hierarchies.

And enormous mother whales lie dreaming suckling their whale-tender
        young

and dreaming with strange whale eyes wide open in the waters of the
    beginning and the end.

And bull-whales gather their women and whale-calves in a ring
when danger threatens, on the surface of the ceaseless flood
and range themselves like great fierce Seraphim[9] facing the threat
encircling their huddled monsters of love.
and all this happiness in the sea, in the salt
where God is also love, but without words: 30
and Aphrodite is the wife of whales
most happy, happy she!

and Venus among the fishes skips and is a she-dolphin
she is the gay, delighted porpoise sporting with love and the sea
she is the female tunny-fish, round and happy among the males
and dense with happy blood, dark rainbow bliss in the sea.

D. H. LAWRENCE

They Say the Sea Is Loveless

They say the sea is loveless, that in the sea
love cannot live, but only bare, salt splinters
of loveless life.

But from the sea
the dolphins leap round Dionysos'[10] ship
whose masts have purple vines,
and up they come with the purple dark of rainbows
and flip! they go! with the nose-dive of sheer delight;
and the sea is making love to Dionysos
in the bouncing of these small and happy whales.

D. H. LAWRENCE

Sea-Weed

Sea-weed sways and sways and swirls
as if swaying were its form of stillness;
and if it flushes against fierce rock
it slips over it as shadows do, without hurting itself.

D. H. LAWRENCE

The Sea

You, you are all unloving, loveless, you;
Restless and lonely, shaken by your own moods,
You are celibate and single, scorning a comrade even,
Threshing your own passions with no woman for the threshing-floor,
Finishing your dreams for your own sake only,
Playing your great game around the world, alone,
Without playmate, or helpmate, having no one to cherish,
No one to comfort, and refusing any comforter.

Not like the earth, the spouse all full of increase
Moiled over with the rearing of her many-mouthed young;   10
You are single, you are fruitless, phosphorescent, cold and callous,
Naked of worship, of love or of adornment,
Scorning the panacea even of labour,
Sworn to a high and splendid purposelessness
Of brooding and delighting in the secret of life's goings,
Sea, only you are free, sophisticated.

You who toil not, you who spin not,
Surely but for you and your like, toiling
Were not worth while, nor spinning worth the effort!

You who take the moon as in a sieve, and sift   20
Her flake by flake and spread her meaning out;
You who roll the stars like jewels in your palm,
So that they seem to utter themselves aloud;
You who steep from out the days their colour,
Reveal the universal tint that dyes
Their web; who shadow the sun's great gestures and expressions
So that he seems a stranger in his passing;
Who voice the dumb night fittingly;
Sea, you shadow of all things, now mock us to death with your
          shadowing.

D. H. LAWRENCE

The Sea

In the midmost of ocean
the water lifts its arms dreaming of spars;
the world is very round, projects its roundness
past all the poles, beyond the one horizon
on that bald ocean overhead, the sky
where swim the worlds like fish in soundless waters.

Imposing its single structure on the sky
and drawing thence its variable mood
of bright confusion, gloom and equable
conformity, the ocean goes scotfree   10
of other obligation but to pay
the moon its due respects, discharged like spouse.

Left to its own enormous devices the sea
in timeless reverie conceives of life,
being itself the world in pantomime.

Predicting past and future in one long
drawn breath it blends its tides with dawn,
rolls in panoramic sleight-of-hand
creation out of chaos endlessly;

all forms revealed in fluid architecture   20
flowing like time as if time were turned back:
undreamed-of wars all happening at once
(what rage pent up in atoms: do the drops
take toll of one another? no the sea
had not dreamed this)
                        but like a savage plays
archaic symmetries and simple shapes:
builds promontories, houses lakes, holds out
mirages of itself, erects straw cliffs
hurdled with ease;   30
                        or lolling all its length
coiled and Niled, in coat of mail tilts evil
complete with scale and hiss, smitten to sculpture,
to iron leaves, to flame, to birds flying
in and out of fluted, spandreled, spired
buildings out of all time swaying, crumpling
in scaffoldings of spray.

                        And then the flowers
all petal and no stem; then finned and ferned,
the leaping swordfish an effrontery   40
to all its backs, all life presumptuous

and those looking too long upon its wake
who thought to make themselves immortal too,
taking it at its word, instruct it now

(old moonface cratered and sunksocketed,
seamywrinkled, picked and pocked with waves,
the waves all faces lifted looking around,
hair dripping across their foreheads or flung back
for a last despairing gasp before they drown)

for now the last least vestige of the air 50
that gave the ocean its free hand with space,
gave fins wings roots and legs to walk the sky,
withdraws and leaves it still.

Now on its sleeve
it wears the heart that every shipwreck finds;
lies flat, unworked by other element

and in this state of utter unbelief
that keeps it what it is, like nothing else,
smoother than glass, stiller than the dead,
its natural supine and spineless self 60
that never will arise but from without
(yet even now protests the least intrusion)

believing not that all its mimicry
has ever come to pass, how perfectly
mirrors God's face, the workings of his mind.

LLOYD FRANKENBERG

Long Trip

The sea is a wilderness of waves,
A desert of water.
We dip and dive,
Rise and roll,
Hide and are hidden
On the sea.
    Day, night,
    Night, day,
The sea is a desert of waves,
A wilderness of water.

LANGSTON HUGHES

Moonlight Night: Carmel

Tonight the waves march
In long ranks
Cutting the darkness
With their silver shanks,
Cutting the darkness
And kissing the moon
And beating the land's
Edge into a swoon.

LANGSTON HUGHES

The Sea

I have seen the sea in many moods
And felt its presence
Even though miles away from it.
I have no Mansfield love for it[11]
And feel no lure to be alone by it.
Nor do I hear its call.
And yet,
The more you think of it—
The sea, I mean—
The more it stirs that tiny itch   10
Inside your brain—
That "almost" understanding of all the reasons why—
Of why we are
And why the sea should be.

On the surface, the sea reflects emotions
Easily reproduced by Kodak—
Lovers' dreams and poets' pens.
Sequined seas,
Jade green between
The mainland and Hong Kong;   20
The wine dark seas—if wine is blue—
Between the islands of the gods;
Frothy seas and frisky seas
And seas with saber teeth;
The queasy heavy heaving sea
Scratching its hoary back against the rocks of Scotland;
The sparkling seas, skittering sunshine
And the silver-paper seas
With palm trees—pasted silhouettes;
Melancholy seas that stretch to infinity   30
And mewky, pewky seas
Lapping up rubbers and orange peels
And belching 'neath the pier;
The brisk, bright sea
With ostrich feathers curling down its cleavage;
And seas so deep that auld lang syne
Sinks like a stone into its depths.

The children's sea, squealingly exciting
And full of slippery wiggles,
Always there to touch-you-last—   40

A handy, sloshing, joshing plaything
That doesn't have to be tidied up or put away—
Bucketable and splashable,
Marred only by its icky taste.

The sailors' sea,
Predictable in its unpredictability,
Charted and yet untouched,
Despite a million keels
And the discipline of countless rudders.
Not cruel, for cruelty needs a reason;   50
Not compassionate,
For compassion needs a depth of understanding.
The sea—
A tool for sailors' trade.

The lovers' sea—
A background for honeymoons,
A cadence for passion,
A chance to play Canute,[12]
A thing to sit and look at
While you dream of other things.   60

And yet it's not romantic,
For romance needs sex for a carrot
To lead it on its merry way.
Not that the sea is sexless—
Heaven knows it writhes
With couplings so complex,
So intricate,
That a piscatorial Kama Sutra[13]
Would be on such a scale
As to give all landlubbers   70
A dry and arid complex,
Even without contemplating
The copulation of the whale!

Down!
Down!
Down!
Under the skin of wave and flotsam—
Green, black ooze
And there is the past—
The very womb of man—   80
A hole in space—
Filled with Pandora's[14] box of goodies,
The sustenance of life,

22

The richness undredged,
The answers to questions as yet unasked.
And yet—
Up,
Up,
Up,
Through the turbulence and jetsam,   90
Through the fruit of plankton to the surface—
Blue,
Bright beneath the moon
Or boiling bent on cold destruction
Or sullenly shouldering the land.

The sea,
Described by metaphors
Or onomatopoetic phrases,
Conjuring visions,
Evoking songs and symphonies,   100
Described in every way but wet.
The sea—
A *koan*[15] without words;
The quintessence of philosophy.
For if you see the sea
And look away
And then look back,
The sea you see
Is not the same sea you saw—
Or, if you prefer,   110
The sea you saw
Is not the same sea
You see.

KEN NOYLE

The Main-Deep

The long rólling,
Steady-póuring,
Deep-trenchéd
Green billow:

The wide-topped,
Unbróken,
Green-glacid,
Slow-sliding.

23

Cold-flushing,
On—on—on—
Chill-rushing,
Hush-hushing,
Hush—hushing. . . .

JAMES STEPHENS

The Shell

And then I pressed the shell
Close to my ear
And listened well,
And straightway like a bell
Came low and clear
The slow, sad murmur of the distant seas,
Whipped by an icy breeze
Upon a shore
Wind-swept and desolate.
It was a sunless strand that never bore   10
The footprint of a man,
Nor felt the weight
Since time began
Of any human quality or stir
Save what the dreary winds and waves incur.
And in the hush of waters was the sound
Of pebbles rolling round,
For ever rolling with a hollow sound.
And bubbling sea-weeds as the waters go
Swish to and fro   20
Their long, cold tentacles of slimy gray.
There was no day,
Nor felt the weight
Setting the stars alight
To wonder at the moon:
Was twilight only and the frightened croon,
Smitten to whimpers, of the dreary wind
And waves that journeyed blind—
And then I loosed my ear ... O, it was sweet
To hear a cart go jolting down the street.

JAMES STEPHENS

Winter Ocean

Many-maned scud-thumper, tub
of male whales, maker of worn wood, shrub-
ruster, sky-mocker, rave!
portly pusher of waves, wind-slave.

JOHN UPDIKE

Man and the Sea

IN THE OPENING CHAPTER of *Moby Dick*, Ishmael speaks of the irresistible force that draws man to the sea. Wherever the ocean meets the shore, says Herman Melville's narrator, man will be found keeping a vigil, watching the sea. Robert Frost comments on the same phenomenon in his poem, *Neither Out Far Nor in Deep*. This strange attraction is further explored in Edna St. Vincent Millay's *Exiled* and in John Masefield's well-known *Sea-Fever*. Darwinists might explain it as man's instinctive gravitation toward his source. Others might cite aesthetic reasons for the lure of the sea, or simply attribute it to man's insatiable curiosity. Whatever the reason, man is drawn to the water's edge and beyond.

Born of this attraction, man's long-standing relationship with the sea has been both complex and multifaceted. The ocean has been seen as temptress and mother, provider and destroyer, womb and grave.

Since at least the time of the ancient Egyptian and Phoenician civilizations, the oceans have been used as a means of travel and commerce. The excerpt from Psalm 107 that opens this chapter speaks of those who go down to the sea in ships and do business upon the waters, and this subject is also treated by Masefield in *Cargoes*. But perhaps even more exciting to the imagination is the idea of a voyage to distant ports, an idea dealt with in the poems of E. E. Cummings, William Empson, and Hart Crane.

Unfortunately, but inevitably, some of the ships that make long journeys across the sea meet with disaster and come to their final rest under the sea. Adrienne Rich's *Diving into the Wreck* and Robert Hayden's *The Diver* both chronicle descents to the underwater graves of once-proud ships. Interestingly, both of these poems employ a unique visual form—short lines arranged in a long vertical column—to portray the diver's descent to the ocean floor.

But if the sea is a graveyard for ships, it is also a graveyard for some of the men who sail them. This theme is evident in Marianne Moore's *A Grave*, Joyce Kilmer's *Mid-Ocean in War-Time*, William Meredith's *The Open Sea*, Stephen Spender's *The Drowned*, Carl Sandburg's *Bones*, and

John Wheelwright's bittersweet *Fish Food*, written in memory of Hart Crane, who disappeared from the ship upon which he was embarked during a voyage from Mexico to New York in 1932—an apparent suicide by drowning.

From **Psalm 107**

23 They that go down to the sea in
ships, that do business in great waters;
24 These see the works of the LORD,
and his wonders in the deep.
25 For he commandeth, and raiseth the
stormy wind, which lifteth up the waves
thereof.
26 They mount up to the heaven, they
go down again to the depths: their soul
is melted because of trouble.
27 They reel to and fro, and stagger
like a drunken man, and are at their
wits' end.
28 Then they cry unto the LORD in their
trouble, and he bringeth them out of their
distresses.
29 He maketh the storm a calm, so that
the waves thereof are still.
30 Then are they glad because they be
quiet; so he bringeth them unto their
desired haven.

The Seafarer[1]

A song I sing   of my sea-adventure,
The strain of peril,   the stress of toil,
Which oft I endured   in anguish of spirit
Through weary hours   of aching woe.
My bark was swept   by the breaking seas;
Bitter the watch   from the bow by night
As my ship drove on   within sound of the rocks.
My feet were numb   with the nipping cold,
Hunger sapped   a sea-weary spirit,
And care weighed heavy   upon my heart.   10
    Little the landlubber,   safe on shore,

27

Knows what I've suffered   in icy seas
Wretched and worn   by the winter storms,
Hung with icicles,   stung by hail,
Lonely and friendless   and far from home.
In my ears no sound   but the roar of the sea,
The icy combers,   the cry of the swan;
In place of the mead-hall   and laughter of men
My only singing   the sea-mew's call,
The scream of the gannet,   the shriek of the gull;   20
Through the wail of the wild gale   beating the bluffs
The piercing cry   of the ice-coated petrel,
The storm-drenched eagle's echoing scream.
In all my wretchedness,   weary and lone,
I had no comfort   of comrade or kin.
   Little indeed can he credit,   whose town-life
Pleasantly passes   in feasting and joy,
Sheltered from peril,   what weary pain
Often I've suffered   in foreign seas.
Night shades darkened   with driving snow   30
From the freezing north,   and the bonds of frost
Firm-locked the land,   while falling hail,
Coldest of kernels,   encrusted earth.
   Yet still, even now,   my spirit within me
Drives me seaward   to sail the deep,
To ride the long swell   of the salt sea-wave.
Never a day   but my heart's desire
Would launch me forth   on the long sea-path,
Fain of far harbors   and foreign shores.
Yet lives no man   so lordly of mood,   40
So eager in giving,   so ardent in youth,
So bold in his deeds,   or so dear to his lord,
Who is free from dread   in his far sea-travel,
Or fear of God's purpose   and plan for his fate.
The beat of the harp,   and bestowal of treasure,
The love of woman,   and worldly hope,
Nor other interest   can hold his heart
Save only the sweep   of the surging billows;
His heart is haunted   by love of the sea.
   Trees are budding   and towns are fair,   50
Meadows kindle   and all life quickens,
All things hasten   the eager-hearted
Who joyeth therein,   to journey afar,
Turning seaward   to distant shores.
The cuckoo stirs him   with plaintive call,

The herald of summer,   with mournful song,
Foretelling the sorrow   that stabs the heart.
Who liveth in luxury,   little he knows
What woe men endure   in exile's doom.
   Yet still, even now,   my desire outreaches,   60
My spirit soars   over tracts of sea,
O'er the home of the whale,   and the world's expanse.
Eager, desirous,   the lone sprite returneth;
It cries in my ears   and it urges my heart
To the path of the whale   and the plunging sea.

ANONYMOUS

From *The Faerie Queene*
Book I, Canto XII, XLII

Now strike your sailes, yee jolly mariners,
For we be come unto a quiet rode,
Where we must land some of our passengers,
And light this weary vessell of her lode.
Here she a while may make her safe abode,
Till she repaired have her tackles spent,
And wants supplide; and then againe abroad
On the long voiage whereto she is bent:
Well may she speede, and fairely finish her intent.

EDMUND SPENSER

From *The Faerie Queene*
Book II, Canto VI, XXIII

'Faire sir,' quoth she, 'be not displeasd at all:
Who fares on sea may not commaund his way,
Ne wind and weather at his pleasure call:
The sea is wide, and easy for to stray;
The wind unstable, and doth never stay.
But here a while ye may in safety rest,
Till season serve new passage to assay:
Better safe port, then be in seas distrest.'
Therewith she laught, and did her earnest end in jest.

EDMUND SPENSER

From *The Tempest*
Act I, Scene II
Lines 1–13

If by your art, my dearest father, you have
Put the wild waters in this roar, allay them.
The sky, it seems, would pour down stinking pitch
But that the sea, mounting to the welkin's° cheek,   sky's
Dashes the fire out. Oh, I have suffered
With those that I saw suffer! A brave vessel,
Who had no doubt some noble creature in her,
Dashed all to pieces. Oh, the cry did knock
Against my very heart! Poor souls, they perished!
Had I been any god of power, I would
Have sunk the sea within the earth or ere
It should the good ship so have swallowed and
The fraughting° souls within her.   freighting

WILLIAM SHAKESPEARE

From *The Tempest*
Act II, Scene I
Lines 114–122

I saw him beat the surges under him,
And ride upon their backs. He trod the water,
Whose enmity he flung aside, and breasted
The surge most swoln° that met him. His bold head   swollen
'Bove the contentious waves he kept, and oared
Himself with his good arms in lusty stroke
To the shore, that o'er his wave-worn basis bowed,
As stooping to relieve him. I not doubt
He came alive to land.

WILLIAM SHAKESPEARE

From *Pericles*
Act III, Scene I
Lines 1–10

Thou God of this great vast, rebuke these surges
Which wash both Heaven and Hell; and thou, that hast
Upon the winds command, bind them in brass,

Having called them from the deep! Oh, still
Thy deafening dreadful thunders! Gently quench
Thy nimble sulfurous flashes! Oh, how, Lychorida,
How does my Queen?—Thou stormest venomously.
Wilt thou spit all thyself? The seaman's whistle
Is as a whisper in the ears of death,
Unheard.

WILLIAM SHAKESPEARE

Bermudas

   Where the remote Bermudas ride,
In th' ocean's bosom unespied,
From a small boat that rowed along,
The listening winds received this song:

   "What should we do but sing His praise,
That led us through the watery maze
Unto an isle so long unknown,
And yet far kinder than our own?
Where He the huge sea monsters wracks,
That lift the deep upon their backs;   10
He lands us on a grassy stage,
Safe from the storms, and prelate's rage.
He gave us this eternal spring
Which here enamels everything,
And sends the fowls to us in care,
On daily visits through the air;
He hangs in shades the orange bright,
Like golden lamps in a green night,
And does in the pomegranates close
Jewels more rich than Ormus² shows;   20
He makes the figs our mouths to meet,
And throws the melons at our feet;
But apples plants of such a price,
No tree could ever bear them twice;
With cedars, chosen by His hand,
From Lebanon, He stores the land;
And makes the hollow seas, that roar,
Proclaim the ambergris on shore;
He cast (of which we rather boast)   30
The Gospel's pearl upon our coast,
And in these rocks for us did frame
A temple, where to sound His name.

O! let our voice His praise exalt,
Till it arrive at heaven's vault,
Which, thence (perhaps) rebounding, may
Echo beyond the Mexique Bay."

   Thus sung they in the English boat,
An holy and a cheerful note;
And all the way, to guide their chime,
With falling oars they kept the time.   40

ANDREW MARVELL

To Lucasta. Going beyond the Seas

If to be absent were to be
     Away from thee;
  Or that when I am gone,
  You and I were alone;
Then, my Lucasta, might I crave
Pity from blust'ring wind, or swallowing wave.

But I'll not sigh one blast or gale
     To swell my sail;
  Or pay a tear to suage
  The foaming blew-god's rage;   10
For whether he will let me pass
Or no, I'm still as happy as I was.

Though seas and land betwixt us both,
     Our faith and troth,
  Like separated souls,
  All time and space controls;
Above the highest sphere we meet
Unseen, unknown, and greet as angels greet.

So then we do anticipate
     Our after-fate,   20
  And are alive i' th' skies,
  If thus our lips and eyes
Can speak like spirits unconfined
In heav'n, their earthy bodies left behind.

RICHARD LOVELACE

Three Sonnets

(i)
To a Fish

You strange, astonished-looking, angle-faced,
Dreary-mouthed, gaping wretches of the sea,
Gulping salt water everlastingly,
Cold-blooded, though with red your blood be graced,
And mute, though dwellers in the roaring waste;
And you, all shapes beside, that fishy be—
Some round, some flat, some long, all devilry,
Legless, unloving, infamously chaste:

O scaly, slippery, wet, swift, staring wights,
What is't ye do? What life lead? eh, dull goggles?
How do ye vary your vile days and nights?
How pass your Sundays? Are ye still but joggles
In ceaseless wash? Still nought but gapes, and bites,
And drinks, and stares, diversified with boggles?

(ii)
A Fish replies

Amazing monster! that, for aught I know,
With the first sight of thee didst make our race
For ever stare! O flat and shocking face,
Grimly divided from the breast below!
Thou that on dry land horribly dost go
With a split body and most ridiculous pace,
Prong after prong, disgracer of all grace,
Long-useless-finned, haired, upright, unwet, slow!

O breather of unbreathable, sword-sharp air,
How canst exist? How bear thyself, thou dry
And dreary sloth? What particle canst share
Of the only blessed life, the watery?
I sometimes see of ye an actual *pair*
Go by, linked fin by fin, most odiously.

(iii)
The Fish turns into a Man, and then into a Spirit, and again speaks

Indulge thy smiling scorn, if smiling still,
O man! and loathe, but with a sort of love;
For difference must its use by difference prove,

And, in sweet clang, the spheres with music fill.
One of the spirits am I, that at his will
Live in whate'er has life—fish, eagle, dove—
No hate, no pride, beneath naught, nor above,
A visitor of the rounds of God's sweet skill.

Man's life is warm, glad, sad, 'twixt loves and graves,
Boundless in hope, honoured with pangs austere,
Heaven-gazing; and his angel-wings he craves:
The fish is swift, small-needing, vague yet clear,
A cold, sweet, silver life, wrapped in round waves,
Quickened with touches of transporting fear.

LEIGH HUNT

O God! Have Mercy in This Dreadful Hour

O God! have mercy in this dreadful hour
On the poor mariner! in comfort here
Safe shelter'd as I am, I almost fear
The blast that rages with resistless power.
What were it now to toss upon the waves,
The madden'd waves, and know no succour near;
The howling of the storm alone to hear.
And the wild sea that to the tempest raves;
To gaze amid the horrors of the night
And only see the billow's gleaming light;
Then in the dread of death to think of her
Who, as she listens sleepless to the gale,
Puts up a silent prayer and waxes pale?...
O God! have mercy on the mariner!

ROBERT SOUTHEY

She Comes Majestic with Her Swelling Sails

She comes majestic with her swelling sails,
The gallant Ship; along her watery way
Homeward she drives before the favouring gales;
Now flirting at their length the streamers play,
And now they ripple with the ruffling breeze.
Hark to the sailors' shouts! the rocks rebound,
Thundering in echoes to the joyful sound.

Long have they voyaged o'er the distant seas,
And what a heart-delight they feel at last,
So many toils, so many dangers past,
To view the port desired, he only knows
Who on the stormy deep for many a day
Hath tost, aweary of his watery way,
And watch'd, all anxious, every wind that blows.

anticipation of home

ROBERT SOUTHEY

With Ships the Sea
Was Sprinkled Far and Nigh

With Ships the sea was sprinkled far and nigh,
Like stars in heaven, and joyously it showed;
Some lying fast at anchor in the road,
Some veering up and down, one knew not why.
A goodly Vessel did I then espy
Come like a giant from a haven broad;
And lustily along the bay she strode,
Her tackling rich, and of apparel high.
This Ship was nought to me, nor I to her,
Yet I pursued her with a Lover's look;
This Ship to all the rest did I prefer:
When will she turn, and whither? She will brook
No tarrying; where She comes the winds must stir:
On went She, and due north her journey took.

WILLIAM WORDSWORTH

Where Lies the Land
to Which Yon Ship Must Go?

Where lies the Land to which yon Ship must go?
Fresh as a lark mounting at break of day,
Festively she puts forth in trim array;
Is she for tropic suns, or polar snow?
What boots the inquiry?—Neither friend nor foe
She cares for; let her travel where she may,
She finds familiar names, a beaten way
Ever before her, and a wind to blow.
Yet still I ask, what haven is her mark?

And, almost as it was when ships were rare,
(From time to time, like Pilgrims, here and there
Crossing the waters) doubt, and something dark,
Of the old Sea some reverential fear,
Is with me at thy farewell, joyous Bark!

WILLIAM WORDSWORTH

Where Lies the Land
to Which the Ship Would Go?

Where lies the land to which the ship would go?
Far, far ahead, is all her seamen know.
And where the land she travels from? Away,
Far, far behind, is all that they can say.

On sunny noons upon the deck's smooth face,
Linked arm in arm, how pleasant here to pace;
Or, o'er the stern reclining, watch below
The foaming wake far widening as we go.

On stormy nights when wild north-westers rave,
How proud a thing to fight with wind and wave!
The dripping sailor on the reeling mast
Exults to bear, and scorns to wish it past.

Where lies the land to which the ship would go?
Far, far ahead, is all her seamen know.
And where the land she travels from? Away,
Far, far behind, is all that they can say.

ARTHUR HUGH CLOUGH

Ode to the West Wind

I

O wild West Wind, thou breath of Autumn's being,
Thou, from whose unseen presence the leaves dead
Are driven, like ghosts from an enchanter fleeing,

Yellow, and black, and pale, and hectic red,
Pestilence-stricken multitudes: O thou,
Who chariotest to their dark wintry bed

The wingèd seeds, where they lie cold and low,

Each like a corpse within its grave, until
Thine azure sister of the Spring shall blow

Her clarion o'er the dreaming earth, and fill   10
(Driving sweet buds like flocks to feed in air)
With living hues and odours plain and hill:

Wild Spirit, which art moving everywhere;
Destroyer and preserver; hear, oh, hear!

II

Thou on whose stream, mid the steep sky's commotion,
Loose clouds like earth's decaying leaves are shed,
Shook from the tangled boughs of Heaven and Ocean,
Angels of rain and lightning: there are spread
On the blue surface of thine aëry surge,   20
Like the bright hair uplifted from the head

Of some fierce Maenad,³ even from the dim verge
Of the horizon to the zenith's height,
The locks of the approaching storm. Thou dirge

Of the dying year, to which this closing night
Will be the dome of a vast sepulchre,
Vaulted with all thy congregated might

Of vapours, from whose solid atmosphere
Black rain, and fire, and hail will burst: oh, hear!

III

Thou who didst waken from his summer dreams
The blue Mediterranean, where he lay,   30
Lulled by the coil of his crystàlline streams,

Beside a pumice isle in Baiae's bay,⁴
And saw in sleep old palaces and towers
Quivering within the wave's intenser day,

All overgrown with azure moss and flowers
So sweet, the sense faints picturing them! Thou
For whose path the Atlantic's level powers

Cleave themselves into chasms, while far below
The sea-blooms and the oozy woods which wear
The sapless foliage of the ocean, know   40

Thy voice, and suddenly grow gray with fear,
And tremble and despoil themselves: oh, hear!

IV

If I were a dead leaf thou mightest bear;
If I were a swift cloud to fly with thee;
A wave to pant beneath thy power, and share

The impulse of thy strength, only less free
Than thou, O uncontrollable! If even
I were as in my boyhood, and could be

The comrade of thy wanderings over Heaven,
As then, when to outstrip thy skiey speed   50
Scarce seemed a vision; I would ne'er have striven

As thus with thee in prayer in my sore need.
Oh, lift me as a wave, a leaf, a cloud!
I fall upon the thorns of life! I bleed!
A heavy weight of hours has chained and bowed
One too like thee: tameless, and swift, and proud.

V

Make me thy lyre, even as the forest is:
What if my leaves are falling like its own!
The tumult of thy mighty harmonies

Will take from both a deep, autumnal tone,   60
Sweet though in sadness. Be thou, Spirit fierce,
My spirit! Be thou me, impetuous one!

Drive my dead thoughts over the universe
Like withered leaves to quicken a new birth!
And, by the incantation of this verse,

Scatter, as from an unextinguished hearth
Ashes and sparks, my words among mankind!
Be through my lips to unawakened earth

The trumpet of a prophecy! O, Wind,
If Winter comes, can Spring be far behind?

PERCY BYSSHE SHELLEY

From the Greek of Moschus⁵

When winds that move not its calm surface sweep
The azure sea, I love the land no more;
The smiles of the serene and tranquil deep
Tempt my unquiet mind.—But when the roar
Of Ocean's gray abyss resounds, and foam
Gathers upon the sea, and vast waves burst,
I turn from the drear aspect to the home
Of Earth and its deep woods, where, interspersed,
When winds blow loud, pines make sweet melody.
Whose house is some lone bark, whose toil the sea,
Whose prey the wandering fish, an evil lot
Has chosen.—But I my languid limbs will fling
Beneath the plane, where the brook's murmuring
Moves the calm spirit, but disturbs it not.

PERCY BYSSHE SHELLEY

From *Childe Harold's Pilgrimage*
Canto II

XVII

He that has sail'd upon the dark blue sea
Has view'd at times, I ween, a full fair sight;
When the fresh breeze is fair as breeze may be,
The white sail set, the gallant frigate tight;
Masts, spires, and strand retiring to the right,
The glorious main expanding o'er the bow,
The convoy spread like wild swans in their flight,
The dullest sailer wearing bravely now,
So gaily curl the waves before each dashing prow.

XVIII

And oh, the little warlike world within!
The well-reeved guns, the netted canopy,
The hoarse command, the busy humming din,
When, at a word, the tops are mann'd on high:
Hark, to the Boatswain's call, the cheering cry!
While through the seaman's hand the tackle glides;
Or schoolboy Midshipman that, standing by,
Strains his shrill pipe as good or ill betides,
And well the docile crew that skillful urchin guides.

39

XIX

White is the glassy deck, without a stain,
Where on the watch the staid Lieutenant walks:
Look on that part which sacred doth remain
For the lone chieftain, who majestic stalks,
Silent and fear'd by all—not oft he talks
With aught beneath him, if he would preserve
That strict restraint, which, broken, ever balks
Conquest and Fame: but Britons rarely swerve
From law, however stern, which tends their strength to nerve.

XX

Blow! swiftly blow, thou keel-compelling gale!
Till the broad sun withdraws his lessening ray;
Then must the pennant-bearer slacken sail,
That lagging barks may make their lazy way.
Ah, grievance sore and listless dull delay,
To waste on sluggish hulks the sweetest breeze!
What leagues are lost before the dawn of day,
Thus loitering pensive on the willing seas,
The flapping sail haul'd down to halt for logs like these!

GEORGE GORDON, LORD BYRON

From *Childe Harold's Pilgrimage*
Canto IV

CLXXVIII

There is a pleasure in the pathless woods
There is a rapture on the lonely shore,
There is society where none intrudes,
By the deep Sea, and music in its roar:
I love not Man the less, but Nature more,
From these our interviews, in which I steal
From all I may be or have been before,
To mingle with the Universe, and feel
What I can ne'er express, yet can not all conceal.

CLXXIX

Roll on, thou deep and dark blue Ocean, roll!
Ten thousand fleets sweep over thee in vain;

Man marks the earth with ruin, his control
Stops with the shore; upon the watery plain
The wrecks are all thy deed, nor doth remain
A shadow of man's ravage, save his own,
When, for a moment, like a drop of rain,
He sinks into thy depths with bubbling groan,
Without a grave, unknell'd, uncoffin'd, and unknown.

CLXXX

His steps are not upon thy paths, thy fields
Are not a spoil for him,—thou dost arise
And shake him from thee; the vile strength he wields
For earth's destruction thou dost all despise,
Spurning him from thy bosom to the skies,
And send'st him, shivering in thy playful spray
And howling, to his Gods, where haply lies
His petty hope in some near port or bay,
And dashest him again to earth:—there let him lay.

CLXXXI

The armaments which thunderstrike the walls
Of rock-built cities, bidding nations quake
And monarchs tremble in their capitals,
The oak leviathans, whose huge ribs make
Their clay creator the vain title take
Of lord of thee and arbiter of war,—
These are thy toys, and, as the snowy flake,
They melt into thy yeast of waves, which mar
Alike the Armada's pride or spoils of Trafalgar.

CLXXXII

Thy shores are empires, changed in all save thee—
Assyria, Greece, Rome, Carthage, what are they?
Thy waters wash'd them power while they were free,
And many a tyrant since; their shores obey
The stranger, slave, or savage; their decay
Has dried up realms to deserts:—not so thou,
Unchangeable save to thy wild waves' play;
Time writes no wrinkle on thine azure brow;
Such as creation's dawn beheld, thou rollest now.

CLXXXIII

Thou glorious mirror, where the Almighty's form
Glasses itself in tempests; in all time,
Calm or convulsed—in breeze, or gale, or storm,
Icing the pole, or in the torrid clime
Dark-heaving;—boundless, endless, and sublime—
The image of Eternity—the throne
Of the Invisible; even from out thy slime
The monsters of the deep are made; each zone
Obeys thee; thou goest forth, dread, fathomless, alone.

CLXXXIV

And I have loved thee, Ocean! and my joy
Of youthful sports was on thy breast to be
Borne, like thy bubbles, onward. From a boy
I wanton'd with thy breakers—they to me
Were a delight; and if the freshening sea
Made them a terror—'t was a pleasing fear,
For I was as it were a child of thee,
And trusted to thy billows far and near,
And laid my hand upon thy mane—as I do here.

                          GEORGE GORDON, LORD BYRON

Eternal Father, Strong to Save[6]

Eternal Father, strong to save,
Whose arm hath bound the restless wave,
Who bidd'st the mighty ocean deep
Its own appointed limits keep:
    O hear us when we cry to thee
    For those in peril on the sea.

O Christ, whose voice the waters heard
And hushed their raging at thy word,
Who walkedst on the foaming deep,   10
And calm amid its rage didst sleep:
    O hear us when we cry to thee
    For those in peril on the sea.

Most Holy Spirit, who didst brood
Upon the chaos dark and rude,
And bid its angry tumult cease,

And give, for wild confusion, peace;
    O hear us when we cry to thee
    For those in peril on the sea.

O Trinity of love and power,
Our brethren shield in danger's hour;   20
From rock and tempest, fire and foe,
Protect them wheresoe'er they go;
    Thus evermore shall rise to thee
    Glad hymns of praise from land and sea.
                  Amen.

WILLIAM WHITING

Rocked in the Cradle of the Deep

Rocked in the cradle of the deep
I lay me down in peace to sleep;
Secure I rest upon the wave,
For thou, O Lord! hast power to save.
I know thou wilt not slight my call,
For Thou dost mark the sparrow's fall;
And calm and peaceful shall I sleep,
Rocked in the cradle of the deep.

When in the dead of night I lie
And gaze upon the trackless sky,   10
The star-bespangled heavenly scroll,
The boundless waters as they roll,—
I feel thy wondrous power to save
From perils of the stormy wave:
Rocked in the cradle of the deep,
I calmly rest and soundly sleep.

And such the trust that still were mine,
Though stormy winds swept o'er the brine,
Or though the tempest's fiery breath
Roused me from sleep to wreck and death.   20
In ocean cave, still safe with Thee
The germ of immortality!
And calm and peaceful shall I sleep,
Rocked in the cradle of the deep.

EMMA HART WILLARD

The Hurricane

Happy the man who, safe on shore,
   Now trims, at home, his evening fire;
Unmov'd, he hears the tempests roar,
   That on the tufted groves expire:
Alas! on us they doubly fall,
Our feeble barque must bear them all.

Now to their haunts the birds retreat,
   The squirrel seeks his hollow tree,
Wolves in their shaded caverns meet,
   All, all are blest but wretched we—   10
Foredoomed a stranger to repose,
No rest the unsettled ocean knows.

While o'er the dark abyss we roam,
   Perhaps, with last departing gleam,
We saw the sun descend in gloom,
   No more to see his morning beam;
But buried low, by far too deep,
On coral beds, unpitied, sleep!

But what a strange, uncoasted strand
   Is that, where fate permits no day—   20
No charts have we to mark that land,
   No compass to direct that way—
What Pilot shall explore that realm,
What new Columbus take the helm!

While death and darkness both surround,
   And tempests rage with lawless power,
Of friendship's voice I hear no sound,
   No comfort in this dreadful hour—
What friendship can in tempests be,
   What comfort on this raging sea?   30

The barque, accustomed to obey,
   No more the trembling pilots guide:
Alone she gropes her trackless way,
   While mountains burst on either side—
Thus, skill and science both must fall;
And ruin is the lot of all.

PHILIP FRENEAU

Calm Morning at Sea

Midocean like a pale blue morning-glory
    Opened wide, wide;
The ship cut softly through the silken surface;
    We watched the white sea-birds ride
Unrocking on the holy virgin water
    Fleckless on every side.

SARA TEASDALE

My Brigantine

                My brigantine!
Just in thy mould and beauteous in thy form,
Gentle in roll and buoyant on the surge,
Light as the sea-fowl rocking in the storm,
In breeze and gale thy onward course we urge,
                My water-queen!

                Lady of mine!
More light and swift than thou none thread the sea,
With surer keel or steadier on its path;
We brave each waste of ocean-mystery
And laugh to hear the howling tempest's wrath,
                For we are thine!

                My brigantine!
Trust to the mystic power that points thy way,
Trust to the eye that pierces from afar,
Trust the red meteors that around thee play,
And, fearless, trust the Sea-Green Lady's Star,
                Thou bark divine!

JAMES FENIMORE COOPER

Commemorative of a Naval Victory

Sailors there are of gentlest breed,
    Yet strong, like every goodly thing;
The discipline of arms refines,
    And the wave gives tempering.
    The damasked blade its beam can fling;

It lends the last grave grace:
The hawk, the hound, and sworded nobleman
   In Titian's picture for a king,
Are of hunter or warrior race.

In social halls a favored guest   10
   In years that follow victory won,
How sweet to feel your festal fame
   In woman's glance instinctive thrown:
   Repose is yours—your deed is known,
It musks the amber wine;
It lives, and sheds a light from storied days
   Rich as October sunsets brown,
Which make the barren place to shine.

But seldom the laurel wreath is seen
   Unmixed with pensive pansies dark;   20
There's a light and a shadow on every man
   Who at last attains his lifted mark—
   Nursing through night the ethereal spark.
Elate he never can be;
He feels that spirits which glad had hailed his worth,
   Sleep in oblivion.—The shark
Glides white through the phosphorus sea.

HERMAN MELVILLE

To Ned

Where is the world we roved, Ned Bunn?[7]
   Hollows thereof lay rich in shade
By voyagers old inviolate thrown
   Ere Paul Pry cruised with Pelf and Trade.[8]
To us old lads some thoughts come home
Who roamed a world young lads no more shall roam.

Nor less the satiate year impends
   When, wearying of routine-resorts,
The pleasure-hunter shall break loose,
   Ned, for our Pantheistic ports:—   10
Marquesas and glenned isles that be
Authentic Edens in a Pagan sea.

The charm of scenes untried shall lure,
    And, Ned, a legend urge the flight—
The Typee-truants under stars
    Unknown to Shakespere's *Midsummer-Night;*
And man, if lost to Saturn's Age,[9]
Yet feeling life no Syrian pilgrimage.

But, tell, shall he the tourist find
    Our isles the same in violet-glow   20
Enamoring us what years and years—
    Ah, Ned, what years and years ago!
Well, Adam advances, smart in pace,
But scarce by violets that advance you trace.

But we, in anchor-watches calm,
    The Indian Psyche's[10] languor won,
And, musing, breathed primeval balm
    From Edens ere yet over-run;
Marvelling mild if mortal twice,
Here and hereafter, touch a Paradise.

                              HERMAN MELVILLE

Break, Break, Break

Break, break, break,
    On thy cold gray stones, O Sea!
And I would that my tongue could utter
    The thoughts that arise in me.

O, well for the fisherman's boy,
    That he shouts with his sister at play!
O, well for the sailor lad,
    That he sings in his boat on the bay!

And the stately ships go on
    To their haven under the hill;
But O for the touch of a vanish'd hand,
    And the sound of a voice that is still!

Break, break, break,
    At the foot of thy crags, O Sea!
But the tender grace of a day that is dead
    Will never come back to me.

                              ALFRED, LORD TENNYSON

From *The Princess*
Part II—Sweet and Low
Lines 456–471

Sweet and low, sweet and low,
    Wind of the western sea,
Low, low, breathe and blow,
    Wind of the western sea!
    Over the rolling waters go,
    Come from the dying moon, and blow,
       Blow him again to me;
While my little one, while my pretty one sleeps.

    Sleep and rest, sleep and rest,
       Father will come to thee soon;
    Rest, rest, on mother's breast,
       Father will come to thee soon;
    Father will come to his babe in the nest,
    Silver sails all out of the west
       Under the silver moon;
Sleep, my little one, sleep, my pretty one, sleep.

ALFRED, LORD TENNYSON

Song for All Seas, All Ships

1

To-day a rude brief recitative,
Of ships sailing the seas, each with its special flag or ship-signal,
Of unnamed heroes in the ships—of waves spreading and spreading far
    as the eye can reach,
Of dashing spray, and the winds piping and blowing,
And out of these a chant for the sailors of all nations,
Fitful, like a surge.

Of sea-captains young or old, and the mates, and of all intrepid sailors,
Of the few, very choice, taciturn, whom fate can never surprise nor
    death dismay,
Pick'd sparingly without noise by thee old ocean, chosen by thee,
Thou sea that pickest and cullest the race in time, and unitest nations,
Suckled by thee, old husky nurse, embodying thee,
Indomitable, untamed as thee.

(Ever the heroes on water or on land, by ones or twos appearing,
Ever the stock preserv'd and never lost, though rare, enough for seed
    preserv'd.)

48

2

Flaunt out O sea your separate flags of nations!
Flaunt out visible as ever the various ship-signals!
But do you reserve especially for yourself and for the soul of man one
      flag above all the rest,
A spiritual woven signal for all nations, emblem of man elate above
      death,
Token of all brave captains and all intrepid sailors and mates,
And all that went down doing their duty,
Reminiscent of them, twined from all intrepid captains young or old,
A pennant universal, subtly waving all time, o'er all brave sailors,
All seas, all ships.

WALT WHITMAN

Patroling Barnegat

Wild, wild the storm, and the sea high running,
Steady the roar of the gale, with incessant undertone muttering,
Shouts of demoniac laughter fitfully piercing and pealing,
Waves, air, midnight, their savagest trinity lashing,
Out in the shadows there milk-white combs careering,
On beachy slush and sand spirits of snow fierce slanting,
Where through the murk the easterly death-wind breasting,
Through cutting swirl and spray watchful and firm advancing,
(That in the distance! is that a wreck? is the red signal flaring?)
Slush and sand of the beach tireless till daylight wending,
Steadily, slowly, through hoarse roar never remitting,
Along the midnight edge by those milk-white combs careering,
A group of dim, weird forms, struggling, the night confronting,
That savage trinity warily watching.

WALT WHITMAN

After the Sea-Ship

After the sea-ship, after the whistling winds,
After the white-gray sails taut to their spars and ropes,
Below, a myriad myriad waves hastening, lifting up their necks,
Tending in ceaseless flow toward the track of the ship,
Waves of the ocean bubbling and gurgling, blithely prying,
Waves, undulating waves, liquid, uneven, emulous waves,
Toward that whirling current, laughing and buoyant, with curves,
Where the great vessel sailing and tacking displaced the surface,

Larger and smaller waves in the spread of the ocean yearnfully flowing,
The wake of the sea-ship after she passes, flashing and frolicsome under
    the sun,
A motley procession with many a fleck of foam and many fragments,
Following the stately and rapid ship, in the wake following.

WALT WHITMAN

The Beauty of the Ship

When, staunchly entering port,
After long ventures, hauling up, worn and old,
Batter'd by sea and wind, torn by many a fight,
With the original sails all gone, replaced, or mended,
I only saw, at last, the beauty of the Ship.

WALT WHITMAN

The Dismantled Ship

In some unused lagoon, some nameless bay,
On sluggish, lonesome waters, anchor'd near the shore,
An old, dismasted, gray and batter'd ship, disabled, done,
After free voyages to all the seas of earth, haul'd up at last
    and hawser'd tight,
Lies rusting, mouldering.

WALT WHITMAN

The Old Ships

I have seen old ships sail like swans asleep
Beyond the village which men still call Tyre,[11]
With leaden age o'ercargoed, dipping deep
For Famagusta[12] and the hidden sun
That rings black Cyprus with a lake of fire;
And all those ships were certainly so old—
Who knows how oft with squat and noisy gun,
Questing brown slaves or Syrian oranges,
The pirate Genoese   10
Hell-raked them till they rolled
Blood, water, fruit and corpses up the hold.
But now through friendly seas they softly run,
Painted the mid-sea blue or shore-sea green,
Still patterned with the vine and grapes in gold.

But I have seen,
Pointing her shapely shadows from the dawn
An image tumbled on a rose-swept bay,
A drowsy ship of some yet older day;
And, wonder's breath indrawn,
Thought I—who knows—who knows—but in that same   20
(Fished up beyond Aeaea,[13] patched up new
—Stern painted brighter blue—)
That talkative, bald-headed seaman came
(Twelve patient comrades sweating at the oar)
From Troy's doom-crimson shore,
And with great lies about his wooden horse
Set the crew laughing, and forgot his course.

It was so old a ship—who knows, who knows?
—And yet so beautiful, I watched in vain
To see the mast burst open with a rose,   30
And the whole deck put on its leaves again.

                              JAMES ELROY FLECKER

The Sea-Limits

Consider the sea's listless chime:
    Time's self it is, made audible,—
    The murmur of the earth's own shell.
Secret continuance sublime
    Is the sea's end: our sight may pass
    No furlong further. Since time was,
This sound hath told the lapse of time.

No quiet, which is death's,—it hath
    The mournfulness of ancient life,
    Enduring always at dull strife.   10
As the world's heart of rest and wrath,
    Its painful pulse is in the sands.
    Last utterly, the whole sky stands,
Grey and not known, along its path.

Listen alone beside the sea,
    Listen alone among the woods;
    Those voices of twin solitudes
Shall have one sound alike to thee:
    Hark where the murmurs of thronged men
    Surge and sink back and surge again,—   20
Still the one voice of wave and tree.

51

Gather a shell from the strown beach
  And listen at its lips: they sigh
  The same desire and mystery,
The echo of the whole sea's speech.
  And all mankind is thus at heart
  Not anything but what thou art:
And Earth, Sea, Man, are all in each.

Dante Gabriel Rossetti

Falmouth

O, Falmouth is a fine town with ships in the bay,
And I wish from my heart it's there I was today;
I wish from my heart I was far away from here,
Sitting in my parlor and talking to my dear.
  For it's home, dearie, home—it's home I want to be.
  Our topsails are hoisted, and we'll away to sea.
  O, the oak and the ash and the bonnie birken° tree   birch
  They're all growing green in the old countrie.

In Baltimore a-walking a lady I did meet
With her babe on her arm, as she came down the street;   10
And I thought how I sailed, and the cradle standing ready
For the pretty little babe that has never seen its daddie.
  And it's home, dearie, home . . .

O, if it be a lass, she shall wear a golden ring;
And if it be a lad, he shall fight for his king:
With his dirk and his hat and his little jacket blue
He shall walk the quarter-deck as his daddie used to do.
  And it's home, dearie, home . . .

O, there's a wind a-blowing, a-blowing from the west,
And that of all the winds is the one I like the best,   20
For it blows at our backs, and it shakes our pennon free,
And it soon will blow us home to the old countrie.
  For it's home, dearie, home—it's home I want to be.
  Our topsails are hoisted, and we'll away to sea.
  O, the oak and the ash and the bonnie birken tree
  They're all growing green in the old countrie.

W. E. Henley

A Man Adrift on a Slim Spar

A man adrift on a slim spar
A horizon smaller than the rim of a bottle
Tented waves rearing lashy dark points
The near whine of froth in circles.
                God is cold.

The incessant raise and swing of the sea
And growl after growl of crest
The sinkings, green, seething, endless
The upheaval half-completed.
                God is cold.   10

The seas are in the hollow of The Hand;
Oceans may be turned to a spray
Raining down through the stars
Because of a gesture of pity toward a babe.
Oceans may become grey ashes,
Die with a long moan and a roar
Amid the tumult of the fishes
And the cries of the ships,
Because The Hand beckons the mice.

A horizon smaller than a doomed assassin's cap,   20
Inky, surging tumults
A reeling, drunken sky and no sky
A pale hand sliding from a polished spar.
                God is cold.

The puff of a coat imprisoning air:
A face kissing the water-death
A weary slow sway of a lost hand
And the sea, the moving sea, the sea.
                God is cold.

STEPHEN CRANE

Over the Sea to Skye

Sing me a song of a lad that is gone,
    Say, could that lad be I?
Merry of soul he sailed on a day
    Over the sea to Skye.

53

Mull was astern, Rum on the port,
    Egg on the starboard bow;[14]
Glory of youth glowed in his soul:
    Where is that glory now?

Sing me a song of a lad that is gone,
    Say, could that lad be I?   10
Merry of soul he sailed on a day
    Over the sea to Skye.

Give me again all that was there,
    Give me the sun that shone!
Give me the eyes, give me the soul,
    Give me the lad that's gone!

Sing me a song of a lad that is gone,
    Say, could that lad be I?
Merry of soul he sailed on a day
    Over the sea to Skye.   20

Billow and breeze, islands and seas,
    Mountains of rain and sun,
All that was good, all that was fair,
    All that was me is gone.

                ROBERT LOUIS STEVENSON

Les Silhouettes

The sea is flecked with bars of grey,
The dull dead wind is out of tune,
And like a withered leaf the moon
Is blown across the stormy bay.

Etched clear upon the pallid sand
Lies the black boat: a sailor boy
Clambers aboard in careless joy
With laughing face and gleaming hand.

And overhead the curlews cry,
Where through the dusky upland grass
The young brown-throated reapers pass,
Like silhouettes against the sky.

                OSCAR WILDE

The Long Trail

There's a whisper down the field where the year has shot her yield,
  And the ricks stand grey to the sun,
Singing: "Over then, come over, for the bee has quit the clover,
  "And your English summer's done."
      You have heard the beat of the off-shore wind,
      And the thresh of the deep-sea rain;
      You have heard the song—how long? how long?
      Pull out on the trail again!
Ha' done with the Tents of Shem,[15] dear lass,
We've seen the seasons through,   10
And it's time to turn on the old trail, our own trail, the out trail,
Pull out, pull out, on the Long Trail—the trail that is always new!

It's North you may run to the rime-ringed sun
  Or South to the blind Horn's hate;
Or East all the way into Mississippi Bay,
  Or West to the Golden Gate—
      Where the blindest bluffs hold good, dear lass,
      And the wildest tales are true,
      And the men bulk big on the old trail, our own trail, the out
        trail,
      And life runs large on the Long Trail—the trail that is always
        new.   20

The days are sick and cold, and the skies are grey and old,
  And the twice-breathed airs blow damp;
And I'd sell my tired soul for the bucking beam-sea roll
  Of a black Bilbao tramp,[16]
      With her load-line over her hatch, dear lass,
      And a drunken Dago crew,
      And her nose held down on the old trail, our own trail, the out
        trail
      From Cadiz south on the Long Trail—the trail that is always
      new.

There be triple ways to take, of the eagle or the snake,
  Or the way of a man with a maid;   30
But the sweetest way to me is a ship's upon the sea
  In the heel of the North-East Trade.
      Can you hear the crash on her bows, dear lass,
      And the drum of the racing screw,
      As she ships it green on the old trail, our own trail, the out trail,
      As she lifts and 'scends on the Long Trail—the trail that is
        always new?

See the shaking funnels roar, with the Peter at the fore,
   And the fenders grind and heave,
And the derricks clack and grate, as the tackle hooks the crate,
   And the fall-rope whines through the sheave;   40
      It's "Gang-plank up and in," dear lass,
      It's "Hawsers warp her through!"
      And it's "All clear aft" on the old trail, our own trail, the out
         trail,
      We're backing down on the Long Trail—the trail that is always
         new.

O the mutter overside, when the port-fog holds us tied,
   And the sirens hoot their dread,
When foot by foot we creep o'er the hueless viewless deep
   To the sob of the questing lead!
      It's down by the Lower Hope, dear lass,
      With the Gunfleet Sands in view,   50
      Till the Mouse swings green on the old trail, our own trail, the
         out trail,
      And the Gull Light lifts on the Long Trail[17]—the trail that is
         always new.

O the blazing tropic night, when the wake's a welt of light
   That holds the hot sky tame,
And the steady fore-foot snores through the planet-powdered floors
   Where the scared whale flukes in flame!
      Her plates are flaked by the sun, dear lass,
      And her ropes are taut with the dew,
      For we're booming down on the old trail, our own trail, the out
         trail,
      We're sagging south on the Long Trail—the trail that is   60
         always new.

Then home, get her home, where the drunken rollers comb,
   And the shouting seas drive by,
And the engines stamp and ring, and the wet bows reel and swing,
   And the Southern Cross rides high!
      Yes, the old lost stars wheel back, dear lass,
      That blaze in the velvet blue.
      They're all old friends on the old trail, our own trail, the out
         trail,
      They're God's own guide on the Long Trail—the trail that is
         always new.

Fly forward, O my heart, from the Foreland to the Start[18]—   70
   We're steaming all too slow,

And it's twenty thousand mile to our little lazy isle
  Where the trumpet-orchids blow!
      You have heard the call of the off-shore wind
      And the voice of the deep-sea rain;
      You have heard the song. How long—how long?
      Pull out on the trail again!

The Lord knows what we may find, dear lass,
And The Deuce knows what we may do—
But we're back once more on the old trail, our own trail, the out trail,
We're down, hull-down, on the Long Trail—the trail that is always
    new!

RUDYARD KIPLING

Dover Beach

The sea is calm to-night.
The tide is full, the moon lies fair
Upon the straits;—on the French coast the light
Gleams and is gone; the cliffs of England stand,
Glimmering and vast, out in the tranquil bay.
Come to the window, sweet is the night-air!

Only, from the long line of spray
Where the sea meets the moon-blanch'd land,
Listen! you hear the grating roar
Of pebbles which the waves draw back, and fling,   10
At their return, up the high strand,
Begin, and cease, and then again begin,
With tremulous cadence slow, and bring
The eternal note of sadness in.

Sophocles[19] long ago
Heard it on the Ægaean, and it brought
Into his mind the turbid ebb and flow
Of human misery; we
Find also in the sound a thought,
Hearing it by this distant northern sea.   20

The Sea of Faith[20]
Was once, too, at the full, and round earth's shore
Lay like the folds of a bright girdle furl'd.
But now I only hear
Its melancholy, long, withdrawing roar,
Retreating, to the breath
Of the night-wind, down the vast edges drear
And naked shingles of the world.

Ah, love, let us be true
To one another! for the world, which seems 30
To lie before us like a land of dreams,
So various, so beautiful, so new,
Hath really neither joy, nor love, nor light,
Nor certitude, nor peace, nor help for pain;
And we are here as on a darkling plain
Swept with confused alarms of struggle and flight,
Where ignorant armies clash by night.

MATTHEW ARNOLD

Ex-Voto

When their last hour shall rise
Pale on these mortal eyes,
Herself like one that dies,
   And kiss me dying
The cold last kiss, and fold
Close round my limbs her cold
Soft shade as raiment rolled
   And leave them lying,

If aught my soul would say
Might move to hear me pray 10
The birth-god of my day
   That he might hearken,
This grace my heart should crave,
To find no landward grave
That worldly springs make brave,
   World's winters darken,

Nor grow through gradual hours
The cold blind seed of flowers
Made by new beams and showers
   From limbs that moulder, 20
Nor take my part with earth,
But find for death's new birth
A bed of larger girth,
   More chaste and colder.

Not earth's for spring and fall,
Not earth's at heart, not all
Earth's making, though men call
   Earth only mother,
Not hers at heart she bare

Me, but thy child, O fair   30
Sea, and thy brother's care,
   The wind thy brother.

Yours was I born, and ye,
The sea-wind and the sea,
Made all my soul in me
   A song for ever,
A harp to string and smite
For love's sake of the bright
Wind and the sea's delight,
   To fail them never: 40

Not while on this side death
I hear what either saith
And drink of either's breath
   With heart's thanksgiving
That in my veins like wine
Some sharp salt blood of thine,
Some springtide pulse of brine,
   Yet leaps up living.

When thy salt lips wellnigh
Sucked in my mouth's last sigh,   50
Grudged I so much to die
   This death as others?
Was it no ease to think
The chalice from whose brink
Fate gave me death to drink
   Was thine—my mother's?

Thee too, the all-fostering earth,
Fair as thy fairest birth,
More than thy worthiest worth,
   We call, we know thee,   60
More sweet and just and dread
Than live men highest of head
Or even thy holiest dead
   Laid low below thee.

The sunbeam on the sheaf,
The dewfall on the leaf,
All joy, all grace, all grief,
   Are thine for giving;
Of thee our loves are born,
Our lives and loves, that mourn   70
And triumph; tares with corn,
   Dead seed with living:

59

All good and ill things done
In eyeshot of the sun
At last in thee made one
　　Rest well contented;
All words of all man's breath
And works he doth or saith,
All wholly done to death,
　　None long lamented.　　　　　　　　　　　　80

A slave to sons of thee,
Thou, seeming, yet art free;
But who shall make the sea
　　Serve even in seeming?
What plough shall bid it bear
Seed to the sun and the air,
Fruit for thy strong sons' fare,
　　Fresh wine's foam streaming?

What oldworld son of thine,
Made drunk with death as wine,　　　　　　90
Hath drunk the bright sea's brine
　　With lips of laughter?
Thy blood they drink; but he
Who hath drunken of the sea
Once deeplier than of thee
　　Shall drink not after.

Of thee thy sons of men
Drink deep, and thirst again;
For wine in feasts, and then
　　In fields for slaughter;　　　　　　　　　100
But thirst shall touch not him
Who hath felt with sense grown dim
Rise, covering lip and limb
　　The wan sea's water.

All fire of thirst that aches
The salt sea cools and slakes
More than all springs or lakes
　　Freshets or shallows;
Wells where no beam can burn
Through frondage of the fern　　　　　　　110
That hides from hart and hern
　　The haunt it hallows.

Peace with all graves on earth
For death or sleep or birth
Be alway, one in worth
   One with another;
But when my time shall be,
O mother, O my sea,
Alive or dead, take me,
   Me too, my mother.

ALGERNON CHARLES SWINBURNE

Who Has Not Walked upon the Shore

Who has not walked upon the shore,
And who does not the morning know,
The day the angry gale is o'er,
The hour the wind has ceased to blow?

The horses of the strong south-west
Are pastured round his tropic tent,
Careless how long the ocean's breast
Sob on and sigh for passion spent.

The frightened birds, that fled inland
To house in rock and tower and tree,
Are gathering on the peaceful strand,
To tempt again the sunny sea;

Whereon the timid ships steal out,
And laugh to find their foe asleep,
That lately scattered them about,
And drove them to the fold like sheep.

The snow-white clouds he northward chased
Break into phalanx, line, and band:
All one way to the south they haste,
The south, their pleasant fatherland.

ROBERT BRIDGES

A Passer-By

Whither, O splendid ship, thy white sails crowding,
    Leaning across the bosom of the urgent West,
That fearest nor sea rising, nor sky clouding,
    Whither away, fair rover, and what thy quest?
    Ah! soon, when Winter has all our vales opprest,
When skies are cold and misty, and hail is hurling,
    Wilt thou glide on the blue Pacific, or rest
In a summer haven asleep, thy white sails furling.

I there before thee, in the country that well thou knowest,
    Already arrived am inhaling the odorous air: 10
I watch thee enter unerringly where thou goest,
    And anchor queen of the strange shipping there,
    Thy sails for awnings spread, thy masts bare;
Nor is aught from the foaming reef to the snow-capped grandest
    Peak, that is over the feathery palms more fair
Than thou, so upright, so stately, and still thou standest.

And yet, O splendid ship, unhailed and nameless,
    I know not if, aiming a fancy, I rightly divine
That thou hast a purpose joyful, a courage blameless,
    Thy port assured in a happier land than mine.   20
    But for all I have given thee, beauty enough is thine,
As thou, aslant with trim tackle and shrouding,
    From the proud nostril curve of a prow's line
In the offing scatterest foam, thy white sails crowding.

                                        ROBERT BRIDGES

The Wreck

Storm and unconscionable winds once cast
On grinding shingle, masking gap-toothed rock,
This ancient hulk. Rent hull, and broken mast,
She sprawls sand-mounded, of sea birds the mock.
Her sailors, drowned, forgotten, rot in mould,
Or hang in stagnant quiet of the deep;
The brave, the afraid into one silence sold;
Their end a memory fainter than of sleep.
She held good merchandise. She paced in pride
The uncharted paths men trace in ocean's foam.

Now laps the ripple in her broken side,
And zephyr in tamarisk softly whispers, Home.
The dreamer scans her in the sea-blue air,
And, sipping of contrast, finds the day more fair.

WALTER DE LA MARE

Never More, Sailor

Never more, Sailor,
Shalt thou be
Tossed on the wind-ridden,
Restless sea.
Its tides may labour;
All the world
Shake 'neath that weight
Of waters hurled:
But its whole shock
Can only stir   10
Thy dust to a quiet
Even quieter.
Thou mock'st at land
Who now art come
To such a small
And shallow home;
Yet bore the sea
Full many a care
For bones that once
A sailor's were.   20
And though the grave's
Deep soundlessness
Thy once sea-deafened
Ear distress,
No robin ever
On the deep
Hopped with his song
To haunt thy sleep.

WALTER DE LA MARE

Sunlight and Sea

Give me the sunlight and the sea
And who shall take my heaven from me?
Light of the Sun, Life of the Sun,
O happy, bold companion,
Whose golden laughters round me run,
Making wine of the blue air
With wild-rose kisses everywhere,
Browning the limb, flushing the cheek,
Apple-fragrant, leopard-sleek,
Dancing from thy red-curtained East   10
Like a Nautch-girl[21] to my feast,
Proud because her lord, the Spring,
Praised the way those anklets ring;
Or wandering like a white Greek maid
Leaf-dappled through the dancing shade,
Where many a green-veined leaf imprints
Breast and limb with emerald tints,
That softly net her silken shape
But let the splendour still escape,
While rosy ghosts of roses flow   20
Over the supple rose and snow.

But sweetest, fairest is thy face,
When we meet, when we embrace,
Where the white sand sleeps at noon
Round that lonely blue lagoon,
Fringed with one white reef of coral
Where the sea-birds faintly quarrel
And the breakers on the reef
Fade into a dream of grief,
And the palm-trees overhead   30
Whisper that all grief is dead.

Sister Sunlight, lead me then
Into thy healing seas again . . .
For when we swim out, side by side,
Like a lover with his bride,
When thy lips are salt with brine,
And thy wild eyes flash in mine,
The music of a mightier sea
Beats with my blood in harmony.
I breast the primal flood of being,   40

Too clear for speech, too near for seeing;
And to his heart, new reconciled,
The Eternal takes his earth-bound child.

Who the essential secret spells
In those gigantic syllables,—
Flowing, ebbing, ebbing, flowing,—
Gathers wisdom past all knowing.
Song of the Sea, I hear, I hear,
That deeper music of the sphere,
Catch the rhythm of sun and star,   50
And know what light and darkness are;
Ay, faint beginnings of a rhyme
That swells beyond the tides of time;
Beat with thy rhythm in blood and breath,
And make one song of life and death.
I hear, I hear, and rest content,
Merged in the primal element,
The old element whence life arose,
The fount of youth, to which it goes.

Give me the sunlight and the sea   60
And who shall take my heaven from me?

ALFRED NOYES

Sea-Fever

I must go down to the seas again, to the lonely sea and the sky,
And all I ask is a tall ship and a star to steer her by,
And the wheel's kick and the wind's song and the white sail's shaking,
And a grey mist on the sea's face and a grey dawn breaking.

I must go down to the seas again, for the call of the running tide
Is a wild call and a clear call that may not be denied;
And all I ask is a windy day with the white clouds flying,
And the flung spray and the blown spume and the sea-gulls crying.

I must go down to the seas again to the vagrant gypsy life,
To the gull's way and the whale's way where the wind's like a whetted
        knife;
And all I ask is a merry yarn from a laughing fellow-rover,
And quiet sleep and a sweet dream when the long trick's over.

JOHN MASEFIELD

Cargoes

Quinquireme of Nineveh from distant Ophir[22]
Rowing home to haven in sunny Palestine,
With a cargo of ivory,
And apes and peacocks,
Sandalwood, cedarwood, and sweet white wine.

Stately Spanish galleon coming from the Isthmus,[23]
Dipping through the Tropics by the palm-green shores,
With a cargo of diamonds,
Emeralds, amethysts,
Topazes, and cinnamon, and gold moidores.

Dirty British coaster with a salt-caked smoke-stack
Butting through the Channel in the mad March days,
With a cargo of Tyne coal,
Road-rail, pig-lead,
Firewood, iron-ware, and cheap tin trays.

JOHN MASEFIELD

D'Avalos' Prayer

When the last sea is sailed, when the last shallow charted,
   When the last field is reaped, and the last harvest stored,
When the last fire is out and the last guest departed,
   Grant the last prayer that I shall pray, Be good to me, O Lord!

And let me pass in a night at sea, a night of storm and thunder,
   In the loud crying of the wind through sail and rope and spar.
Send me a ninth great peaceful wave to drown and roll me under
   To the cold tunny-fishes' home where the drowned galleons are.

And in the dim green quiet place far out of sight and hearing,
   Grant I may hear at whiles the wash and thresh of the sea-foam
About the fine keen bows of the stately clippers steering
   Towards the lone northern star and the fair ports of home.

JOHN MASEFIELD

Sea Lullaby

The old moon is tarnished
With smoke of the flood,
The dead leaves are varnished
With colour like blood,

A treacherous smiler
With teeth white as milk,
A savage beguiler
In sheathings of silk,

The sea creeps to pillage,
She leaps on her prey;   10
A child of the village
Was murdered today.

She came up to meet him
In a smooth golden cloak,
She choked him and beat him
To death, for a joke.

Her bright locks were tangled,
She shouted for joy,
With one hand she strangled
A strong little boy.   20

Now in silence she lingers
Beside him all night
To wash her long fingers
In silvery light.

ELINOR WYLIE

Mid-Ocean in War-Time
(For My Mother)

The fragile splendour of the level sea,
    The moon's serene and silver-veilèd face,
    Make of this vessel an enchanted place
Full of white mirth and golden sorcery.
Now, for a time, shall careless laughter be
    Blended with song, to lend song sweeter grace,
    And the old stars, in their unending race,
Shall heed and envy young humanity.

And yet to-night, a hundred leagues away,
    These waters blush a strange and awful red.

Before the moon, a cloud obscenely grey
　　Rises from decks that crash with flying lead.
And these stars smile their immemorial way
　　On waves that shroud a thousand newly dead!

A Grave

Man looking into the sea,
taking the view from those who have as much right to
　　　　it as you have to it yourself,
it is human nature to stand in the middle of a thing,
but you cannot stand in the middle of this;
the sea has nothing to give but a well excavated grave.
The firs stand in a procession, each with an emerald
　　　　turkey-foot at the top,
reserved as their contours, saying nothing;
repression, however, is not the most obvious characteristic
　　　　of the sea;
the sea is a collector, quick to return a rapacious look.
There are others besides you who have worn that look—　　　　　10
whose expression is no longer a protest; the fish no longer
　　　　investigate them
for their bones have not lasted:
men lower nets, unconscious of the fact that they are desecrating a
　　　　grave,
and row quickly away—the blades of the oars
moving together like the feet of water-spiders as if there
　　　　were no such thing as death.
The wrinkles progress upon themselves in a phalanx—
　　　　beautiful under networks of foam,
and fade breathlessly while the sea rustles in and out
　　　　of the seaweed;
the birds swim through the air at top speed, emitting
　　　　cat-calls as heretofore—　　　　　　　　　　　　　　　　　　20
the tortoise-shell scourges about the feet of the cliffs, in
　　　　motion beneath them;
and the ocean, under the pulsation of lighthouses and
　　　　noise of bell-buoys,
advances as usual, looking as if it were not that ocean
　　　　in which dropped things are bound to sink—
in which if they turn and twist, it is neither with volition
　　　　nor consciousness.

MARIANNE MOORE

68

The Open Sea

We say the sea is lonely; better say
Ourselves are lonesome creatures whom the sea
Gives neither yes nor no for company.

Oh, there are people, all right, settled in the sea;
It is as populous as Maine today,
But no one who will give you the time of day.

A man who asks there of his family
Or a friend or teacher gets a cold reply
Or finds him dead against that vast majority.

Nor does it signify that people who stay
Very long, bereaved or not, at the edge of the sea
Hear the drowned folk call: that is mere fancy,

They are speechless. And the famous noise of sea
Which a poet has beautifully told us in our day
Is hardly a sound to speak comfort to the lonely.

Although not yet a man given to prayer, I pray
For each creature lost since the start at sea,
And give thanks it was not I, nor yet one close to me.

WILLIAM MEREDITH

Passage Steamer

Upon the decks they take beef tea
   Who are so free, so free, so free,
But down the ladder in the engine-room
   (Doom, doom, doom, doom)
The great cranks rise and fall, repeat,
The great cranks plod with their Assyrian feet
   To match the monotonous energy of the sea.

Back from a journey I require
   Some new desire, desire, desire,
But find in the open sea and sun   10
   None, none, none, none;
The gulls that bank around the mast
Insinuate that nothing we pass is past,
   That all our beginnings were long since begun.

69

And when I think of you, my dear,
   Who were so near, so near, so near,
The barren skies from wall to wall
   Appal, appal, pall, pall,
The spray no longer gilds the wave,
The sea looks nothing more nor less than a grave   20
   And the world and the day are grey and that is all.

Louis MacNeice

what is

what is
a
voyage
?

up
upup:go
ing

downdowndown

com;ing won
der
ful sun

moon stars the all,& a

(big
ger than
big

gest could even

begin to be)dream
of;a thing:of
a creature who's

O

cean
(everywhere
nothing

but light and dark;but

never forever
& when)un
til one strict

here of amazing most

now,with what
thousands of(hundreds
of)millions of

CriesWhichAreWings

　　　e. e. cummings

Sea Voyage

Re-plyed, extorted, oft transposed, and fleeting,
Tune from plucked cotton, the cat's-cradle pattern
Dances round fingers that would scratch in meeting
And dures and fosters their abandoned kitten.
Drawn taut, this flickering of wit would freeze,
And grave, knot-diamond, its filigrees.

Pillowed on gulfs between exiguous bobbins
The Son of Spiders, crucified to lace,
Suspends a red rag to a thousand dobbins
And sails so powered to a better place.
All his gained ports, thought's inter-reached trapeze,
Map-sail, transport him towards Hercules,[24]

Earth-bound. Blue-sea-bound, the crisp silver foam,
Forbad be crystal, a lace eringo,[25]
Flaps from the haunch seven petticoats at home,
Wards, silk, in ocean overskirt, her rainbow.
Sand-rope, the sodden goblet of the seas
Holds, concentrate, her liquid pedigrees.
We sum in port her banquet of degrees.

WILLIAM EMPSON

Voyages

I

Above the fresh ruffles of the surf
Bright striped urchins flay each other with sand.
They have contrived a conquest for shell shucks,
And their fingers crumble fragments of baked weed
Gaily digging and scattering.

71

And in answer to their treble interjections
The sun beats lightning on the waves,
The waves fold thunder on the sand;
And could they hear me I would tell them:

O brilliant kids, frisk with your dog,   10
Fondle your shells and sticks, bleached
By time and the elements; but there is a line
You must not cross nor ever trust beyond it
Spry cordage of your bodies to caresses
Too lichen-faithful from too wide a breast.
The bottom of the sea is cruel.

II

—And yet this great wink of eternity,
Of rimless floods, unfettered leewardings,
Samite sheeted and processioned where
Her undinal vast belly moonward bends,   20
Laughing the wrapt inflections of our love;

Take this Sea,²⁶ whose diapason knells
On scrolls of silver snowy sentences,
The sceptered terror of whose session rends
As her demeanors motion well or ill,
All but the pieties of lovers' hands.

And onward, as bells off San Salvador
Salute the crocus lusters of the stars,
In these poinsettia meadows of her tides,—
Adagios²⁷ of islands, O my Prodigal,   30
Complete the dark confessions her veins spell.

Mark how her turning shoulders wind the hours,
And hasten while her penniless rich palms
Pass superscription of bent foam and wave,—
Hasten, while they are true,—sleep, death, desire,
Close round one instant in one floating flower.

Bind us in time, O seasons clear, and awe.
O minstrel galleons of Carib fire,
Bequeath us to no earthly shore until
Is answered in the vortex of our grave   40
The seal's wide spindrift gaze toward paradise.

HART CRANE

72

Fish Food

As you[28] drank deep as Thor, did you think of milk or wine?
Did you drink blood, while you drank the salt deep?
Or see through the film of light, that sharpened your rage with its stare,
a shark, dolphin, turtle? Did you not see the Cat
who, when Thor lifted her, unbased the cubic ground?
You would drain fathomless flagons to be slaked with vacuum—
The sea's teats have suckled you, and you are sunk far
in bubble-dreams, under swaying translucent vines
of thundering interior wonder. Eagles can never now
carry parts of your body, over cupped mountains   10
as emblems of their anger, embers to fire self-hate
to other wonders, unfolding white flaming vistas.
Fishes now look upon you, with eyes which do not gossip.
Fishes are never shocked. Fishes will kiss you, each
fish tweak you; every kiss takes bits of you away,
till your bones alone will roll, with the Gulf Stream's swell.
So has it been already, so have the carpers and puffers
nibbled your carcass of fame, each to his liking. Now
in tides of noon, the bones of your thought-suspended structures
gleam as you intended. Noon pulled your eyes with small   20
magnetic headaches; the will seeped from your blood. Seeds
of meaning popped from the pods of thought. And you fall. And the
          unseen
churn of Time changes the pearl-hued ocean;
like a pearl-shaped drop, in a huge water-clock
falling; from *came* to *go,* from *come* to *went.* And you fell.
Waters received you. Waters of our Birth in Death dissolve you.
Now you have willed it, may the Great Wash take you.
As the Mother-Lover takes your woe away, and cleansing
grief and you away, you sleep, you do not snore.   30
Lie still. Your rage is gone on a bright flood
away; as, when a bad friend held out his hand
you said, "Do not talk any more. I know you meant no harm."
What was the soil whence your anger sprang, who are deaf
as the stones to the whispering flight of the Mississippi's rivers?
What did you see as you fell? What did you hear as you sank?
Did it make you drunken with hearing?
I will not ask any more. You saw or heard no evil.

JOHN WHEELWRIGHT

The Drowned

They still vibrate with the sound
Of electric bells,
The sailors who drown
While their mouths and ships fill
With wells of silence
And horizons of distance.

Kate and Mary were cities
Where they lingered on shore
Mingling with the cuties
Who danced on duty there   10
—With no Sergeant Numb come
To shut down the bar.

No letters reach wrecks
Corpses have no telephone;
Cold tides cut the nerves;
The desires are frozen,
While the blurred sky
Rubs salt medals on the eyes.

Jack sees her with another
And he knows how she smiles   20
At the light facile rival
Who so simply beguiles
Dancing and doing
What *he* never will now.

Cut off unfairly
By the doom of doom
Which makes heroes and serious
Skulls of us all.
Under waves we now roll
Whose one dream was to play   30
And forget these bones all day.

STEPHEN SPENDER

Seascape

In Memoriam, M.A.S.[29]

There are some days the happy ocean lies
Like an unfingered harp, below the land.
Afternoon gilds all the silent wires
Into a burning music for the eyes.
On mirrors flashing between fine-strung fires
The shore, heaped up with roses, horses, spires,
Wanders on water, walking above ribbed sand.

The motionlessness of the hot sky tires
And a sigh, like a woman's, from inland
Brushes the instrument with shadowing hand   10
Drawing across its wires some gull's sharp cries
Or bell, or shout, from distant, hedged-in shires;
These, deep as anchors, the hushing wave buries.

Then from the shore, two zig-zag butterflies,
Like errant dog-roses, cross the bright strand
Spiralling over sea in foolish gyres
Until they fall into reflected skies.
They drown. Fishermen understand
Such wings sunk in such ritual sacrifice,

Recalling legends of undersea, drowned cities.   20
What voyagers, oh what heroes, flamed like pyres
With helmets plumed, have set forth from some island
And them the sea engulfed. Their eyes,
Contorted by the cruel waves' desires
Glitter with coins through the tide scarcely scanned,
While, above them, that harp assumes their sighs.

STEPHEN SPENDER

Seascape

This celestial seascape, with white herons got up as angels,
flying as high as they want and as far as they want sidewise
in tiers and tiers of immaculate reflections;
the whole region, from the highest heron
down to the weightless mangrove island
with bright green leaves edged neatly with bird-droppings
like illumination in silver,
and down to the suggestively Gothic arches of the mangrove roots
and the beautiful pea-green back-pasture
where occasionally a fish jumps, like a wild-flower   10
in an ornamental spray of spray;
this cartoon by Raphael[30] for a tapestry for a Pope:
it does look like heaven.
But a skeletal lighthouse standing there
in black and white clerical dress,
who lives on his nerves, thinks he knows better.
He thinks that hell rages below his iron feet,
that that is why the shallow water is so warm,
and he knows that heaven is not like this.
Heaven is not like flying or swimming,   20
but has something to do with blackness and a strong glare
and when it gets dark he will remember something
strongly worded to say on the subject.

Elizabeth Bishop

Half-Tide Ledge

Sunday the sea made morning worship, sang
Venite, Kyrie, and a long Amen,[31]
over a flowing cassock did put on
glittering blindness, surplice of the sun.
Towards high noon her eldest, high-run tide
rebelled at formal song and in the Sanctus[32]
made heavy mockery of God,
and I, almost before I knew it, saw
the altar ledges of the Lord awash.
These are the obsequies I think on most.

R. P. Blackmur

Sea Gods

I

They say there is no hope—
sand—drift—rocks—rubble of the sea—
the broken hulk of a ship,
hung with shreds of rope,
pallid under the cracked pitch.

they say there is no hope
to conjure you—
no whip of the tongue to anger you—
no hate of words
you must rise to refute.   10

They say you are twisted by the sea,
you are cut apart
by wave-break upon wave-break,
that you are misshapen by the sharp rocks,
broken by the rasp and after-rasp.

That you are cut, torn, mangled,
torn by the stress and beat,
no stronger than the strips of sand
along your ragged beach.

III

For you will come,   20
you will yet haunt men in ships,
you will trail across the fringe of strait
and circle the jagged rocks.

You will trail across the rocks
and wash them with your salt,
you will curl between sand-hills—
you will thunder along the cliff—
break—retreat—get fresh strength—
gather and pour weight upon the beach.

You will draw back,   30
and the ripple on the sand-shelf
will be witness of your track.
O privet-white, you will paint
the lintel of wet sand with froth.

You will bring myrrh-bark
and drift laurel-wood from hot coasts!
when you hurl high—high—
we will answer with a shout.

For you will come,
you will come,   40
you will answer our taut hearts,
you will break the lie of men's thoughts,
and cherish and shelter us.

                                    H. D.

Pasa Thalassa Thalassa

"The sea is everywhere the sea."

I

Gone—faded out of the story, the sea-faring friend I remember?
Gone for a decade, they say: never a word or a sign.
Gone with his hard red face that only his laughter could wrinkle,
Down where men go to be still, by the old way of the sea.

Never again will he come, with rings in his ears like a pirate,
Back to be living and seen, here with his roses and vines;
Here where the tenants are shadows and echoes of years uneventful,
Memory meets the event, told from afar by the sea.

Smoke that floated and rolled in the twilight away from the chimney
Floats and rolls no more. Wheeling and falling, instead,   10
Down with a twittering flash go the smooth and inscrutable swallows,
Down to the place made theirs by the cold work of the sea.

Roses have had their day, and the dusk is on yarrow and wormwood—
Dusk that is over the grass, drenched with memorial dew;
Trellises lie like bones in a ruin that once was a garden,
Swallows have lingered and ceased, shadows and echoes are all.

II

Where is he lying to-night, as I turn away down to the valley,
Down where the lamps of men tell me the streets are alive?
Where shall I ask, and of whom, in the town or on land or on water,
News of a time and a place buried alike and with him?   20

Few now remain who may care, nor may they be wiser for caring,
Where or what manner the doom, whether by day or by night;
Whether in Indian deeps or on flood-laden fields of Atlantis,
Or by the roaring Horn, shrouded in silence he lies.

Few now remain who return by the weed-weary path to his cottage,
Drawn by the scene as it was—met by the chill and the change;
Few are alive who report, and few are alive who remember,
More of him now than a name carved somewhere on the sea.

"Where is he lying?" I ask, and the lights in the valley are nearer;
Down to the streets I go, down to the murmur of men.   30
Down to the roar of the sea in a ship may be well for another—
Down where he lies to-night, silent, and under the storms.

EDWIN ARLINGTON ROBINSON

Exiled

Searching my heart for its true sorrow,
    This is the thing I find to be:
That I am weary of words and people,
    Sick of the city, wanting the sea;

Wanting the sticky, salty sweetness
    Of the strong wind and shattered spray;
Wanting the loud sound and the soft sound
    Of the big surf that breaks all day.

Always before about my dooryard,
    Marking the reach of the winter sea,   10
Rooted in sand and dragging drift-wood,
    Straggled the purple wild sweet-pea;

Always I climbed the wave at morning,
    Shook the sand from my shoes at night,
That now am caught beneath great buildings,
    Stricken with noise, confused with light.

If I could hear the green piles groaning
    Under the windy wooden piers,
See once again the bobbing barrels,
    And the black sticks that fence the weirs,   20

If I could see the weedy mussels
    Crusting the wrecked and rotting hulls,
Hear once again the hungry crying
    Overhead, of the wheeling gulls,

79

Feel once again the shanty straining
  Under the turning of the tide,
Fear once again the rising freshet,
  Dread the bell in the fog outside,

I should be happy,—that was happy
  All day long on the coast of Maine!   30
I have a need to hold and handle
  Shells and anchors and ships again!

I should be happy, that am happy
  Never at all since I came here.
I am too long away from water.
  I have a need of water near.

EDNA ST. VINCENT MILLAY

Neither Out Far Nor In Deep

The people along the sand
All turn and look one way.
They turn their back on the land.
They look at the sea all day.

As long as it takes to pass
A ship keeps raising its hull;
The wetter ground like glass
Reflects a standing gull.

The land may vary more;
But wherever the truth may be—
The water comes ashore,
And the people look at the sea.

They cannot look out far.
They cannot look in deep.
But when was that ever a bar
To any watch they keep?

ROBERT FROST

The Sea Hold

The sea is large.
The sea hold on a leg of land in the Chesapeake hugs an early sunset
    and a last morning star over the oyster beds and the late clam boats
    of lonely men.
Five white houses on a half-mile strip of land ... five white dice rolled
    from a tube.

Not so long ago ... the sea was large ...
And today the sea has lost nothing ... it keeps all.

I am a loon about the sea.
I make so many sea songs, I cry so many sea cries, I forget so many sea
    songs and sea cries.

I am a loon about the sea.
So are five men I had a fish fry with once in a tar-paper shack
    trembling in a sand storm.
The sea knows more about them than they know themselves.
They know only how the sea hugs and will not let go.

The sea is large.
The sea must know more than any of us.

CARL SANDBURG

Young Sea

The sea is never still.
It pounds on the shore
Restless as a young heart,
Hunting.

The sea speaks
And only the stormy hearts
Know what it says:
It is the face
      of a rough mother speaking.

The sea is young.   10
One storm cleans all the hoar
And loosens the age of it.
I hear it laughing, reckless.

They love the sea,
Men who ride on it
And know they will die
Under the salt of it.

Let only the young come,
  Says the sea.
Let them kiss my face   20
  And hear me.
I am the last word
  And I tell
Where storms and stars come from.

CARL SANDBURG

Bones

Sling me under the sea.
Pack me down in the salt and wet.
No farmer's plow shall touch my bones.
No Hamlet hold my jaws and speak
How jokes are gone and empty is my mouth.
Long, green-eyed scavengers shall pick my eyes,
Purple fish play hide-and-seek,
And I shall be song of thunder, crash of sea,
Down on the floors of salt and wet.
      Sling me ... under the sea.

CARL SANDBURG

North Atlantic

When the sea is everywhere
from horizon to horizon ...
  when the salt and blue
  fill a circle of horizons ...
I swear again how I know
the sea is older than anything else
and the sea younger than anything else.

My first father was a landsman.
My tenth father was a sea-lover,
  a gypsy sea-boy, a singer of chanties.   10
  (Oh Blow the Man Down!)

The sea is always the same:
and yet the sea always changes.

    The sea gives all,
    and yet the sea keeps something back.

The sea takes without asking.
The sea is a worker, a thief and a loafer.
    Why does the sea let go so slow?
    Or never let go at all?

    The sea always the same   20
    day after day,
    the sea always the same
    night after night,
    fog on fog and never a star,
    wind on wind and running white sheets,
    bird on bird always a sea-bird—
    so the days get lost:
    it is neither Saturday nor Monday,
    it is any day or no day,
    it is a year, ten years.   30

    Fog on fog and never a star,
    what is a man, a child, a woman,
    to the green and grinding sea?
The ropes and boards squeak and groan.

On the land they know a child they have named Today.
On the sea they know three children they have named:
            Yesterday, Today, Tomorrow.

I made a song to a woman:—it ran:
    I have wanted you.
    I have called to you   40
    on a day I counted a thousand years.

In the deep of a sea-blue noon
many women run in a man's head,
phantom women leaping from a man's forehead
        ... to the railings ... into the sea ... to the
        sea rim ...
        ... a man's mother ... a man's wife ... other
        women ...
I asked a sure-footed sailor how and he said:
    I have known many women but there is only one sea.

I saw the North Star once
and our old friend, The Big Dipper,   50
    only the sea between us:
    "Take away the sea
    and I lift The Dipper,
    swing the handle of it,
    drink from the brim of it."

I saw the North Star one night
and five new stars for me in the rigging ropes,
and seven old stars in the cross of the wireless
            plunging by night,
            plowing by night—   60
Five new cool stars, seven old warm stars.

I have been let down in a thousand graves
            by my kinfolk.
I have been left alone with the sea and the sea's
    wife, the wind, for my last friends
And my kinfolk never knew anything about it at all.

Salt from an old work of eating our graveclothes is here.
    The sea-kin of my thousand graves,
    The sea and the sea's wife, the wind,
They are all here tonight   70
            between the circle of horizons,
            between the cross of the wireless
            and the seven old warm stars.
Out of a thousand sea-holes I came yesterday.
Out of a thousand sea-holes I come tomorrow.

I am kin of the changer.
            I am a son of the sea
            and the sea's wife, the wind.

                          CARL SANDBURG

84

Crossing the Atlantic

We sail out of season into an oyster-gray wind,
over a terrible hardness.
Where Dickens crossed with *mal de mer*
in twenty weeks or twenty days
I cross toward him in five.
Wrapped in robes—
not like Caesar but like liver with bacon—
I rest on the stern
burning my mouth with a wind-hot ash,
watching my ship   10
bypass the swells
as easily as an old woman reads a palm.
I think, as I look North, that a field of mules
lay down to die.

The ship is 27 hours out.
I have entered her.
She might be a whale,
sleeping 2000 and ship's company,
the last 40¢ martini
and steel staterooms where night goes on forever.   20
Being inside them is, I think,
the way one would dig into a planet
and forget the word *light*.
I have walked cities,
miles of mole alleys with carpets.
Inside I have been ten girls who speak French.
They languish everywhere like bedsheets.

Oh my Atlantic of the cracked shores,
those blemished gates of Rockport and Boothbay,
those harbor smells like the innards of animals!   30
Old childish Queen, where did you go,
you bayer at wharfs and Victorian houses?

I have read each page of my mother's voyage.
I have read each page of her mother's voyage.
I have learned their words as they learned Dickens'.
I have swallowed these words like bullets.
But I have forgotten the last guest—terror.
Unlike them, I cannot toss in the cabin
as in childbirth.

Now always leaving me in the West
is the wake,
a ragged bridal veil, unexplained,
seductive, always rushing down the stairs,
never detained, never enough.   40

The ship goes on
as though nothing else were happening.
Generation after generation,
I go her way.
She will run East, knot by knot, over an old bloodstream,
stripping it clear,   50
each hour ripping it, pounding, pounding,
forcing through as through a virgin.
Oh she is so quick!
This dead street never stops!

ANNE SEXTON

The Slow Pacific Swell

Far out of sight forever stands the sea,
Bounding the land with pale tranquillity.
When a small child, I watched it from a hill
At thirty miles or more. The vision still
Lies in the eye, soft blue and far away:
The rain has washed the dust from April day;
Paint-brush and lupine lie against the ground;
The wind above the hill-top has the sound
Of distant water in unbroken sky;
Dark and precise the little steamers ply—   10
Firm in direction they seem not to stir.
That is illusion. The artificer
Of quiet, distance holds me in a vise
And holds the ocean steady to my eyes.

Once when I rounded Flattery,[33] the sea
Hove its loose weight like sand to tangle me
Upon the washing deck, to crush the hull;
Subsiding, dragged flesh at the bone. The skull
Felt the retreating wash of dreaming hair.
Half drenched in dissolution, I lay bare.   20
I scarcely pulled myself erect; I came
Back slowly, slowly knew myself the same.
That was the ocean. From the ship we saw

Gray whales for miles: the long sweep of the jaw,
The blunt head plunging clean above the wave.
And one rose in a tent of sea and gave
A darkening shudder; water fell away;
The whale stood shining, and then sank in spray.

A landsman, I. The sea is but a sound.
I would be near it on a sandy mound,   30
And hear the steady rushing of the deep
While I lay stinging in the sand with sleep.
I have lived inland long. The land is numb.
It stands beneath the feet, and one may come
Walking securely, till the sea extends
Its limber margin, and precision ends.
By night a chaos of commingling power,
The whole Pacific hovers hour by hour.
The slow Pacific swell stirs on the sand,
Sleeping to sink away, withdrawing land,   40
Heaving and wrinkled in the moon, and blind;
Or gathers seaward, ebbing out of mind.

YVOR WINTERS

The Mediterranean

Quem das finem, rex magne, dolorum?[34]

Where we went in the boat was a long bay
A slingshot wide, walled in by towering stone—
Peaked margin of antiquity's delay,
And we went there out of time's monotone:

Where we went in the black hull no light moved
But a gull white-winged along the feckless wave,
The breeze, unseen but fierce as a body loved,
That boat drove onward like a willing slave:

Where we went in the small ship the seaweed
Parted and gave to us the murmuring shore   10
And we made feast and in our secret need
Devoured the very plates Æneas[35] bore:

Where derelict you see through the low twilight
The green coast that you, thunder-tossed, would win,
Drop sail, and hastening to drink all night
Eat dish and bowl—to take that sweet land in!

Where we feasted and caroused on the sandless
Pebbles, affecting our day of piracy,
What prophecy of eaten plates could landless
Wanderers fulfil by the ancient sea?   20

We for that time might taste the famous age
Eternal here yet hidden from our eyes
When lust of power undid its stuffless rage;
They, in a wineskin, bore earth's paradise.

Let us lie down once more by the breathing side
Of Ocean, where our live forefathers sleep
As if the Known Sea still were a month wide—
Atlantis howls but is no longer steep!

What country shall we conquer, what fair land
Unman our conquest and locate our blood?   30
We've cracked the hemispheres with careless hand!
Now, from the Gates of Hercules[36] we flood

Westward, westward till the barbarous brine
Whelms us to the tired land where tasseling corn,
Fat beans, grapes sweeter than muscadine
Rot on the vine: in that land were we born.

                                        ALLEN TATE

Diving into the Wreck

First having read the book of myths,
and loaded the camera,
and checked the edge of the knife-blade,
I put on
the body-armor of black rubber
the absurd flippers
the grave and awkward mask.
I am having to do this
not like Cousteau with his
assiduous team   10
aboard the sun-flooded schooner
but here alone.

There is a ladder.
The ladder is always there
hanging innocently
close to the side of the schooner.
We know what it is for,

88

we who have used it.
otherwise   20
it is a piece of maritime floss
some sundry equipment.

I go down.
Rung after rung and still
the oxygen immerses me
the blue light
the clear atoms
of our human air.
I go down.
My flippers cripple me,
I crawl like an insect down the ladder   30
and there is no one
to tell me when the ocean
will begin.

First the air is blue and then
it is bluer and then green and then
black I am blacking out and yet
my mask is powerful
it pumps my blood with power
the sea is another story
the sea is not a question of power   40
I have to learn alone
to turn my body without force
in the deep element.

And now: it is easy to forget
what I came for
among so many who have always
lived here
swaying their crenellated fans
between the reefs
and besides   50
you breathe differently down here.

I came to explore the wreck.
The words are purposes.
The words are maps.
I came to see the damage that was done
and the treasures that prevail.
I stroke the beam of my lamp
slowly along the flank
of something more permanent
than fish or weed   60

the thing I came for:
the wreck and not the story of the wreck
the thing itself and not the myth
the drowned face always staring
toward the sun
the evidence of damage
worn by salt and sway into this threadbare beauty
the ribs of the disaster
curving their assertion
among the tentative haunters.   70

This is the place.
And I am here, the mermaid whose dark hair
streams black, the merman in his armored body.
We circle silently
about the wreck
we dive into the hold.
I am she; I am he

whose drowned face sleeps with open eyes
whose breasts still bear the stress
whose silver, copper, vermeil cargo lies   80
obscurely inside barrels
half-wedged and left to rot
we are the half-destroyed instruments
that once held to a course
the water-eaten log
the fouled compass

We are, I am, you are
by cowardice or courage
the one who find our way
back to this scene   90
carrying a knife, a camera
a book of myths
in which
our names do not appear.

ADRIENNE RICH

The Diver

Sank through easeful
azure. Flower
creatures flashed and
shimmered there—
lost images
fadingly remembered.
Swiftly descended
into canyon of cold
nightgreen aloneness.
Freefalling, weightless   10
as in dreams of
wingless flight,
plunged through infra-
space and came to the
dead ship,
carcass that swarmed with
voracious life.
Angelfish, their
lively blue and
yellow prised from   20
darkness by the
flashlight's beam,
thronged her portholes.
Moss of bryozoans
blurred, obscured her
metal. Snappers
gold groupers explored her,
fearless of bubbling
manfish. I entered the
wreck, awed by her silence,   30
feeling more keenly
now the iron cold. With
flashlight probing
fogs of water
saw the sad slow
dance of gilded
chairs: the ecto-
plasmic swirl of
garments; drowned   40
instruments of
buoyancy;
drunken shoes. Then

livid gesturings,
eldritch hide and
seek of watching
faces. I yearned to
find those hiding
ones, to fling aside the
mask and call to them,   50
yield to rapturous
whisperings, have
done with self and
every dinning
vain complexity.
Yet in languid
frenzy strove, as
one freezing fights off
sleep desiring sleep;
strove against the
cancelling arms that   60
suddenly surrounded
me, fled the
numbing kisses
that I craved.
Reflex of life-wish?
Regulator's brittle
belling? Swam from the
ship somehow;
somehow began the
measured rise.   70

ROBERT HAYDEN

Full Fathom Five

Old man, you surface seldom.
Then you come in with the tide's coming
When seas wash cold, foam-

Capped: white hair, white beard, far-flung,
A dragnet, rising, falling, as waves
Crest and trough. Miles long

Extend the radial sheaves
Of your spread hair, in which wrinkling skeins
Knotted, caught, survives

The old myth of origins
Unimaginable. You float near
As keeled ice-mountains

Of the north, to be steered clear
Of, not fathomed. All obscurity
Starts with a danger:

Your dangers are many. I
Cannot look much but your form suffers
Some strange injury

And seems to die: so vapors
Ravel to clearness on the dawn sea.
The muddy rumors

Of your burial move me
To half-believe: your reappearance
Proves rumors shallow,

For the archaic trenched lines
Of your grained face shed time in runnels:
Ages beat like rains

On the unbeaten channels
Of the ocean. Such sage humor and
Durance are whirlpools

To make away with the ground-
Work of the earth and the sky's ridgepole.
Waist down, you may wind

One labyrinthine tangle
To root deep among knuckles, shinbones,
Skulls. Inscrutable,

Below shoulders not once
Seen by any man who kept his head,
You defy questions;

You defy other godhood.
I walk dry on your kingdom's border
Exiled to no good.

Your shelled bed I remember.
Father, this thick air is murderous.
I would breathe water.

SYLVIA PLATH

The Quaker Graveyard in Nantucket

(For Warren Winslow, Dead at Sea)

*Let man have dominion over the fishes of the sea and the fowls of the air
and the beasts and the whole earth, and every creeping creature that moveth
upon the earth.*

I

A brackish reach of shoal off Madaket,[37]—
The sea was still breaking violently and night
Had steamed into our North Atlantic Fleet,
When the drowned sailor clutched the drag-net. Light
Flashed from his matted head and marble feet,
He grappled at the net
With the coiled, hurdling muscles of his thighs:
The corpse was bloodless, a botch of reds and whites,
Its open, staring eyes
Were lustreless dead-lights   10
Or cabin-windows on a stranded hulk
Heavy with sand. We weight the body, close
Its eyes and heave it seaward whence it came,
Where the heel-headed dogfish barks its nose
On Ahab's[38] void and forehead; and the name
Is blocked in yellow chalk.
Sailors, who pitch this portent at the sea
Where dreadnaughts shall confess
Its hell-bent deity,
When you are powerless   20
To sand-bag this Atlantic bulwark, faced
By the earth-shaker, green, unwearied, chaste
In his steel scales: ask for no Orphean[39] lute
To pluck life back. The guns of the steeled fleet
Recoil and then repeat
The hoarse salute.

II

Whenever winds are moving and their breath
Heaves at the roped-in bulwarks of this pier,
The terns and sea-gulls tremble at your death
In these home waters. Sailor, can you hear   30
The Pequod's sea wings, beating landward, fall
Headlong and break on our Atlantic wall

94

Off 'Sconset,[40] where the yawing S-boats splash
The bellbuoy, with ballooning spinnakers,
As the entangled, screeching mainsheet clears
The blocks: off Madaket, where lubbers lash
The heavy surf and throw their long lead squids
For blue-fish? Sea-gulls blink their heavy lids
Seaward. The winds' wings beat upon the stones,
Cousin, and scream for you and the claws rush   40
At the sea's throat and wring it in the slush
Of this old Quaker graveyard where the bones
Cry out in the long night for the hurt beast
Bobbing by Ahab's whaleboats in the East.

III

All you recovered from Poseidon died
With you, my cousin, and the harrowed brine
Is fruitless on the blue beard of the god,
Stretching beyond us to the castles in Spain,
Nantucket's westward haven. To Cape Cod
Guns, cradled on the tide,   50
Blast the eelgrass about a waterclock
Of bilge and backwash, roil the salt and sand
Lashing earth's scaffold, rock
Our warships in the hand
Of the great God, where time's contrition blues
Whatever it was these Quaker sailors lost
In the mad scramble of their lives. They died
When time was open-eyed,
Wooden and childish; only bones abide
There, in the nowhere, where their boats were tossed   60
Sky-high, where mariners had fabled news
Of IS, the whited monster. What it cost
Them is their secret. In the sperm-whale's slick
I see the Quakers drown and hear their cry:
"If God himself had not been on our side,
If God himself had not been on our side,
When the Atlantic rose against us, why,
Then it had swallowed us up quick."

IV

This is the end of the whaleroad and the whale
Who spewed Nantucket bones on the thrashed swell   70

95

And stirred the troubled waters to whirlpools
To send the Pequod packing off to hell:
This is the end of them, three-quarters fools,
Snatching at straws to sail
Seaward and seaward on the turntail whale,
Spouting out blood and water as it rolls,
Sick as a dog to these Atlantic shoals:
Clamavimus,[41] O depths. Let the sea-gulls wail
For water, for the deep where the high tide
Mutters to its hurt self, mutters and ebbs.   80
Waves wallow in their wash, go out and out,
Leave only the death-rattle of the crabs,
The beach increasing, its enormous snout
Sucking the ocean's side.
This is the end of running on the waves;
We are poured out like water. Who will dance
The mast-lashed master of Leviathans
Up from this field of Quakers in their unstoned graves?

V

When the whale's viscera go and the roll
Of its corruption overruns this world   90
Beyond tree-swept Nantucket and Wood's Hole
And Martha's Vineyard,[42] Sailor, will your sword
Whistle and fall and sink into the fat?
In the great ash-pit of Jehoshaphat[43]
The bones cry for the blood of the white whale,
The fat flukes arch and whack about its ears,
The death-lance churns into the sanctuary, tears
The gun-blue swingle, heaving like a flail,
And hacks the coiling life out: it works and drags
And rips the sperm-whale's midriff into rags,   100
Gobbets of blubber spill to wind and weather,
Sailor, and gulls go round the stoven timbers
Where the morning stars sing out together
And thunder shakes the white surf and dismembers
The red flag hammered in the mast-head. Hide,
Our steel, Jonas Messias,[44] in Thy side.

VI

OUR LADY OF WALSINGHAM[45]

There once the penitents took off their shoes

96

And then walked barefoot the remaining mile;
And the small trees, a stream and hedgerows file
Slowly along the munching English lane,   110
Like cows to the old shrine, until you lose
Track of your dragging pain.
The stream flows down under the druid tree,
Shiloah's[46] whirlpools gurgle and make glad
The castle of God. Sailor, you were glad
And whistled Sion[47] by that stream. But see:
Our Lady, too small for her canopy,
Sits near the altar. There's no comeliness
At all or charm in that expressionless
Face with its heavy eyelids. As before,   120
This face, for centuries a memory,
Non est species, neque decor,[48]
Expressionless, expresses God: it goes
Past castled Sion. She knows what God knows,
Not Calvary's Cross nor crib at Bethlehem
Now, and the world shall come to Walsingham.

VII

The empty winds are creaking and the oak
Splatters and splatters on the cenotaph,
The boughs are trembling and a gaff
Bobs on the untimely stroke   130
Of the greased wash exploding on a shoal-bell
In the old mouth of the Atlantic. It's well;
Atlantic, you are fouled with the blue sailors,
Sea-monsters, upward angel, downward fish:
Unmarried and corroding, spare of flesh
Mart once of supercilious, winged clippers,
Atlantic, where your bell-trap guts its spoil
You could cut the brackish winds with a knife
Here in Nantucket, and cast up the time
When the Lord God formed man from the sea's slime   140
And breathed into his face the breath of life,
And blue-lunged combers lumbered to the kill.
The Lord survives the rainbow of His will.

ROBERT LOWELL

97

Tales of the Sea

ONE OF THE MOST IMPORTANT LEGACIES of the classical tradition in literature is the narrative form of poetry. Some of the earliest extant verse was apparently written for the primary purpose of telling a tale. Whereas lyric poems often focus on a single point in time, the narrative usually has a beginning, a middle, and an end, and progresses in chronological order. As a result, narratives tend to be longer than lyrics and are often cast in the form of epics or ballads. Subjects for classic sea narratives include the sailor, separation from loved ones, storms and shipwrecks, and naval battles.

The sailors who appear in such poetry range all the way from the simple Breton seaman in Robert Browning's *Hervé Riel* to the dauntless admiral in Joaquin Miller's popular *Columbus*. In *John Winter,* Laurence Binyon uses the ballad stanza to tell how a sailor finds the lure of the sea more powerful than that of family life ashore. On the other hand, the narrator in Robert Louis Stevenson's *Christmas at Sea* longs for the companionship of his family when he finds himself at sea during yuletide. In his dramatic narrative, *Black-Eyed Susan,* John Gay depicts the sorrows of a sailor taking leave of his sweetheart; however, Gay's seaman tells his love, "We only part to meet again," a theme also explored by Browning in *Meeting at Night* and *Parting at Morning.*

It should come as no surprise that a sailor's loved ones looked upon his departures with no little trepidation. An awareness of the dangers of a life at sea is revealed by the large number of poems written about storms and shipwrecks. John Donne's *The Storme* tells what it feels like to be battered about by the sea, and the ferocity of the tempest described is heightened when contrasted with the serenity of *The Calme.* Yet, while the sea may be Janus-faced, it is not malevolent; rather, it is chillingly indifferent. With baffling inconsistency, it claims a life in one instance and spares a life in the next. Thus, the son of Alec Yeaton in Thomas Bailey Aldrich's poem and the daughter of the skipper of Henry Wadsworth Longfellow's schooner *Hesperus* are placed in practically identical circumstances, but come to antipodal ends.

Perhaps more sea poems deal with naval battles than with any other subject. Indeed, it almost seems as if having a commemorative poem written was at one time the final step in most battle plans. As a result, we have a plethora of narratives memorializing naval battles, many of which, however, are by minor poets, and, while full of genuine emotion, tend to be short on literary merit. Therefore, only well-written examples of the genre are included here, such as *The Night of Trafalgar* by Thomas Hardy and Walt Whitman's *The Battle of the* Bonhomme Richard *and the* Serapis.

Finally, we have included in this chapter a poem that saved a ship. *Old Ironsides* was written by a youthful Oliver Wendell Holmes after he read about plans to scrap the frigate *Constitution*. In a matter of days the poem was reprinted in newspapers across the country and in broadsides, and it aroused the public sentiment that led to the preservation of what is today the oldest warship afloat in any navy in the world.

From *The Canterbury Tales*
General Prologue—The Shipman
Lines 390–412

A Shipman was ther, woning° fer by weste—	dwelling
For ought I woot,° he was of Dertemouthe.[1]	know
He rood upon a rouncy° as he couthe,	large nag
In a gowne of falding° to the knee.	heavy wool
A daggere hanging on a laas° hadde he	strap
Aboute his nekke, under his arm adown.	
The hote somer hadde maad his hewe° al brown;	color
And certainly he was a good felawe.	
Ful many a draughte of win hadde he drawe	
Fro Burdeuxward,[2] whil that the chapman sleep:	
Of nice° conscience took he no keep;°	fastidious/heed 400
If that he faught and hadde the hyer hand,	
By water he sente hem hoom to every land.	
But of his craft, to rekene wel his tides,	
His stremes and his daungers him bisides,	
His herbewe° and his moone, his lodemenage,°	anchorage/pilotage
There was noon swich from Hulle to Cartage.[3]	
Hardy he was and wis to undertake;	
With many a tempest hadde his beerd been shake;	
He knew alle the havenes as they were	
Fro Gotlond to the Cape of Finistere,[4]	410
And every crike in Britaine and in Spaine.	
His barge ycleped was the Maudeline.°	Magdalene

GEOFFREY CHAUCER

Sir Patrick Spens

The king sits in Dumferline town,
 Drinking the blude-reid° wine: blood-red
"O whar will I get a guid sailor
 To sail this ship of mine?"

Up and spak an eldern° knicht,   ancient
 Sat at the king's richt knee:
"Sir Patrick Spens is the best sailor
 That sails upon the sea."

The king has written a braid° letter   broad 10
 And signed it wi' his hand,
And sent it to Sir Patrick Spens,
 Was walking on the sand.

The first line that Sir Patrick read,
 A loud lauch° lauched he;   laugh
The next line that Sir Patrick read,
 The tear blinded his ee.°   eye

"O wha° is this has done this deed,   who
 This ill deed done to me,
To send me out this time o' the year,   20
 To sail upon the sea?

"Make haste, make haste, my mirry men all,
 Our guid ship sails the morn."
"O say na sae,° my master dear,   not so
 For I fear a deadly storm.

"Late late yestre'en I saw the new moon
 Wi' the auld moon in her arm,
And I fear, I fear, my dear master,
 That we will come to harm."

O our Scots nobles were richt laith°   loath
 To weet° their cork-heeled shoon,°   wet/shoes 30
But lang owre° a' the play were played   ere
 Their hats they swam aboon.°   above

O lang, lang may their ladies sit,
 Wi' their fans into their hand,
Or e'er they see Sir Patrick Spens
 Come sailing to the land.

O lang, lang may the ladies stand,
 Wi' their gold kembs° in their hair,   combs

Waiting for their ain° dear lords,   own
  For they'll see thame na mair.°   more

Half o'er, half o'er to Aberdour
  It's fifty fadom° deep,   fathoms
And there lies guid Sir Patrick Spens,
  Wi' the Scots lords at his feet.

ANONYMOUS

From *Henry V*
Prologue to Act III
Lines 3–17

               ... Suppose that you have seen
The well-appointed King at Hampton pier
Embark his royalty, and his brave fleet
With silken streamers the young Phoebus[5] fanning.
Play with your fancies, and in them behold
Upon the hempen tackle ship boys climbing.
Hear the shrill whistle which doth order give
To sounds confused. Behold the threaden sails,
Borne with the invisible and creeping wind,
Draw the huge bottoms through the furrowed sea,
Breasting the lofty surge. Oh, do but think
You stand upon the rivage° and behold   shore
A city on the inconstant billows dancing,
For so appears this fleet majestical,
Holding due course to Harfleur.[6]

WILLIAM SHAKESPEARE

From *Annus Mirabilis*
Digression Concerning Shipping and Navigation
Lines 617–656

By viewing Nature, Natures Hand-maid, Art,
  Makes mighty things from small beginnings grow:
Thus fishes first to shipping did impart
  Their tail the Rudder, and their head the Prow.   620

Some Log, perhaps, upon the waters swam
  An useless drift, which, rudely cut within,
And hollow'd, first a floating trough became,
  And cross some Riv'let passage did begin.

In shipping such as this the *Irish Kern,*
   And untaught *Indian,* on the stream did glide:
Ere sharp-keel'd Boats to stem the floud did learn,
   Or fin-like Oars did spread from either side.

Adde but a Sail, and *Saturn* so appear'd,
   When, from lost Empire, he to Exile went,   630
And with the Golden age to *Tyber*[7] steer'd,
   Where Coin & first Commerce he did invent.

Rude as their Ships was Navigation, then;
   No useful Compass or Meridian known:
Coasting, they kept the Land within their ken,°   sight
   And knew no North but when the Pole-star shone.

Of all who since have us'd the open Sea,
   Then the bold *English* none more fame have won:
Beyond the Year, and out of Heav'ns high-way,
   They make discoveries where they see no Sun.   640

But what so long in vain, and yet unknown,
   By poor man-kinds benighted wit is sought,
Shall in this Age to *Britain* first be shown,
   And hence be to admiring Nations taught.

The Ebbs of Tydes, and their mysterious flow,
   We, as Arts Elements shall understand:
And as by Line upon the Ocean go,
   Whose paths shall be familiar as the Land.

Instructed ships shall sail to quick Commerce;
   By which remotest Regions are alli'd: 650
Which makes one City of the Universe,
   Where some may gain, and all may be suppli'd.

Then, we upon our Globes last verge shall go,
   And view the Ocean leaning on the sky:
From thence our rolling Neighbours we shall know,
   And on the Lunar world securely pry.

                                          JOHN DRYDEN

The Storme

Thou which art I, ('tis nothing to be soe)
Thou which art still thy selfe, by these shalt know
Part of our passage; And, a hand, or eye
By *Hilliard*[8] drawne, is worth an history,
By a worse painter made; and (without pride)
When by thy judgment they are dignifi'd,
My lines are such. 'Tis the preheminence
Of friendship onely to'impute excellence.
England to whom we'owe, what we be, and have,
Sad that her sonnes did seeke a forraine° grave   foreign 10
(For, Fates, or Fortunes drifts none can soothsay,
Honour and misery have one face and way.)
From out her pregnant intrailes sigh'd a winde
Which at th'ayres middle marble roome did finde
Such strong resistance, that it selfe it threw
Downeward againe; and so when it did view
How in the port, our fleet deare time did leese,°   lose
Withering like prisoners, which lye but for fees,
Mildly it kist our sailes, and, fresh, and sweet,
As, to a stomack sterv'd, whose insides meete,   20
Meate comes, it came; and swole our sailes, when wee
So joyd, as *Sara*'her swelling joy'd to see.[9]
But 'twas but so kinde, as our countrimen,
Which bring friends one dayes way, and leave them then.
Then like two mighty Kings, which dwelling farre
Asunder, meet against a third to warre,
The South and West winds joyn'd, and, as they blew,
Waves like a rowling trench before them threw.
Sooner then you read this line, did the gale,
Like shot, not fear'd, till felt, our sailes assaile;   30
And what at first was call'd a gust, the same
Hath now a stormes, anon a tempests name.
Ionas, I pitty thee, and curse those men,
Who when the storm rag'd most, did wake thee[10] then;
Sleepe is paines easiest salve, and doth fullfill
All offices of death, except to kill.
But when I wakt, I saw, that I saw not.
I, and the Sunne, which should teach mee'had forgot
East, West, day, night, and I could onely say,
If'the world had lasted, now it had beene day.   40
Thousands our noyses were, yet wee 'mongst all
Could none by his right name, but thunder call:

Lightning was all our light, and it rain'd more
Then if the Sunne had drunke the sea before;
Some coffin'd in their cabbins lye,'equally
Griev'd that they are not dead, and yet must dye.
And as sin-burd'ned soules from graves will creepe,
At the last day, some forth their cabbins peepe:
And tremblingly'aske what newes, and doe heare so,
Like jealous husbands, what they would not know.   50
Some sitting on the hatches, would seeme there,
With hideous gazing to feare away feare.
Then note they the ships sicknesses, the Mast
Shak'd with this ague, and the Hold and Wast¹¹
With a salt dropsie° clog'd, and all our tacklings   water
Snapping, like too-high-stretched treble strings.
And from our totterd° sailes, ragges drop downe so,   tattered
As from one hang'd in chaines, a yeare agoe.
Even our Ordinance plac'd for our defence,
Strive to breake loose, and scape away from thence.   60
Pumping hath tir'd our men, and what's the gaine?
Seas into seas throwne, we suck in againe;
Hearing hath deaf'd our saylers; and if they
Knew how to heare, there's none knowes what to say.
Compar'd to these stormes, death is but a qualme,
Hell somewhat lightsome, and the'Bermuda calme.
Darknesse, lights elder brother, his birth-right
Claims o'r this world, and to heaven hath chas'd light.
All things are one, and that one none can be,
Since all formes, uniforme deformity   70
Doth cover, so that wee, except God say
Another *Fiat,*¹² shall have no more day.
So violent, yet long these furies bee,
That though thine absence sterve me,'I wish not thee.

                                          JOHN DONNE

104

The Calme

Our storme is past, and that storms tyrannous rage,
A stupid calme, but nothing it, doth swage.
The fable[13] is inverted, and farre more
A blocke afflicts, now, then a storke before.
Stormes chafe, and soone weare out themselves, or us;
In calmes, Heaven laughs to see us languish thus.
As steady'as I can wish, that my thoughts were,
Smooth as thy mistresse glasse, or what shines there,
The sea is now. And, as the Iles which wee
Seeke, when wee can move, our ships rooted bee.   10
As water did in stormes, now pitch runs out
As lead, when a fir'd Church becomes one spout.
And all our beauty, and our trimme, decayes,
Like courts removing, or like ended playes.
The fighting place now seamens ragges supply;
And all the tackling is a frippery.[14]
No use of lanthornes;° and in one place lay   lanterns
Feathers and dust, to day and yesterday.
Earths hollownesses, which the worlds lungs are,
Have no more winde then the'upper valt of aire.   20
We can nor lost friends, nor sought foes recover,
But meteorlike, save that wee move not, hover.
Onely the Calenture° together drawes   delirium
Deare friends, which meet dead in great fishes jawes:
And on the hatches as on Altars lyes
Each one, his owne Priest, and owne Sacrifice.
Who live, that miracle do multiply
Where walkers in hot Ovens,[15] doe not dye.
If in despite of these, wee swimme, that hath
No more refreshing, then our brimstone Bath,   30
But from the sea, into the ship we turne,
Like parboyl'd wretches, on the coales to burne.
Like *Bajazet*[16] encag'd, the sheepheards scoffe,
Or like slacke sinew'd *Sampson,*[17] his haire off,
Languish our ships. Now, as a Miriade
Of Ants, durst th'Emperours lov'd snake invade,[18]
The crawling Gallies, Sea-gaoles, finny chips,
Might brave our Pinnaces,[19] now bed-ridde ships.
Whether a rotten state, and hope of gaine,
Or, to disuse mee° from the queasie paine   separate myself 40
Of being belov'd, and loving, or the thirst

105

Of honour, or faire death, out pusht mee first,
I lose my end: for here as well as I
A desperate may live, and a coward die.
Stagge, dogge, and all which from, or towards flies,
Is paid with life, or pray, or doing dyes.
Fate grudges us all, and doth subtly lay
A scourge, 'gainst which wee all forget to pray,
He that at sea prayes for more winde, as well
Under the poles may begge cold, heat in hell.   50
What are wee then? How little more alas
Is man now, then before he was? he was
Nothing; for us, wee are for nothing fit;
Chance, or our selves still disproportion it.
Wee have no power, no will, no sense; I lye,
I should not then thus feele this miserie.

JOHN DONNE

From *The Shipwreck*
Canto II
Lines 142–185

Four hours the sun his high meridian throne
Had left, and o'er Atlantic regions shone.
Still blacker clouds, that all the skies invade,
Draw o'er his sullied orb a dismal shade:
A lowering squall obscures the southern sky,
Before whose sweeping breath the waters fly.
Its weight the top-sails can no more sustain—
Reef top-sails, reef! the master calls again.
The halyards and top-bow-lines soon are gone,   150
To clue-lines and reef-tackles next they run:
The shivering sails descend; the yards are square;
Then quick aloft the ready crew repair:
The weather-earings and the lee they past,
The reefs enroll'd, and every point made fast.
Their task above thus finished, they descend,
And vigilant the approaching squall attend.
It comes resistless! and with foaming sweep
Upturns the whitening surface of the deep:
In such a tempest, borne to deeds of death,   160
The wayward sisters scour the blasted heath.
The clouds, with ruin pregnant, now impend,
And storm and cataracts tumultuous blend.

Deep on her side the reeling vessel lies:
Brail up the mizzen quick! the master cries,
Man the clue-garnets! let the main-sheet fly!
It rends in thousand shivering shreds on high!
The main-sail all in streaming ruins tore,
Loud fluttering, imitates the thunder's roar:
The ship still labours in the oppressive strain,   170
Low bending, as if ne'er to rise again.
Bear up the helm a-weather! Rodmond cries:
Swift at the word the helm a-weather flies;
She feels its guiding power, and veers apace,
And now the fore-sail right athwart they brace:
With equal sheets restrain'd, the bellying sail
Spreads a broad concave to the sweeping gale.
While o'er the foam the ship impetuous flies,
The helm the attentive timoneer applies:
As in pursuit along the aërial way   180
With ardent eye the falcon marks his prey,
Each motion watches of the doubtful chase,
Obliquely wheeling through the fluid space;
So, govern'd by the steersman's glowing hands,
The regent helm her motion still commands.

Lines 236–338

As the proud horse with costly trappings gay,
Exulting, prances to the bloody fray;
Spurning the ground he glories in his might,
But reels tumultuous in the shock of fight;
E'en so, caparison'd in gaudy pride,   240
The bounding vessel dances on the tide.
   Fierce and more fierce the gathering tempest grew;
South, and by west, the threatening demon blew;
Auster's resistless force all air invades,
And every rolling wave more ample spreads.
The ship no longer can her top-sails bear;
No hopes of milder weather now appear.
Bow-lines and halyards are cast off again,
Clue-lines haul'd down, and sheets let fly amain:
Embrail'd each top-sail, and by braces squared,   250
The seamen climb aloft, and man each yard.
They furl'd the sails, and pointed to the wind
The yards, by rolling tackles then confined,
While o'er the ship the gallant boatswain flies;

Like a hoarse mastiff through the storm he cries,
Prompt to direct the unskilful still appears,
The expert he praises, and the timid cheers.
Now some, to strike top-gallant-yards attend,
Some, travellers up the weather-back-stays send,
At each mast-head the top-ropes others bend: 260
The parrels, lifts, and clue-lines soon are gone,
Topp'd and unrigg'd, they down the back-stays run;
The yards secure along the booms were laid,
And all the flying ropes aloft belay'd.
Their sails reduced, and all the rigging clear,
Awhile the crew relax from toils severe;
Awhile their spirits with fatigue opprest,
In vain expect the alternate hour of rest.
But with redoubling force the tempests blow,
And watery hills in dread succession flow: 270
A dismal shade o'ercasts the frowning skies;
New troubles grow, fresh difficulties rise;
No season this from duty to descend;
All hands on deck must now the storm attend.
     His race perform'd, the sacred lamp of day
Now dipt in western clouds his parting ray:
His languid fires, half lost in ambient haze,
Refract along the dusk a crimson blaze;
Till deep immerged the sickening orb descends,
And cheerless night o'er heaven her reign extends: 280
Sad evening's hour, how different from the past!
No flaming pomp, no blushing glories cast,
No ray of friendly light is seen around;
The moon and stars in hopeless shade are drown'd.
     The ship no longer can whole courses bear,
To reef them now becomes the master's care;
The sailors, summon'd aft, all ready stand,
And man the enfolding brails at his command.
But here the doubtful officers dispute,
Till skill, and judgment, prejudice confute: 290
For Rodmond, to new methods still a foe,
Would first, at all events, the sheet let go;
To long-tried practice obstinately warm,
He doubts conviction, and relies on form.
This Albert and Arion disapprove,
And first to brail the tack up firmly move:
"The watchful seaman, whose sagacious eye
On sure experience may with truth rely,

Who from the reigning cause foretells the effect,
This barbarous practice ever will reject;   300
For, fluttering loose in air, the rigid sail
Soon flits to ruins in the furious gale;
And he who strives the tempest to disarm,
Will never first embrail the lee yard-arm."
So Albert spoke; to windward, at his call,
Some seamen the clue-garnet stand to haul;
The tack's eased off, while the involving clue
Between the pendent blocks ascending flew.
The sheet and weather-brace they now stand by,
The lee clue-garnet and the bunt-lines ply: 310
Then, all prepared, Let go the sheet! he cries—
Loud rattling, jarring, through the blocks it flies!
Shivering at first, till by the blast impell'd,
High o'er the lee yard-arm the canvas swell'd;
By spilling lines embraced, with brails confined,
It lies at length unshaken by the wind.
The fore-sail then secured with equal care,
Again to reef the main-sail they repair;
While some above the yard o'er-haul the tye,
Below, the down-haul tackle others ply;   320
Jears, lifts, and brails, a seaman each attends,
And down the mast its mighty yard descends.
When lower'd sufficient they securely brace,
And fix the rolling tackle in its place;
The reef-lines and their earings now prepared,
Mounting on pliant shrouds they man the yard.
Far on the extremes appear two able hands,
For no inferior skill this task demands:
To windward, foremost, young Arion strides,
The lee yard-arm the gallant boatswain rides.   330
Each earing to its cringle first they bend,
The reef-band then along the yard extend;
The circling earings round the extremes entwined,
By outer and by inner turns they bind;
The reef-lines next from hand to hand received,
Through eyelet-holes and roban-legs were reeved;
The folding reefs in plaits inroll'd they lay,
Extend the worming lines, and ends belay.

                          WILLIAM FALCONER

109

The Castaway

Obscurest night involved the sky,
   The Atlantic billows roared,
When such a destined wretch as I,
Washed headlong from on board,
Of friends, of hope, of all bereft,
His floating home forever left.

No braver chief could Albion[20] boast
   Than he with whom he went,
Nor ever ship left Albion's coast,
   With warmer wishes sent.   10
He loved them both, but both in vain,
Nor him beheld, nor her again.

Not long beneath the whelming brine,
   Expert to swim, he lay;
Nor soon he felt his strength decline,
   Or courage die away;
But waged with death a lasting strife,
Supported by despair of life.

He shouted; nor his friends had failed
   To check the vessel's course,   20
But so the furious blast prevailed,
   That, pitiless perforce,
They left their outcast mate behind,
And scudded still before the wind.

Some succor yet they could afford;
   And, such as storms allow,
The cask, the coop, the floated cord,
   Delayed not to bestow.
But he (they knew) nor ship, nor shore,   30
Whate'er they gave, should visit more.

Nor, cruel as it seemed, could he
   Their haste himself condemn,
Aware that flight, in such a sea,
   Alone could rescue them;
Yet bitter felt it still to die
Deserted, and his friends so nigh.

He long survives, who lives an hour
   In ocean, self-upheld;
And so long he, with unspent power,   40
   His destiny repelled;

And ever, as the minutes flew,
Entreated help, or cried, "Adieu!"

At length, his transient respite past,
    His comrades, who before
Had heard his voice in every blast,
    Could catch the sound no more.
For then, by toil subdued, he drank
The stifling wave, and then he sank.

No poet wept him; but the page   50
    Of narrative sincere,
That tells his name, his worth, his age,
    Is wet with Anson's tear.
And tears by bards or heroes shed
Alike immortalize the dead.

I therefore purpose not, or dream,
    Descanting on his fate,
To give the melancholy theme
    A more enduring date:
But misery still delights to trace   60
Its semblance in another's case.

No voice divine the storm allayed,
    No light propitious shone,
When, snatched from all effectual aid,
    We perished, each alone;
But I beneath a rougher sea,
And whelmed in deeper gulfs than he.

WILLIAM COWPER

A Vision of the Sea

'Tis the terror of tempest. The rags of the sail
Are flickering in ribbons within the fierce gale:
From the stark night of vapours the dim rain is driven,
And when lightning is loosed, like a deluge from Heaven,
She sees the black trunks of the waterspouts spin
And bend, as if Heaven was ruining in,
Which they seemed to sustain with their terrible mass
As if ocean had sunk from beneath them: they pass
To their graves in the deep with an earthquake of sound,
And the waves and the thunders, made silent around,   10

Leave the wind to its echo. The vessel, now tossed
Through the low-trailing rack of the tempest, is lost
In the skirts of the thunder-cloud: now down the sweep
Of the wind-cloven wave to the chasm of the deep
It sinks, and the walls of the watery vale
Whose depths of dread calm are unmoved by the gale,
Dim mirrors of ruin, hang gleaming about;
While the surf, like a chaos of stars, like a rout
Of death-flames, like whirlpools of fire-flowing iron,
With splendour and terror the black ship environ,   20
Or like sulphur-flakes hurled from a mine of pale fire
In fountains spout o'er it. In many a spire
The pyramid-billows with white points of brine
In the cope of the lightning inconstantly shine,
As piercing the sky from the floor of the sea.
The great ship seems splitting! it cracks as a tree,
While an earthquake is splintering its root, ere the blast
Of the whirlwind that stripped it of branches has passed.
The intense thunder-balls which are raining from Heaven
Have shattered its mast, and it stands black and riven.   30
The chinks suck destruction. The heavy dead hulk
On the living sea rolls an inanimate bulk,
Like a corpse on the clay which is hungering to fold
Its corruption around it. Meanwhile, from the hold,
One deck is burst up by the waters below,
And it splits like the ice when the thaw-breezes blow
O'er the lakes of the desert! Who sit on the other?
Is that all the crew that lie burying each other,
Like the dead in a breach, round the foremast? Are those
Twin tigers, who burst, when the waters arose,   40
In the agony of terror, their chains in the hold;
(What now makes them tame, is what then made them bold;)
Who crouch, side by side, and have driven, like a crank,
The deep grip of their claws through the vibrating plank:—
Are these all? Nine weeks the tall vessel had lain
On the windless expanse of the watery plain,
Where the death-darting sun cast no shadow at noon,
And there seemed to be fire in the beams of the moon,
Till a lead-coloured fog gathered up from the deep,
Whose breath was quick pestilence; then, the cold sleep   50
Crept, like blight through the ears of a thick field of corn,
O'er the populous vessel. And even and morn,
With their hammocks for coffins the seamen aghast
Like dead men the dead limbs of their comrades cast

Down the deep, which closed on them above and around,
And the sharks and the dogfish their grave-clothes unbound,
And were glutted like Jews with this manna rained down
From God on their wilderness.²¹ One after one
The mariners died; on the eve of this day,
When the tempest was gathering in cloudy array,   60
But seven remained. Six the thunder has smitten,
And they lie black as mummies on which Time has written
His scorn of the embalmer; the seventh, from the deck
An oak-splinter pierced through his breast and his back,
And hung out to the tempest, a wreck on the wreck.
No more? At the helm sits a woman more fair
Than Heaven, when, unbinding its star-braided hair,
It sinks with the sun on the earth and the sea.
She clasps a bright child on her upgathered knee;
It laughs at the lightning, it mocks the mixed thunder   70
Of the air and the sea, with desire and with wonder
It is beckoning the tigers to rise and come near,
It would play with those eyes where the radiance of fear
Is outshining the meteors; its bosom beats high,
The heart-fire of pleasure has kindled its eye,
While its mother's is lustreless. 'Smile not, my child,
But sleep deeply and sweetly, and so be beguiled
Of the pang that awaits us, whatever that be,
So dreadful since thou must divide it with me!
Dream, sleep! This pale bosom, thy cradle and bed,   80
Will it rock thee not, infant? 'Tis beating with dread!
Alas! what is life, what is death, what are we,
That when the ship sinks we no longer may be?
What! to see thee no more, and to feel thee no more?
To be after life what we have been before?
Not to touch those sweet hands? Not to look on those eyes,
Those lips, and that hair,—all the smiling disguise
Thou yet wearest, sweet Spirit, which I, day by day,
Have so long called my child, but which now fades away
Like a rainbow, and I the fallen shower?'—Lo! the ship   90
Is settling, it topples, the leeward ports dip;
The tigers leap up when they feel the slow brine
Crawling inch by inch on them; hair, ears, limbs, and eyne,
Stand rigid with horror; a loud, long, hoarse cry
Bursts at once from their vitals tremendously,
And 'tis borne down the mountainous vale of the wave,
Rebounding, like thunder, from crag to cave,
Mixed with the clash of the lashing rain,

Hurried on by the might of the hurricane:
The hurricane came from the west, and passed on 100
By the path of the gate of the eastern sun,
Transversely dividing the stream of the storm;
As an arrowy serpent, pursuing the form
Of an elephant, bursts through the brakes of the waste.
Black as a cormorant the screaming blast,
Between Ocean and Heaven, like an ocean, passed,
Till it came to the clouds on the verge of the world
Which, based on the sea and to Heaven upcurled,
Like columns and walls did surround and sustain
The dome of the tempest; it rent them in twain, 110
As a flood rends its barriers of mountainous crag:
And the dense clouds in many a ruin and rag,
Like the stones of a temple ere earthquake has passed,
Like the dust of its fall, on the whirlwind are cast;
They are scattered like foam on the torrent; and where
The wind has burst out through the chasm, from the air
Of clear morning the beams of the sunrise flow in,
Unimpeded, keen, golden, and crystalline,
Banded armies of light and of air, at one gate
They encounter, but interpenetrate. 120
And that breach in the tempest is widening away,
And the caverns of cloud are torn up by the day,
And the fierce winds are sinking with weary wings,
Lulled by the motion and murmurings
And the long glassy heave of the rocking sea,
And overhead glorious, but dreadful to see,
The wrecks of the tempest, like vapours of gold,
Are consuming in sunrise. The heaped waves behold
The deep calm of blue Heaven dilating above,
And, like passions made still by the presence of Love, 130
Beneath the clear surface reflecting it slide
Tremulous with soft influence; extending its tide
From the Andes to Atlas, round mountain and isle,
Round sea-birds and wrecks, paved with Heaven's azure smile,
The wide world of waters is vibrating. Where
Is the ship? On the verge of the wave where it lay
One tiger is mingled in ghastly affray
With a sea-snake. The foam and the smoke of the battle
Stain the clear air with sunbows: the jar, and the rattle
Of solid bones crushed by the infinite stress 140
Of the snake's adamantine voluminousness;
And the hum of the hot blood that spouts and rains

Where the gripe of the tiger has wounded the veins
Swollen with rage, strength, and effort; the whirl and the splash
As of some hideous engine whose brazen teeth smash
The thin winds and soft waves into thunder; the screams
And hissings crawl fast o'er the smooth ocean-streams,
Each sound like a centipede. Near this commotion,
A blue shark is hanging within the blue ocean,
The fin-wingèd tomb of the victor. The other   150
Is winning his way from the fate of his brother
To his own with the speed of despair. Lo! a boat
Advances: twelve rowers with the impulse of thought
Urge on the keen keel,—the brine foams. At the stern
Three marksmen stand levelling. Hot bullets burn
In the breast of the tiger, which yet bears him on
To his refuge and ruin. One fragment alone,—
'Tis dwindling and sinking, 'tis now almost gone,—
Of the wreck of the vessel peers out of the sea.
With her left hand she grasps it impetuously.   160
With her right she sustains her fair infant. Death, Fear,
Love, Beauty, are mixed in the atmosphere,
Which trembles and burns with the fervour of dread
Around her wild eyes, her bright hand, and her head,
Like a meteor of light o'er the waters! her child
Is yet smiling, and playing, and murmuring; so smiled
The false deep ere the storm. Like a sister and brother
The child and the ocean still smile on each other,
Whilst[22]—

PERCY BYSSHE SHELLEY

Alec Yeaton's Son

Gloucester, August, 1720

The wind it wailed, the wind it moaned,
    And the white caps flecked the sea;
"An' I would to God," the skipper groaned,
    "I had not my boy with me!"

Snug in the stern-sheets, little John
    Laughed as the scud swept by;
But the skipper's sunburnt cheek grew wan
    As he watched the wicked sky.

115

"Would he were at his mother's side!"
    And the skipper's eyes were dim.   10
"Good Lord in heaven, if ill betide,
    What would become of him!

"For me—my muscles are as steel,
    For me let hap what may:
I might make shift upon the keel
    Until the break o' day.

"But he, he is so weak and small,
    So young, scarce learned to stand—
O pitying Father of us all,
    I trust him in Thy hand!   20

"For Thou, who markest from on high
    A sparrow's fall—each one!—
Surely, O Lord, thou'lt have an eye
    On Alec Yeaton's son!"

Then, steady, helm! Right straight he sailed
    Towards the headland light:
The wind it moaned, the wind it wailed,
    And black, black fell the night.

Then burst a storm to make one quail
    Though housed from winds and waves—   30
They who could tell about that gale
    Must rise from watery graves!

Sudden it came, as sudden went;
    Ere half the night was sped,
The winds were hushed, the waves were spent,
    And the stars shone overhead.

Now, as the morning mist grew thin,
    The folk on Gloucester shore
Saw a little figure floating in
    Secure, on a broken oar!   40

Up rose the cry, "A wreck! a wreck!
    Pull, mates, and waste no breath!"—
They knew it, though 't was but a speck
    Upon the edge of death!

Long did they marvel in the town
    At God His strange decree,
That let the stalwart skipper drown
    And the little child go free!

THOMAS BAILEY ALDRICH

The Wreck of the *Hesperus*[23]

It was the schooner *Hesperus,*
    That sailed the wintry sea;
And the skipper had taken his little daughtèr,
    To bear him company.

Blue were her eyes as the fairy-flax,
    Her cheeks like the dawn of day,
And her bosom white as the hawthorn buds,
    That ope in the month of May.

The skipper he stood beside the helm,
    His pipe was in his mouth,   10
And he watched how the veering flaw did blow
    The smoke now West, now South.

Then up and spake an old Sailòr,
    Had sailed to the Spanish Main,
"I pray thee, put into yonder port,
    For I fear a hurricane.

"Last night, the moon had a golden ring,
    And to-night no moon we see!"
The skipper, he blew a whiff from his pipe,
    And a scornful laugh laughed he.   20

Colder and louder blew the wind,
    A gale from the Northeast,
The snow fell hissing in the brine,
    And the billows frothed like yeast.

Down came the storm, and smote amain
    The vessel in its strength;
She shuddered and paused, like a frighted steed,
    Then leaped her cable's length.

"Come hither! come hither! my little daughtèr,
    And do not tremble so;   30
For I can weather the roughest gale
    That ever wind did blow."

He wrapped her warm in his seaman's coat
    Against the stinging blast;
He cut a rope from a broken spar,
    And bound her to the mast.

"O father! I hear the church-bells ring,
    Oh say, what may it be?"

" 'Tis a fog-bell on a rock-bound coast!"—
  And he steered for the open sea.   40

"O father! I hear the sound of guns,
  Oh say, what may it be?"
"Some ship in distress, that cannot live
  In such an angry sea!"

"O father! I see a gleaming light,
  Oh say, what may it be?"
But the father answered never a word,
  A frozen corpse was he.

Lashed to the helm, all stiff and stark,
  With his face turned to the skies,   50
The lantern gleamed through the gleaming snow
  On his fixed and glassy eyes.

Then the maiden clasped her hands and prayed
  That savèd she might be;
And she thought of Christ, who stilled the wave,
  On the Lake of Galilee.

And fast through the midnight dark and drear,
  Through the whistling sleet and snow,
Like a sheeted ghost, the vessel swept
  Tow'rds the reef of Norman's Woe.   60

And ever the fitful gusts between
  A sound came from the land;
It was the sound of the trampling surf
  On the rocks and the hard sea-sand.

The breakers were right beneath her bows,
  She drifted a dreary wreck,
And a whooping billow swept the crew
  Like icicles from her deck.

She struck where the white and fleecy waves
  Looked soft as carded wool,   70
But the cruel rocks, they gored her side
  Like the horns of an angry bull.

Her rattling shrouds, all sheathed in ice,
  With the masts went by the board;
Like a vessel of glass, she stove and sank,
  Ho! ho! the breakers roared!

At daybreak, on the bleak sea-beach,
  A fisherman stood aghast,
To see the form of a maiden fair,
  Lashed close to a drifting mast.   80

118

The salt sea was frozen on her breast,
    The salt tears in her eyes;
And he saw her hair, like the brown seaweed,
    On the billows fall and rise.

Such was the wreck of the *Hesperus,*
    In the midnight and the snow!
Christ save us all from a death like this,
    On the reef of Norman's Woe!

HENRY WADSWORTH LONGFELLOW

The Convergence of the Twain

Lines on the loss of the Titanic[24]

I

    In a solitude of the sea
    Deep from human vanity,
And the Pride of Life that planned her, stilly couches she.

II

    Steel chambers, late the pyres
    Of her salamandrine fires,
Cold currents thrid, and turn to rhythmic tidal lyres.

III

    Over the mirrors meant
    To glass the opulent
The sea-worm crawls—grotesque, slimed, dumb, indifferent.

IV

    Jewels in joy designed
    To ravish the sensuous mind
Lie lightless, all their sparkles bleared and black and blind.

V

    Dim moon-eyed fishes near
    Gaze at the gilded gear
And query: "What does this vaingloriousness down here?"...

VI

       Well: while was fashioning
       This creature of cleaving wing,
The Immanent Will that stirs and urges everything

VII

       Prepared a sinister mate
       For her—so gaily great—
A Shape of Ice, for the time far and dissociate.

VIII

       And as the smart ship grew
       In stature, grace, and hue,
In shadowy silent distance grew the Iceberg too.

IX

       Alien they seemed to be:
       No mortal eye could see
The intimate welding of their later history,

X

       Or sign that they were bent
       By paths coincident
On being anon twin halves of one august event,

XI

       Till the Spinner of the Years
       Said "Now!" And each one hears,
And consummation comes, and jars two hemispheres.

THOMAS HARDY

From *The Dynasts*
The Night of Trafalgár[25]

In the wild October night-time, when the wind raved round the land,
And the Back-sea met the Front-sea, and our doors were blocked with
      sand,
And we heard the drub of Dead-man's Bay, where bones of thousands
      are,[26]
We knew not what the day had done for us at Trafalgár.
          Had done,
          Had done,
        For us at Trafalgár!

"Pull hard, and make the Nothe,[27] or down we go!" one says, says he.
We pulled; and bedtime brought the storm; but snug at home slept we.
Yet all the while our gallants after fighting through the day,
Were beating up and down the dark, sou'-west of Cadiz Bay.
          The dark,
          The dark,
        Sou'-west of Cadiz Bay!

The victors and the vanquished then the storm it tossed and tore,
As hard they strove, those worn-out men, upon that surly shore;
Dead Nelson and his half-dead crew, his foes from near and far,
Were rolled together on the deep that night at Trafalgár!
          The deep,
          The deep,
       That night at Trafalgár!

THOMAS HARDY

Black-Eyed Susan

All in the Downs[28] the fleet was moor'd,
  The streamers waving in the wind,
When black-eyed Susan came on board:
  "Oh! where shall I my true love find?
Tell me, ye jovial sailors, tell me true,
If my sweet William sails among your crew?"

William, who, high upon the yard,
  Rock'd by the billows to and fro,
Soon as her well-known voice he heard,
  He sighed and cast his eyes below: 10
The cord glides swiftly through his glowing hands,
And quick as lightning on the deck he stands.

So the sweet lark, high-pois'd in air,
  Shuts close his pinions to his breast,
If chance his mate's shrill call he hear,
  And drops at once into her nest:
The noblest captain in the British fleet
Might envy William's lips those kisses sweet.

"O Susan, Susan, lovely dear,
  My vows shall ever true remain!   20
Let me kiss off that falling tear,—
  We only part to meet again:
Change as ye list, ye winds, my heart shall be
The faithful compass that still points to thee!

"Believe not what the landsmen say,
  Who tempt, with doubts, thy constant mind:
They'll tell thee, sailors, when away,
  At every port a mistress find.—
Yes, yes!—believe them when they tell thee so;
For thou art present wheresoe'er I go.   30

"If to fair India's coast we sail,
  Thine eyes are seen in diamonds bright;
Thy breath is Afric's spicy gale,—
  Thy skin is ivory so white:
Thus every beauteous object that I view
Wakes in my soul some charm of lovely Sue.

"Though battle calls me from thy arms,
  Let not my pretty Susan mourn;
Though cannons roar, yet, free from harms,
  William shall to his dear return: 40

Love turns aside the balls that round me fly,
Lest precious tears should drop from Susan's eye."

The boatswain gives his dreadful word,—
   The sails their swelling bosoms spread;
No longer may she stay on board:
   They kiss: She sighs: He hangs his head.
Her lessening boat unwilling rows to land:
"Adieu!" she cries, and waves her lily hand.

JOHN GAY

Admirals All

Effingham, Grenville, Raleigh, Drake,
   Here's to the bold and free!
Benbow, Collingwood, Byron, Blake,
   Hail to the Kings of the Sea!
Admirals all, for England's sake,
   Honour be yours and fame!
And honour, as long as waves shall break,
   To Nelson's peerless name![29]

Admirals all, for England's sake,   10
   Honour be yours and fame!
And honour, as long as waves shall break,
   To Nelson's peerless name!

Essex was fretting in Cadiz Bay
   With the galleons fair in sight;
Howard at last must give him his way,[30]
   And the word was passed to fight.
Never was schoolboy gayer than he,
   Since holidays first began:
He tossed his bonnet to wind and sea,   20
   And under the guns he ran.

Drake[31] nor devil nor Spaniard feared,
   Their cities he put to the sack;
He singed his Catholic Majesty's beard,
   And harried his ships to wrack.
He was playing at Plymouth a rubber of bowls
   When the great Armada came;
But he said, 'They must wait their turn, good souls,'
   And he stooped, and finished the game.

Fifteen sail were the Dutchmen bold,
　　Duncan[32] he had but two; 30
But he anchored them fast where the Texel shoaled
　　And his colours aloft he flew.
'I've taken the depth to a fathom,' he cried,
　　'And I'll sink with a right good will,
For I know when we're all of us under the tide,
　　My flag will be fluttering still.'

Splinters were flying above, below,
　　When Nelson sailed the Sound:
'Mark you, I wouldn't be elsewhere now,'
　　Said he, 'for a thousand pound!' 40
The Admiral's signal bade him fly,
　　But he wickedly wagged his head,
He clapped the glass to his sightless eye
　　And 'I'm damned if I see it!' he said.[33]

Admirals all, they said their say
　　(The echoes are ringing still),
Admirals all, they went their way
　　To the haven under the hill.
But they left us a kingdom none can take,
　　The realm of the circling sea, 50
To be ruled by the rightful sons of Blake
　　And the Rodneys[34] yet to be.

Admirals all, for England's sake,
　　Honour be yours and fame!
And honour, as long as waves shall break,
　　To Nelson's peerless name!

HENRY NEWBOLT

The Captain Stood on the Carronade

The Captain stood on the carronade—"First lieutenant," says he,
"Send all my merry men aft here, for they must list to me:
I haven't the gift of the gab, my sons—because I'm bred to the sea;
That ship there is a Frenchman, who means to fight with we.
　　Odds blood, hammer and tongs, long as I've been to sea,
　　I've fought 'gainst every odds—but I've gain'd the victory.

"That ship there is a Frenchman, and if we don't take *she*,
'Tis a thousand bullets to one, that she will capture *we*;
I haven't the gift of the gab, my boys; so each man to his gun;
If she's not mine in half an hour, I'll flog each mother's son.   10
   Odds bobs, hammer and tongs, long as I've been to sea,
   I've fought 'gainst every odds—and I've gain'd the victory."

We fought for twenty minutes, when the Frenchmen had enough;
"I little thought," said he, "that your men were of such stuff;"
The captain took the Frenchman's sword, a low bow made to he;
"I haven't the gift of the gab, monsieur, but polite I wish to be.
   Odds bobs, hammer and tongs, long as I've been to sea,
   I've fought 'gainst every odds—and I've gain'd the victory."

Our captain sent for all of us; "My merry men," said he,
"I haven't the gift of the gab, my lads, but yet I thankful be;   20
You've done your duty handsomely, each man stood to his gun;
If you hadn't, you villains, as sure as day, I'd have flogg'd each mother's
    son.
   Odds bobs, hammer and tongs, as long as I'm at sea,
   I'll fight 'gainst every odds—and I'll gain the victory."

FREDERICK MARRYAT

Captain Jones' Invitation

Thou, who on some dark mountain's brow
Hast toil'd thy life away till now,
And often from that rugged steep
Beheld the vast extended deep,
Come from thy forest, and with me
Learn what it is to go to sea.

There endless plains the eye surveys
As far from land the vessel strays;
No longer hill nor dale is seen,
The realms of death intrude between,   10
But fear no ill; resolve, with me
To share the dangers of the sea.

But look not there for verdant fields—
Far different prospects Neptune yields;
Green seas shall only greet the eye,
Those seas encircled by the sky,
Immense and deep—come then with me
And view the wonders of the sea.

Yet sometimes groves and meadows gay
Delight the seamen on their way;
From the deep seas that round us swell
With rocks the surges to repel
Some verdant isle, by waves embrac'd,
Swells, to adorn the wat'ry waste.

Though now this vast expanse appear
With glassy surface, calm and clear;
Be not deceiv'd—'tis but a show,
For many a corpse is laid below—
Even Britain's lads—it cannot be—
They were the *masters* of the sea!

Now combating upon the brine,
Where ships in flaming squadrons join,
At every blast the brave expire
'Midst clouds of smoke, and streams of fire;
But scorn all fear; advance with me—
'Tis but the custom of the sea.

Now we the peaceful wave divide,
On broken surges now we ride,
Now every eye dissolves with woe
As on some lee-ward coast we go—
Half lost, half buried in the main
Hope scarcely beams on life again.

Above us storms distract the sky,
Beneath us depths unfathom'd lie,
Too near we see, a ghastly sight,
The realms of everlasting night,
A wat'ry tomb of ocean-green
And only one frail plank between!

But winds must cease, and storms decay,
Not always lasts the gloomy day,
Again the skies are warm and clear,
Again soft zephyrs fan the air,
Again we find the long lost shore,
The winds oppose our wish no more.

If thou hast courage to despise
The various changes of the skies,
To disregard the ocean's rage,
Unmov'd when hostile ships engage,
Come from thy forest, and with me
Learn what it is to go to sea.

PHILIP FRENEAU

Old Ironsides[35]

Ay, tear her tattered ensign down!
    Long has it waved on high,
And many an eye has danced to see
    That banner in the sky;
Beneath it rung the battle shout,
    And burst the cannon's roar;—
The meteor of the ocean air
    Shall sweep the clouds no more.

Her deck, once red with heroes' blood,
    Where knelt the vanquished foe,   10
When winds were hurrying o'er the flood,
    And waves were white below,
No more shall feel the victor's tread,
    Or know the conquered knee;—
The harpies of the shore shall pluck
    The eagle of the sea!

Oh, better that her shattered hulk
    Should sink beneath the wave;
Her thunders shook the mighty deep,
    And there should be her grave;   20
Nail to the mast her holy flag,
    Set every threadbare sail,
And give her to the god of storms,
    The lightning and the gale!

             OLIVER WENDELL HOLMES

From *Song of Myself*
Battle of the *Bonhomme Richard* and the *Serapis*[36]

35

Would you hear of an old-time sea-fight?
Would you learn who won by the light of the moon and stars?
List to the yarn, as my grandmother's father the sailor told it to me.

Our foe was no skulk in his ship I tell you, (said he,)   900
His was the surly English pluck, and there is no tougher or truer,
    and never was, and never will be;
Along the lower'd eve he came horribly raking us.

127

We closed with him, the yards entangled, the cannon touch'd,
My captain lash'd fast with his own hands.

We had receiv'd some eighteen pound shots under the water,
On our lower-gun-deck two large pieces had burst at the first fire,
    killing all around and blowing up overhead.

Fighting at sun-down, fighting at dark,
Ten o'clock at night, the full moon well up, our leaks on the gain,
    and five feet of water reported,
The master-at-arms loosing the prisoners confined in the afterhold to
    give them a chance for themselves.

The transit to and from the magazine is now stopt by the sentinels,   910
They see so many strange faces they do not know whom to trust.

Our frigate takes fire,
The other asks if we demand quarter?
If our colors are struck and the fighting done?

Now I laugh content for I hear the voice of my little captain,
We have not struck, he composedly cries, *we have just begun our
    part of the fighting.*

Only three guns are in use,
One is directed by the captain himself against the enemy's main-mast,
Two well serv'd with grape and canister silence his musketry and clear
    his decks.

The tops alone second the fire of this little battery, especially the
    main-top,   920
They hold out bravely during the whole of the action.

Not a moment's cease,
The leaks gain fast on the pumps, the fire eats toward the powder-
    magazine.

One of the pumps has been shot away, it is generally thought we are
    sinking.

Serene stands the little captain,
He is not hurried, his voice is neither high nor low,
His eyes give more light to us than our battle-lanterns.

Toward twelve there in the beams of the moon they surrender to us.

36

Stretch'd and still lies the midnight,
Two great hulls motionless on the breast of the darkness,   930
Our vessel riddled and slowly sinking, preparations to pass to the one
    we have conquer'd,

The captain on the quarter-deck coldly giving his orders through a
    countenance white as a sheet,
Near by the corpse of the child that serv'd in the cabin,
The dead face of an old salt with long white hair and carefully curl'd
    whiskers,
The flames spite of all that can be done flickering aloft and below,
The husky voices of the two or three officers yet fit for duty,
Formless stacks of bodies and bodies by themselves, dabs of flesh upon
    the masts and spars,
Cut of cordage, dangle of rigging, slight shock of the soothe of waves,
Black and impassive guns, litter of powder-parcels, strong scent,
A few large stars overhead, silent and mournful shining,   940
Delicate sniffs of sea-breeze, smells of sedgy grass and fields by the
    shore, death-messages given in charge to survivors,
The hiss of the surgeon's knife, the gnawing teeth of his saw,
Wheeze, cluck, swash of falling blood, short wild scream, and long,
    dull tapering groan,
These so, these irretrievable.

WALT WHITMAN

On Board the '76

Our ship lay tumbling in an angry sea,
    Her rudder gone, her mainmast o'er the side;
Her scuppers, from the waves' clutch staggering free,
    Trailed threads of priceless crimson through the tide;
Sails, shrouds, and spars with pirate cannon torn,
    We lay, awaiting morn.

Awaiting morn, such morn as mocks despair;
    And she that bare the promise of the world
Within her sides, now hopeless, helmless, bare,
    At random o'er the wildering waters hurled;   10
The reek of battle drifting slow alee
    Not sullener than we.

Morn came at last to peer into our woe,
    When lo, a sail! Now surely help was nigh;
The red cross flames aloft, Christ's pledge; but no,
    Her black guns grinning hate, she rushes by
And hails us:—"Gains the leak! Ay, so we thought!
    Sink, then, with curses fraught!"

I leaned against my gun still angry-hot,
    And my lids tingled with the tears held back: 20
This scorn methought was crueller than shot:
    The manly death-grip in the battle-wrack,
Yard-arm to yard-arm, were more friendly far
    Than such fear-smothered war.

There our foe wallowed, like a wounded brute
    The fiercer for his hurt. What now were best?
Once more tug bravely at the peril's root,
    Though death came with it? Or evade the test
If right or wrong in this God's world of ours
    Be leagued with mightier powers?   30

Some, faintly loyal, felt their pulses lag
    With the slow beat that doubts and then despairs;
Some, caitiff, would have struck the starry flag
    That knits us with our past, and makes us heirs
Of deeds high-hearted as were ever done
    'Neath the all-seeing sun.

But there was one, the Singer of our crew,
    Upon whose head Age waved his peaceful sign,
But whose red heart's-blood no surrender knew;   40
    And couchant under brows of massive line,
The eyes, like guns beneath a parapet,
    Watched, charged with lightnings yet.

The voices of the hills did his obey;
    The torrents flashed and tumbled in his song;
He brought our native fields from far away,
    Or set us 'mid the innumerable throng
Of dateless woods, or where we heard the calm
    Old homestead's evening psalm.

But now he sang of faith to things unseen,   50
    Of freedom's birthright given to us in trust;
And words of doughty cheer he spoke between,
    That made all earthly fortune seem as dust,
Matched with that duty, old as Time and new,
    Of being brave and true.

We, listening, learned what makes the might of words,—
    Manhood to back them, constant as a star;
His voice rammed home our cannon, edged our swords,
    And sent our boarders shouting; shroud and spar
Heard him and stiffened; the sails heard, and wooed   60
    The winds with loftier mood.

In our dark hours he manned our guns again;
    Remanned ourselves from his own manhood's stores;
Pride, honor, country, throbbed through all his strain;
    And shall we praise? God's praise was his before;
And on our futile laurels he looks down,
        Himself our bravest crown.

                                JAMES RUSSELL LOWELL

The Captain

A Legend of the Navy

He that only rules by terror
    Doeth grievous wrong.
Deep as Hell I count his error.
    Let him hear my song.
Brave the Captain was; the seamen
    Made a gallant crew,
Gallant sons of English freemen,
    Sailors bold and true.
But they hated his oppression,
    Stern he was and rash;   10
So for every light transgression
    Doom'd them to the lash.
Day by day more harsh and cruel
    Seem'd the Captain's mood.
Secret wrath like smother'd fuel
    Burnt in each man's blood.
Yet he hoped to purchase glory,
    Hoped to make the name
Of his vessel great in story,
    Wheresoe'er he came.   20
So they past by capes and islands,
    Many a harbour-mouth,
Sailing under palmy highlands
    Far within the South.
On a day when they were going
    O'er the lone expanse,
In the north, her canvas flowing,
    Rose a ship of France.
Then the Captain's colour heighten'd,
    Joyful came his speech;   30

But a cloudy gladness lighten'd
  In the eyes of each.
'Chase,' he said: the ship flew forward,
  And the wind did blow;
Stately, lightly, went she Norward,
  Till she near'd the foe.
Then they look'd at him they hated,
  Had what they desired;
Mute with folded arms they waited—
  Not a gun was fired.   40
But they heard the foeman's thunder
  Roaring out their doom;
All the air was torn in sunder,
  Crashing went the boom,
Spars were splinter'd, decks were shatter'd,
  Bullets fell like rain;
Over mast and deck were scatter'd
  Blood and brains of men.
Spars were splinter'd; decks were broken;
  Every mother's son—   50
Down they dropt—no word was spoken—
  Each beside his gun.
On the decks as they were lying,
  Were their faces grim.
In their blood, as they lay dying,
  Did they smile on him.
Those, in whom he had reliance
  For his noble name,
With one smile of still defiance
  Sold him unto shame.   60
Shame and wrath his heart confounded,
  Pale he turn'd and red,
Till himself was deadly wounded
  Falling on the dead.
Dismal error! fearful slaughter!
  Years have wander'd by,
Side by side beneath the water
  Crew and Captain lie;
There the sunlit ocean tosses
  O'er them mouldering,   70
And the lonely seabird crosses
  With one waft of the wing.

          ALFRED, LORD TENNYSON

Hervé Riel

I

On the sea and at the Hogue,[37] sixteen hundred ninety-two,
  Did the English fight the French,—woe to France!
And, the thirty-first of May, helter-skelter through the blue,
Like a crowd of frightened porpoises a shoal of sharks pursue,
  Came crowding ship on ship to Saint Malo on the Rance,[38]
With the English fleet in view.

II

'T was the squadron that escaped, with the victor in full chase;
  First and foremost of the drove, in his great ship, Damfreville;
    Close on him fled, great and small,
    Twenty-two good ships in all;   10
And they signalled to the place
"Help the winners of a race!
  Get us guidance, give us harbor, take us quick—or, quicker still,
  Here's the English can and will!"

III

Then the pilots of the place put out brisk and leapt on board;
  "Why, what hope or chance have ships like these to pass?" laughed
        they:
"Rocks to starboard, rocks to port, all the passage scarred and scored,
Shall the 'Formidable' here with her twelve and eighty guns
  Think to make the river-mouth by the single narrow way,
Trust to enter where 't is ticklish for a craft of twenty tons,   20
    And with flow at full beside?
    Now, 't is slackest ebb of tide.
  Reach the mooring? Rather say,
While rock stands or water runs,
  Not a ship will leave the bay!"

IV

Then was called a council straight.
Brief and bitter the debate:
"Here's the English at our heels; would you have them take in tow
All that's left us of the fleet, linked together stern and bow,

133

For a prize to Plymouth Sound? 30
Better run the ships aground!"
  (Ended Damfreville his speech).
"Not a minute more to wait!
  Let the Captains all and each
  Shove ashore, then blow up, burn the vessels on the beach!
France must undergo her fate.

V

"Give the word!" But no such word
Was ever spoke or heard;
  For up stood, for out stepped, for in struck amid all these
—A Captain? A Lieutenant? A Mate—first, second, third? 40
  No such man of mark, and meet
  With his betters to compete!
  But a simple Breton sailor pressed by Tourville for the fleet,
A poor coasting-pilot he, Hervé Riel the Croisickese.

VI

And "What mockery or malice have we here?" cries Hervé Riel:
  "Are you mad, you Malouins? Are you cowards, fools, or rogues?
Talk to me of rocks and shoals, me who took the soundings, tell
On my fingers every bank, every shallow, every swell
  'Twixt the offing here and Grève[39] where the river disembogues?
Are you bought by English gold? Is it love the lying's for? 50
  Morn and eve, night and day,
  Have I piloted your bay,
Entered free and anchored fast at the foot of Solidor.[40]
  Burn the fleet and ruin France? That were worse than fifty Hogues!
  Sirs, they know I speak the truth! Sirs, believe me there's a way!
Only let me lead the line,
  Have the biggest ship to steer,
  Get this 'Formidable' clear,
Make the others follow mine,
And I lead them, most and least, by a passage I know well, 60
  Right to Solidor past Grève,
    And there lay them safe and sound;
    And if one ship misbehave,
    —Keel so much as grate the ground,
Why, I've nothing but my life,—here's my head!" cries Hervé Riel.

VII

Not a minute more to wait.
"Steer us in, then, small and great!
    Take the helm, lead the line, save the squadron!" cried its chief.
Captains, give the sailor place!
    He is Admiral, in brief.   70
Still the north-wind, by God's grace!
See the noble fellow's face
As the big ship, with a bound,
Clears the entry like a hound,
Keeps the passage as its inch of way were the wide sea's profound!
    See, safe through shoal and rock,
    How they follow in a flock,
Not a ship that misbehaves, not a keel that grates the ground,
    Not a spar that comes to grief!
The peril, see, is past,   80
All are harbored to the last,
And just as Hervé Riel hollas "Anchor!"—sure as fate,
Up the English come—too late!

VIII

So, the storm subsides to calm:
    They see the green trees wave
    On the heights o'erlooking Grève.
Hearts that bled are stanched with balm.
"Just our rapture to enhance,
    Let the English rake the bay,
Gnash their teeth and glare askance   90
    As they cannonade away!
'Neath rampired Solidor pleasant riding on the Rance!"
How hope succeeds despair on each Captain's countenance!
Out burst all with one accord,
    "This is Paradise for Hell!
        Let France, let France's King
        Thank the man that did the thing!"
What a shout, and all one word,
    "Hervé Riel!"
As he stepped in front once more,   100
    Not a symptom of surprise
    In the frank blue Breton eyes,
Just the same man as before.

IX

Then said Damfreville, "My friend,
I must speak out at the end,
   Though I find the speaking hard.
Praise is deeper than the lips:
You have saved the King his ships,
   You must name your own reward.   110
'Faith, our sun was near eclipse!
Demand whate'er you will,
France remains your debtor still.
Ask to heart's content and have! or my name's not Damfreville."

X

Then a beam of fun outbroke
On the bearded mouth that spoke,
As the honest heart laughed through
Those frank eyes of Breton blue:
"Since I needs must say my say,
   Since on board the duty's done,
   And from Malo Roads to Croisic Point, what is it but a run?—   120
Since 't is ask and have, I may—
   Since the others go ashore—
Come! A good whole holiday!
   Leave to go and see my wife, whom I call the Belle Aurore!"
   That he asked and that he got,—nothing more.

XI

Name and deed alike are lost:
Not a pillar nor a post
   In his Croisic keeps alive the feat as it befell;
Not a head in white and black
On a single fishing-smack,   130
In memory of the man but for whom had gone to wrack
   All that France saved from the fight whence England bore the bell.
Go to Paris: rank on rank
   Search the heroes flung pell-mell
On the Louvre, face and flank!
   You shall look long enough ere you come to Hervé Riel.
So, for better and for worse,
Hervé Riel, accept my verse!
In my verse, Hervé Riel, do thou once more
Save the squadron, honor France, love thy wife the Belle Aurore!

ROBERT BROWNING

Meeting at Night

The gray sea and the long black land;
And the yellow half-moon large and low;
And the startled little waves that leap
In fiery ringlets from their sleep,
As I gain the cove with pushing prow,
And quench its speed i' the slushy sand.

Then a mile of warm sea-scented beach;
Three fields to cross till a farm appears;
A tap at the pane, the quick sharp scratch
And blue spurt of a lighted match,
And a voice less loud, through its joys and fears,
Than the two hearts beating each to each!

ROBERT BROWNING

Parting at Morning

Round the cape of a sudden came the sea,
And the sun looked over the mountain's rim:
And straight was a path of gold for him,
And the need of a world of men for me.

ROBERT BROWNING

Home-Thoughts, from the Sea

Nobly, nobly Cape Saint Vincent to the Northwest died away;
Sunset ran, one glorious blood-red, reeking into Cadiz Bay;
Bluish 'mid the burning water, full in face Trafalgar lay;[41]
In the dimmest Northeast distance dawned Gibraltar grand and gray;
"Here and here did England help me: how can I help England?"—say,
Whoso turns as I, this evening, turn to God to praise and pray,
While Jove's planet rises yonder, silent over Africa.

ROBERT BROWNING

Lepanto[42]

White founts falling in the Courts of the sun,
And the Soldan of Byzantium[43] is smiling as they run;
There is laughter like the fountains in that face of all men feared,
It stirs the forest darkness, the darkness of his beard;
It curls the blood-red crescent, the crescent of his lips;
For the inmost sea of all the earth is shaken with his ships.
They have dared the white republics up the capes of Italy,
They have dashed the Adriatic round the Lion of the Sea,
And the Pope has cast his arms abroad for agony and loss,
And called the kings of Christendom for swords about the Cross.   10
The cold queen of England is looking in the glass;
The shadow of the Valois[44] is yawning at the Mass;
From evening isles fantastical rings faint the Spanish gun,
And the Lord upon the Golden Horn[45] is laughing in the sun.

Dim drums throbbing, in the hills half heard,
Where only on a nameless throne a crownless prince has stirred,
Where, risen from a doubtful seat and half-attainted stall,
The last knight of Europe takes weapons from the wall,
The last and lingering troubadour to whom the bird has sung,
That once went singing southward when all the world was young.   20
In that enormous silence, tiny and unafraid,
Comes up along a winding road the noise of the Crusade.
Strong gongs groaning as the guns boom far,
Don John of Austria is going to the war;
Stiff flags straining in the night-blasts cold
In the gloom black-purple, in the glint old-gold,
Torchlight crimson on the copper kettle-drums,
Then the tuckets, then the trumpets, then the cannon, and he comes.
Don John laughing in the brave beard curled,
Spurning of his stirrups like the thrones of all the world,   30
Holding his head up for a flag of all the free.
Love-light of Spain—hurrah!
Death-light of Africa!
Don John of Austria
Is riding to the sea.

Mahound[46] is in his paradise above the evening star,
(*Don John of Austria is going to the war.*)
He moves a mighty turban on the timeless houri's knees,
His turban that is woven of the sunsets and the seas.
He shakes the peacock gardens as he rises from his ease,   40
And he strides among the tree-tops and is taller than the trees;

And his voice through all the garden is a thunder sent to bring
Black Azrael and Ariel and Ammon on the wing.
Giants and the Genii,[47]
Multiplex of wing and eye,
Whose strong obedience broke the sky
When Solomon was king.

They rush in red and purple from the red clouds of the morn,
From the temples where the yellow gods shut up their eyes in scorn;
They rise in green robes roaring from the green hells of the sea   50
Where fallen skies and evil hues and eyeless creatures be,
On them the sea-valves cluster and the gray sea-forests curl,
Splashed with a splendid sickness, the sickness of the pearl;
They swell in sapphire smoke out of the blue cracks of the ground,—
They gather and they wonder and give worship to Mahound.
And he saith, "Break up the mountains where the hermit-folk can hide,
And sift the red and silver sands lest bone of saint abide,
And chase the Giaours[48] flying night and day, not giving rest,
For that which was our trouble comes again out of the west.
We have set the seal of Solomon on all things under sun,   60
Of knowledge and of sorrow and endurance of things done.
But a noise is in the mountains, in the mountains; and I know
The voice that shook our palaces—four hundred years ago:
It is he that saith not 'Kismet';[49] it is he that knows not Fate;
It is Richard, it is Raymond, it is Godfrey at the gate!
It is he whose loss is laughter when he counts the wager worth,
Put down your feet upon him, that our peace be on the earth."
For he heard drums groaning and he heard guns jar,
(*Don John of Austria is going to the war.*)
Sudden and still—hurrah!   70
Bolt from Iberia!
Don John of Austria
Is gone by Alcalar.[50]

St. Michael's on his Mountain[51] in the sea-roads of the north
(*Don John of Austria is girt and going forth.*)
Where the gray seas glitter and the sharp tides shift
And the sea-folk labor and the red sails lift.
He shakes his lance of iron and he claps his wings of stone;
The noise is gone through Normandy; the noise is gone alone;
The North is full of tangled things and texts and aching eyes,   80
And dead is all the innocence of anger and surprise,
And Christian killeth Christian in a narrow dusty room,
And Christian dreadeth Christ that hath a newer face of doom,
And Christian hateth Mary that God kissed in Galilee,—

But Don John of Austria is riding to the sea.
Don John calling through the blast and the eclipse,
Crying with the trumpet, with the trumpet to his lips,
Trumpet that sayeth *ha!*
   Domino Gloria![52]
Don John of Austria
Is shouting to the ships.   90

King Philip's in his closet with the Fleece about his neck
(*Don John of Austria is armed upon the deck.*)
The walls are hung with velvet that is black and soft as sin,
And little dwarfs creep out of it and little dwarfs creep in.
He holds a crystal phial that has colors like the moon,
He touches, and it tingles, and he trembles very soon,
And his face is as a fungus of a leprous white and gray
Like plants in the high houses that are shuttered from the day,
And death is in the phial and the end of noble work,   100
But Don John of Austria has fired upon the Turk.
Don John's hunting, and his hounds have bayed—
Booms away past Italy the rumor of his raid.
Gun upon gun, ha! ha!
Gun upon gun, hurrah!
Don John of Austria
Has loosed the cannonade.

The Pope was in his chapel before day or battle broke,
(*Don John of Austria is hidden in the smoke.*)
The hidden room in man's house where God sits all the year,   110
The secret window whence the world looks small and very dear.
He sees as in a mirror on the monstrous twilight sea
The crescent of his cruel ships whose name is mystery;
They fling great shadows foe-wards, making Cross and Castle dark,
They veil the plumèd lions on the galleys of St. Mark;
And above the ships are palaces of brown, black-bearded chiefs,
And below the ships are prisons, where with multitudinous griefs,
Christian captives, sick and sunless, all a laboring race repines
Like a race in sunken cities, like a nation in the mines.
They are lost like slaves that swat, and in the skies of morning hung
The stair-ways of the tallest gods when tyranny was young.   121
They are countless, voiceless, hopeless as those fallen or fleeing on
Before the high Kings' horses in the granite of Babylon.
And many a one grows witless in his quiet room in hell
Where a yellow face looks inward through the lattice of his cell,
And he finds his God forgotten, and he seeks no more a sign—
(*But Don John of Austria has burst the battle-line!*)

Don John pounding from the slaughter-painted poop,
Purpling all the ocean like a bloody pirate's sloop,
Scarlet running over on the silvers and the golds, 130
Breaking of the hatches up and bursting of the holds,
Thronging of the thousands up that labor under sea
White for bliss and blind for sun and stunned for liberty.
Vivat Hispania![53]
Domino Gloria!
Don John of Austria
Has set his people free!

Cervantes[54] on his galley sets the sword back in the sheath
(*Don John of Austria rides homeward with a wreath.*)
And he sees across a weary land a straggling road in Spain, 140
Up which a lean and foolish knight for ever rides in vain,
And he smiles, but not as Sultans smile, and settles back the blade ...
(*But Don John of Austria rides home from the Crusade.*)

G. K. CHESTERTON

Columbus

Behind him lay the gray Azores,
    Behind the Gates of Hercules;
Before him not the ghost of shores,
    Before him only shoreless seas.
The good mate said: "Now must we pray,
    For lo! the very stars are gone.
Brave Admiral, speak, what shall I say?"
    "Why, say, 'Sail on! sail on! and on!'"

"My men grow mutinous day by day;
    My men grow ghastly wan and weak." 10
The stout mate thought of home; a spray
    Of salt wave washed his swarthy cheek.
"What shall I say, brave Admiral, say,
    If we sight naught but seas at dawn?"
"Why, you shall say at break of day,
    'Sail on! sail on! sail on! and on!'"

They sailed and sailed, as winds might blow,
    Until at last the blanched mate said:
"Why, now not even God would know
    Should I and all my men fall dead. 20
These very winds forget their way,
    For God from these dread seas is gone.
Now speak, brave Admiral, speak and say"—
    He said: "Sail on! sail on! and on!"

They sailed. They sailed. Then spake the mate:
  "This mad sea shows his teeth tonight.
He curls his lip, he lies in wait,
  With lifted teeth, as if to bite!
Brave Admiral, say but one good word:
  What shall we do when hope is gone?"   30
The words leapt like a leaping sword:
  "Sail on! sail on! sail on! and on!"

Then, pale and worn, he kept his deck,
  And peered through darkness. Ah, that night
Of all dark nights! And then a speck—
  A light! A light! A light! A light!
It grew, a starlit flag unfurled!
  It grew to be Time's burst of dawn.
He gained a world; he gave that world
  Its grandest lesson: "On! sail on!"

JOAQUIN MILLER

Christmas at Sea

The sheets were frozen hard, and they cut the naked hand;
The decks were like a slide, where a seaman scarce could stand;
The wind was a nor'wester, blowing squally off the sea;
And cliffs and spouting breakers were the only things a-lee.

They heard the surf a-roaring before the break of day;
But 't was only with the peep of light we saw how ill we lay.
We tumbled every hand on deck instanter, with a shout,
And we gave her the maintops'l, and stood by to go about.

All day we tacked and tacked between the South Head and the North;
All day we hauled the frozen sheets, and got no further forth;   10
All day as cold as charity, in bitter pain and dread,
For very life and nature we tacked from head to head.

We gave the South a wider berth, for there the tide race roared;
But every tack we made we brought the North Head close aboard:
So's we saw the cliffs and houses, and the breakers running high,
And the coastguard in his garden, with his glass against his eye.

The frost was on the village roofs as white as ocean foam;
The good red fires were burning bright in every 'longshore home;
The windows sparkled clear, and the chimneys volleyed out;
And I vow we sniffed the victuals as the vessel went about.   20

The bells upon the church were rung with a mighty jovial cheer;
For it's just that I should tell you how (of all days in the year)
This day of our adversity was blessèd Christmas morn,
And the house above the coastguard's was the house where I was born.

O well I saw the pleasant room, the pleasant faces there,
My mother's silver spectacles, my father's silver hair;
And well I saw the firelight, like a flight of homely elves,
Go dancing round the china-plates that stand upon the shelves.

And well I knew the talk they had, the talk that was of me,
Of the shadow on the household and the son that went to sea;   30
And O the wicked fool I seemed, in every kind of way,
To be here and hauling frozen ropes on blessèd Christmas Day.

They lit the high sea-light, and the dark began to fall.
"All hands to loose topgallant sails," I heard the captain call.
"By the Lord, she'll never stand it," our first mate, Jackson, cried.
...."It's the one way or the other, Mr. Jackson," he replied.

She staggered to her bearings, but the sails were new and good.
And the ship smelt up to windward just as though she understood.
As the winter's day was ending, in the entry of the night,
We cleared the weary headland, and passed below the light.   40

And they heaved a mighty breath, every soul on board but me,
As they saw her nose again pointing handsome out to sea;
But all that I could think of, in the darkness and the cold,
Was just that I was leaving home and my folks were growing old.

ROBERT LOUIS STEVENSON

The Sad Shepherd

There was a man whom Sorrow named his friend,
And he, of his high comrade Sorrow dreaming,
Went walking with slow steps along the gleaming
And humming sands, where windy surges wend:
And he called loudly to the stars to bend
From their pale thrones and comfort him, but they
Among themselves laugh on and sing alway:
And then the man whom Sorrow named his friend
Cried out, *Dim sea, hear my most piteous story!*
The sea swept on and cried her old cry still,   10
Rolling along in dreams from hill to hill.
He fled the persecution of her glory

And, in a far-off, gentle valley stopping,
Cried all his story to the dewdrops glistening,
But naught they heard, for they are always listening.
The dewdrops, for the sound of their own dropping.
And then the man whom Sorrow named his friend
Sought once again the shore, and found a shell
And thought, *I will my heavy story tell*
Till my own words, re-echoing, shall send   20
Their sadness through a hollow, pearly heart;
And my own tale again for me shall sing,
And my own whispering words be comforting,
And lo! my ancient burden may depart.
Then he sang softly nigh the pearly rim;
But the sad dweller by the sea-ways lone
Changed all he sang to inarticulate moan
Among her wildering whirls, forgetting him.

WILLIAM BUTLER YEATS

John Winter

What ails John Winter, that so oft
　　Silent he sits apart?
The neighbours cast their looks on him;
　　But deep he hides his heart.

In Deptford streets the houses small
　　Huddle forlorn together.
Whether the wind blow or be still,
　　'Tis soiled and sorry weather.

But over these dim roofs arise
　　Tall masts of ocean ships.   10
Whenever John Winter looked on them,
　　The salt blew on his lips.

He cannot pace the street about,
　　But they stand before his eyes!
The more he shuns them, the more proud
　　And beautiful they rise.

He turns his head, but in his ear
　　The steady trade-winds run,
And in his eye the endless waves
　　Ride on into the sun.   20

His little child at evening said,
   'Now tell us, Dad, a tale
Of naked men that shoot with bows,
   Tell of the spouting whale!'

He told old tales, his eyes were bright,
   His wife looked up to see
And smiled on him: but in the midst
   He ended suddenly.

He bade his boys good-night, and kissed
   And held them to his breast.   30
They wondered and were still, to feel
   Their lips so fondly pressed.

He sat absorbed in silent gloom.
   His wife lifted her head
From sewing, and stole up to him,
   'What ails you, John?' she said.

He spoke no word. A silent tear
   Fell softly down her cheek.
She knelt beside him, and his hand
   Was on her forehead meek.   40

But even as his tender touch
   Her dumb distress consoled,
The mighty waves danced in his eyes
   And through the silence rolled.

There fell a soft November night,
   Restless with gusts that shook
The chimneys, and beat wildly down
   The flames in the chimney nook.

John Winter lay beside his wife,
   'Twas past the mid of night.   50
Softly he rose, and in dead hush
   Stood stealthily upright.

Softly he came where slept his boys,
   And kissed them in their bed.
One stretched his arms out in his sleep;
   At that he turned his head.

And now he bent above his wife,
   She slept a sleep serene,
Her patient soul was in the peace
   Of breathing slumber seen.   60

At last he kissed one aching kiss,
    Then shrank again in dread,
And from his own home guiltily
    And like a thief he fled.

But now with darkness and the wind
    He breathes a breath more free,
And walks with calmer steps like one
    Who goes with destiny.

And see, before him the great masts
    Tower with all their spars   70
Black on the dimness, soaring bold
    Among the mazy stars.

In stormy rushings through the air
    Wild scents the darkness filled,
And with a fierce forgetfulness
    His drinking nostril thrilled.

He hasted with quick feet, he hugged
    The wildness to his breast,
As one who goes the only way
    To set his heart at rest.   80

When morning glimmered, a great ship
    Dropt gliding down the shore.
John Winter coiled the anchor ropes
    Among his mates once more.

LAURENCE BINYON

From Pacific Sonnets

(Three Memorial Sonnets for two young seamen lost overboard in a storm in Mid-Pacific, January 6, 1940)

VII

The seagull, spreadeagled, splayed on the wind,
Span backwards shrieking, belly facing upward,
Fled backwards with a gimlet in its heart
To see the two youths swimming hand in hand
Through green eternity. O swept overboard
Not could the thirty-foot jaws them part,
Or the flouncing skirts that swept them over
Separate what death pronounced was love.

146

I saw them, the hand flapping like a flag,
And another like a dolphin with a child   10
Supporting him. Was I the shape of Jesus
When to me hopeward their eyeballs swivelled,
Saw I was standing in the posture of vague
Horror, oh paralyzed with mere pity's peace?

VIII

From thorax of storms the voices of verbs
Shall call to me without sound, like the vowel
Round which cyclones rage, to nurse my nerve,
My shaken, my broken, my oh I shall grovel
Heart. I taste sea swilling in my bowels,
As now I sit shivering in the swing of waves   20
Like a face in a bubble. As the hull heaves
I and my mind go walking over hell.

The greedy bitch with sailors in her guts,
Green as a dream and formidable as God,
Spitting at stars, gnawing at shores, mad, randy,
Riots with us on her abdomen and puts
Eternity in our cabins, pitches our pod
To the mouth of the death for which no one is ready.

IX

At midday they looked up and saw their death
Standing up overhead as loud as thunder   30
As white as angels and formidable as God:
Then, then the shock, the last gasp of breath,
As grazing the bulwarks they swept over and under,
All the green arms around them that load
Their eyes, their ears, their stomachs with eternals,
Whirled away in a white pool to the stern.

But the most possible of all miracles
Is that the useful tear that did not fall
From the corner of their eyes, was the prize,
The flowers, the gifts, the crystal sepulcher,   40
The funeral contribution and memorial,
The perfect and non-existent obsequies.

GEORGE BARKER

Epitaph

One whom I knew, a student and a poet,
makes his way shorewards tonight out of the sea
blown to a houseless coast near Bettystown
where along sleeping miles the sea is laying
printless meadows of sand, and beyond them to seaward
endless untrodden fields louder than corn. These nets
follow the long beaches. Tonight a guest
noses his way to shore. They wait for him
where the sand meets the grass—and one unmarried holds
her spine's long intricate necklace for his shoulders
pillows his broken face, his for another's
for she died waiting. He will learn much
of roots and the way of sand and the small stones,
and that the shoreward dead are friends to all
at whose heels yell the clock-faced citizens.
So like a ship the dead man comes to shore.

ALEX COMFORT

The Laughter of the Waves

ANY BODY OF WRITING dealing with a particular subject, be it love, war, religion, politics, or the sea, will eventually include works that treat that subject with humor. Along with man's desire to express his deepest thoughts and to tell his most important stories in poetic form, there exists a corresponding need for humor; no part of man's life is so serious, so sacrosanct, that it has escaped humorous treatment by poets, a form widely enjoyed by readers of poetry. So it is with poetry of the sea.

Humorous poetry about the sea not surprisingly concerns itself with the same subjects as does serious sea poetry—the sea itself and the creatures therein, man's relation to the sea, sea stories, and legends of the sea. But, whereas serious poems treat high, socially acceptable subjects with an underlying moral seriousness, humorous poems treat low subjects, or the lower and conventionally less acceptable aspects of a subject, in a way that is usually light and playful. Thus a humorous sea poem, although perhaps written on the same subject and in the same form as a serious one, has an altogether different effect on the reader.

The sea and its creatures are the topics of much humorous sea poetry: in the sea itself, where many poets find evidence of God's handiwork, Lewis Carroll, in *A Sea Dirge,* finds only wetness, nausea, cold, and salt-polluted water; in *To the Immortal Memory of the Halibut on Which I Dined This Day,* William Cowper mocks the idea of grandeur in the creatures of the sea, seeing only the glory of providing a meal for the poet; and Ogden Nash does not think of the creatures in *The Sea-Gull* and *The Octopus* as soaring spirits and awesome beasts, but wonders about their gender and number. Man's relation to the sea is similarly treated. In Cowper's poem, the relationship between man and sea denizen is merely gastronomic; in Oliver Wendell Holmes's *A Sea Dialogue,* the reaction of a salty old helmsman to a passenger's romantic vision of the sea is thoroughly unsympathetic and workmanlike; in *Sea-Chill,* Arthur Guiterman parodies John Masefield's *Sea-Fever* by imitating the language and verse form and pointing out the irony of a man whose reputation is founded on poems that express a love and need for the sea suffering from seasickness as a passenger on a large liner.

The humorous stories of sea poetry follow the same patterns as serious ones. Sailors and seamen are portrayed, but not as heroes; nor are their admirable characteristics immortalized. Instead, the poets address their other traits: Thomas Hood, in *A Sailor's Apology for Bow-Legs*, reveals that the bow-legged gait of the sailor comes not from the rolling sea but from riding a horse; William Falconer, in his mock-heroic *The Midshipman*, uses the conventions of epic poetry—the heroic couplet, an appeal to the muse, frequent allusions, and overstatement—to detail the thoroughly unheroic aspects of a midshipman's life aboard ship; in *A Sea Dialogue*, Holmes's helmsman has none of the fanciful, imaginative impressions of the sea that many poets have; Frederick Marryat's *Port Admiral* is content to send others to face the winter sea while he sits before his fire, comfortable and well fed; James Roche's *A Sailor's Yarn* is about a liar, a teller of tales, with himself as the hero; and in *A Ship of Rio*, Walter de la Mare shows that even monkeys make perfectly adequate sailors.

Narratives of storm and shipwreck do not deal with heroism. For instance, the act common to the shipwrecked men in Lord Byron's *Don Juan*, William Makepeace Thackeray's *Little Billee*, and W. S. Gilbert's *The Yarn of the "Nancy Bell,"* is cannibalism. The poems that treat of love and separation do so in either a ribald or mocking manner: in the excerpt from William Shakespeare's *The Tempest*, the girl Kate has a sharp tongue and will not lower herself to be a sailor's lover, although to sleep with a landsman is quite acceptable to her; W. H. Auden's *Song of the Master and Boatswain* echoes Shakespeare's words, with the difference that it is the seaman, fearing marriage, who spurns the girls; Hood's *Sally Simpkin's Lament* portrays a girl who, as she awaits her lover's return from the sea, can see only half of him in her mind, the lower half having been devoured by a shark; and Rupert Brooke, in *A Channel Passage*, effectively parodies all sentimental poems of parted lovers by having the lover's attempts to reflect on his love repeatedly thwarted by bouts of nausea. War at sea is the subject of Marryat's *Port Admiral* and of Rudyard Kipling's *Soldier An' Sailor Too*.

Humorous poems concerning legends of the sea are of two types. Some poets create their own legends, such as Hood's sailor who has "the whole/ Atlantic for my waist," Roche's second mate who swims a league through stormy seas with the ship's anchor on his back, Kipling's universal mariner in *Poseidon's Law* who is bound by oath never to tell a falsehood at sea but who makes up for lost lies when on shore, and Edward Lear's nonsensical tale of *The Jumblies* who manage to navigate the seas in a sieve. Other poets make use of existing legend: Byron retells the story of *Don Juan*, but depicts him as an ineffectual buffoon; both Holmes in *The Ballad of the Oysterman* and Byron in *Written after Swimming from Sestos to Abydos* make use of the legend of Hero and Leander, Holmes's latter-day Leander drowning from cramp and Byron contracting the ague.

Many poets have tried their hands at humorous writing, and a measure of the widespread popularity of sea poetry is the number of excellent poets, from Shakespeare to Auden, who, although they did not confine themselves to writing of the sea, have been drawn to the laughter of the waves.

From *The Tempest*
Act II, Scene II
Lines 47–56

The master, the swabber, the boatswain and I,
   The gunner and his mate,
Loved Mall, Meg, and Marian and Margery,
   But none of us cared for Kate;
   For she had a tongue with a tang,
   Would cry to a sailor, 'Go hang!'
She loved not the savour of tar nor of pitch,
Yet a tailor might scratch her where'er she did itch:
   Then to sea, boys, and let her go hang.

WILLIAM SHAKESPEARE

A Sailor's Apology for Bow-Legs

There's some is born with their legs straight by natur—
And some is born with bow-legs from the first—
And some that should have growed a good deal straighter,
   But they were badly nursed,
And set, you see, like Bacchus, with their pegs
   Astride of casks and kegs.
I've got myself a sort of bow to larboard
   And starboard,
And this is what it was that warped my legs:

'Twas all along of Poll, as I may say,   10
That fouled my cable when I ought to slip;
   But on the tenth of May,
   When I gets under weigh,
Down there in Hartfordshire, to join by ship.
   I sees the mail
   Get under sail,
The only one there was to make the trip.
   Well, I gives chase
   But as she run
   Two knots to one,   20
There warn't no use in keeping on the race!

Well, casting round about, what next to try on,
   And how to spin,
I spies an ensign with a Bloody Lion,
And bears away to leeward for the inn,
   Beats round the gable,
And fetches up before the coach-horse stable.

Well, there they stand, four kickers in a row,
        And so
I just makes free to cut a brown 'un's cable.
But riding isn't in a seaman's natur;
So I whips out a toughish end of yarn,
And gets a kind of sort of a land-waiter
        To splice me heel to heel,
        Under the she-mare's keel,
And off I goes, and leaves the inn a-starn!

        My eyes! how she did pitch!
And wouldn't keep her own to go in no line,
Tho' I kept bowsing, bowsing at her bow-line,
But always making leeway to the ditch,
And yawed her head about all sorts of ways.
        The devil sink the craft!
And wasn't she tremendous slack in stays!
We couldn't, no how, keep the inn abaft!
        Well, I suppose
We hadn't run a knot—or much beyond—
(What will you have on it?)—but off she goes,
Up to her bends in a fresh-water pond!
        There I am! all a-back!
So I looks forward for her bridal-gears,
To heave her head round on the t'other tack;
        But when I starts,
        The leather parts,
And goes away right over by the ears!

        What could a fellow do,
Whose legs, like mine, you know, were in the bilboes,
But trim myself upright for bringing-to,
And square his yard-arms and brace up his elbows,
        In rig all snug and clever,
Just while his craft was taking in her water?
I didn't like my berth though, howsomdever,
Because the yarn, you see, kept getting tauter.
        Says I—I wish this job was rayther shorter!
        The chase had gained a mile
A-head, and still the she-mare stood a drinking:
        Now, all the while

Her body didn't take, of course, to shrinking.
Says I, she's letting out her reefs, I'm thinking;
        And so she swelled and swelled,
        And yet the tackle held,

30

40

50

60

70

Till both my legs began to bend like winkin'.
My eyes! but she took in enough to founder!
And there's my timbers straining every bit,
      Ready to split,
And her tarnation hull a-growing rounder!

      Well, there—off Hartford Ness,
We lay both lashed and water-logged together,
      And can't contrive a signal of distress.
Thinks I, we must ride out this here foul weather,
Tho' sick of riding out, and nothing less;   80
When, looking round, I sees a man a-starn:
"Hallo!" says I, "come underneath her quarters!"
And hands him out my knife to cut the yarn.
So I gets off, and lands upon the road,
And leaves the she-mare to her own consarn,
      A-standing by the water.
If I get on another, I'll be blowed!
And that's the way, you see, my legs got bowed!

                 THOMAS HOOD

Sally Simpkin's Lament

'Oh! what is that comes gliding in,
   And quite in middling haste?
It is the picture of my Jones,
   And painted to the waist.

'It is not painted to the life,
   For where's the trowsers blue?
Oh Jones, my dear!—Oh dear! my Jones,
   What is become of you?'

'Oh! Sally dear, it is too true,—
   The half that you remark   10
Is come to say my other half
   Is bit off by a shark!

'Oh! Sally, sharks do things by halves
   Yet most completely do!
A bite in one place seems enough,
   But I've been bit in two.

'You know I once was all your own,
   But now a shark must share!
But let that pass—for now to you
   I'm neither here nor there.   20

153

'Alas! death has a strange divorce
   Effected in the sea.
It has divided me from you,
   And even me from me.

'Don't fear my ghost will walk o' nights
   To haunt as people say;
My ghost *can't* walk, for, oh! my legs
   Are many leagues away!

'Lord! think when I am swimming round,
   And looking where the boat is,
A shark just snaps away a *half*
   Without "a *quarter's* notice."

'One half is here, the other half
   Is near Columbia placed:
Oh! Sally, I have got the whole
   Atlantic for my waist.

'But now, adieu—a long adieu!
   I've solved death's awful riddle.
And would say more, but I am doomed
   To break off in the middle.'

                THOMAS HOOD

30

To the Immortal Memory of the Halibut on Which I Dined This Day

Where hast thou floated, in what seas pursued
Thy pastime? When wast thou an egg new-spawned,
Lost in th' immensity of ocean's waste?
Roar as they might, the overbearing winds
That rocked the deep, thy cradle, thou wast safe—
And in thy minnikin° and embryo state,   tiny
Attached to the firm leaf of some salt weed,
Didst outlive tempests, such as wrung and racked
The joints of many a stout and gallant bark,
And whelmed them in the unexplored abyss.   10
Indebted to no magnet and no chart,
Nor under guidance of the polar fire,
Thou wast a voyager on many coasts,
Grazing at large in meadows submarine,
Where flat Batavia just emerging peeps
Above the brine,—where Caledonia's rocks

Beat back the surge,—and where Hibernia shoots[1]
Her wondrous causeway far into the main.
—Wherever thou hast fed, thou little thought'st;
And I not more, that I should feed on thee.   20
Peace therefore, and good health, and much good fish,
To him who sent thee! and success, as oft
As it descends into the billowy gulph,
To the same drag that caught thee!—Fare thee well!
Thy lot thy brethren of the slimy fin
Would envy, could they know that thou wast doomed
To feed a bard, and to be praised in verse.

WILLIAM COWPER

The Midshipman

Aid me, kind Muse, so whimsical a theme,
No poet ever yet pursued for fame:
Boldly I venture on a naval scene,
Nor fear the critic's frown, the pedant's spleen.
Sons of the ocean, we their rules disdain;
Our bosom's honest, and our style is plain.
Let Homer's heroes and his gods delight;
Let Milton with infernal legions fight;
His favourite warrior polish'd Virgil show;
With love and wine luxurious Horace glow: 10
Be such their subjects,—I another choose,
As yet neglected by the laughing Muse.[2]

Deep in that fabric, where Britannia boasts
O'er seas to waft her thunder and her hosts,
A cavern! —unknown to cheering day;
Where one small taper lends a feeble ray;
Where wild disorder holds her wanton reign,
And careless mortals frolic in her train—
Bending beneath a hammock's friendly shade,
See Æsculapius[3] all in arms display'd;   20
In his right hand th' impending steel he holds,
The other round the trembling victim folds;
His gaping myrmidon[4] the deed attends,
While in the pot the crimson stream descends:
Unawed young Galen bears the hostile brunt,
Pills in his rear, and Cullen in his front;[5]

Whilst, muster'd round the medicinal pile,
Death's grim militia stand in rank and file.

In neighbouring mansions —lo! what clouds arise;
It half-conceals its owner from our eyes.
One penny light with feeble lustre shines,
To prove the MID in high Olympus dines.
Let us approach—the preparation view,—
A Cockpit Bean is surely something new!
To him Japan her varnished joys denies,
Nor bloom for him the sweets of eastern skies;
His rugged limbs no lofty mirror shows,
No tender couch invites him to repose;
A pigmy glass upon his toilet stands,
Cracked o'er and o'er by awkward, clumsy hands;
Chesterfield's page polite, the "Seaman's Guide,"
A half-eat biscuit, Congreve's "Mourning Bride,"[6]
Bestrew'd with powder, in confusion lie,
And form a chaos to th' intruding eye.
At length this meteor of an hour is dressed,
And rises, an Adonis,[7] from his chest:
Cautious he treads, lest some unlucky slip
Defile his clothes with burgoo—or with flip:
These rocks escaped, arrives *in status quo;*
Bows; dines and bows; then sinks again below.

Not far from hence a joyous group are met,
For social mirth and sportive pastime set;
In cheering grog the rapid course goes round,
And not a care in all the circle's found,—
Promotion, mess-debts, absent friends, and love
Inspired by hope, in turn their topics prove:
To proud superiors then they each look up,
And curse all discipline in ample cup.

Hark! yonder voice in hollow murmur falls:
Hark! yonder voice the MID to duty calls.
Thus summoned by the gods, he deigns to go,
But first makes known his consequence below,—
At slavery rails, scorns lawless sway to hell,
And damns the powers allow'd a white lapel;
Vows that he's free!—to stoop, to cringe disdains,
Ascends the ladder and resumes his chains.
In canvas'd berth, profoundly deep in thought,
His busy mind with sins and tangents fraught,
A MID reclines—in calculation lost,
His efforts still by some intruder cross'd.

30

40

50

60

70

Now to the longitude's vast height he soars,
And now formation of lobscouse[8] explores;
Now o'er a field of logarithms bends,
And now to make a pudding he pretends:
At once the sage, the hero and the cook,
He wields the sword, the saucepan and the book.
Opposed to him a sprightly messmate lolls,
Declaims with Garrick, or with Shuter drolls:
Sometimes his breast great Cato's virtue warms,
And then his task the gay Lothario charms;   80
Cleone's griefs his tragic feelings wake;
With Richard's pangs th' Orlopian caverns shake![9]
No more the mess for other joys repine,
When pea-soup entering, shows 'tis time to dine.

But think not meanly of this humble seat,
Whence sprung the guardians of the British fleet;
Revere the sacred spot, however low,
Which form'd to martial acts a Hawke, a Howe.[10]

WILLIAM FALCONER

Port Admiral

'Twas at the landing-place that's just below Mount Wyse,
Poll lean'd against the sentry's box, a tear in both her eyes;
Her apron twisted round her arms, all for to keep them warm,
Being a windy Christmas Day, and also a snowstorm.
        And Bet and Sue
        Both stood there too,
            A-shivering by her side;
        They both were dumb,
        And both look'd glum,
            As they watch'd the ebbing tide.   10
        Poll put her arms a-kimbo,
            At the admiral's house look'd she,
        To thoughts before in limbo
            She now a vent gave free.
        You have sent the ship in a gale to work,
            On a lee shore to be jamm'd,
        I'll give you a piece of my mind, old Turk,
            Port Admiral, you be d——d.

157

We'll give you a piece of our mind, old Turk,
　Port Admiral, you be d——d.　　　　　　　　　20

Who ever heard in the sarvice of a frigate made to sail
On Christmas Day, it blowing hard, with sleet, and snow, and hail?
I wish I had the fishing of your back that is so bent,
I'd use the galley poker hot unto your heart's content.
　　Here Bet and Sue
　　Are with me too,
　　　A-shivering by my side;
　　They both are dumb,
　　And both look glum,
　　　And watch the ebbing tide.　　　　　　　30
　　Poll put her arms a-kimbo,
　　　At the admiral's house look'd she,
　　To thoughts that were in limbo
　　　She now a vent gave free.
　　You've got a roaring fire, I'll bet,
　　　In it your toes are jamm'd:
　　Let's give him a piece of our mind, my Bet,
　　　Port Admiral, you be d——d.

Let's give him a piece of our mind, my Bet,
　Port Admiral, you be d——d.　　　　　　　　40

I had the flour and plums all pick'd, and suet all chopp'd fine,
To mix into a pudding rich for all the mess to dine;
I pawn'd my ear-rings for the beef, it weigh'd at least a stone,
Now my fancy man is sent to sea, and I am left alone.
　　Here's Bet and Sue
　　Who stand here too,
　　　A-shivering by my side;
　　They both are dumb,
　　They both look glum,
　　　And watch the ebbing tide.　　　　　　　50
　　Poll put her arms a-kimbo,
　　　At the admiral's house look'd she,
　　To thoughts that were in limbo,
　　　She now a vent gave free.
　　You've got a turkey, I'll be bound,
　　　With which you will be cramm'd;
　　I'll give you a bit of my mind, old hound,
　　　Port Admiral, you be d——d.

I'll give you a bit of my mind, old hound,
    Port Admiral, you be d——d.   60

I'm sure that in this weather they cannot cook their meat,
To eat it raw on Christmas Day will be a pleasant treat;
But let us all go home, girls; it's no use waiting here,
We'll hope that Christmas Day to come they will have better cheer.
    So Bet and Sue,
    Don't stand here too,
      A-shivering by my side:
    Don't keep so dumb,
    Don't look so glum,
      Nor watch the ebbing tide.   70
    Poll put her arms a-kimbo,
      At the admiral's house look'd she,
    To thoughts that were in limbo
      She now a vent gave free.
    So while they cut their raw salt junks,
      With dainties you'll be cramm'd,
    Here's once for all my mind, old hunks,
    Port Admiral, you be d——d.

Chorus

So once for all our mind, old hunks,
    Port Admiral, you be d——d.

FREDERICK MARRYAT

Epistle to a Desponding Sea-Man

    Your men of the land, from the king to Jack Ketch
All join in supposing the sailor a wretch,
That his life is a round of vexation and woe,
With always too much or too little to do:
In the dead of the night, when other men sleep,
He, starboard and larboard, his watches must keep;
Imprison'd by Neptune, he lives like a dog,
And to know where he is, must depend on a LOG,
Must fret in a calm, and be sad in a storm;
In winter much trouble to keep himself warm: 10
Through the heat of the summer pursuing his trade,
No trees, but his topmasts, to yield him a shade:
Then, add to the list of the mariner's evils,
The water corrupted, the bread full of weevils,

Salt junk to be eat, be it better or worse,
And, often bull-beef of an Irishman's horse:
Whosoever is free, he must still be a slave,
(Despotic is always the rule on the wave;)
Not relish'd on water, your lads of the main
Abhor the republican doctrines of PAINE,[11]   20
And each, like the despot of Prussia,[12] may say
That his crew has no right, but the right to obey.
  Such things say the lubbers, and sigh when they've said 'em,
But things are not so bad as their fancies persuade 'em:
There ne'er was a task but afforded some ease,
Nor a calling in life, but had somewhat to please.
If the sea has its storms, it has also its calms,
A time to sing songs and a time to sing psalms.—
Yes—give me a vessel well timber'd and sound,
Her bottom good plank, and in rigging well found,   30
If her spars are but staunch and her oakham swell'd tight,
From tempests and storms I'll extract some delight—
At sea I would rather have Neptune my jailor
Than a lubber on shore, that despises a sailor.
Do they ask me what pleasure I find on the sea?—
Why, absence from land is a pleasure to me:
A hamper of porter, and plenty of grog,
A friend, when too sleepy, to give me a jog,
A coop that will always some poultry afford,
Some bottles of gin, and no parson on board,   40
A crew that is brisk when it happens to blow,
One compass on deck and another below,
A girl, with more sense than the girl at the head,
To read me a novel, or make up my bed—
The man that has these, has a treasure in store
That millions possess not, who live upon shore:
But if it should happen that commerce grew dull,
Or Neptune, ill-humour'd, should batter my hull,
Should damage my cargo, or heave me aground,
Or pay me with farthings instead of a pound: 50
Should I always be left in the rear of the race,
And this be forever—forever the case;
Why then, if the honest plain truth I may tell,
I would clew up my topsails, and bid him farewell.

PHILIP FRENEAU

160

The Ballad of the Oysterman

It was a tall young oysterman lived by the river-side,
His shop was just upon the bank, his boat was on the tide;
The daughter of a fisherman, that was so straight and slim,
Lived over on the other bank, right opposite to him.

It was the pensive oysterman that saw a lovely maid,
Upon a moonlight evening, a sitting in the shade:
He saw her wave her handkerchief, as much as if to say,
"I'm wide awake, young oysterman, and all the folks away."

Then up arose the oysterman, and to himself said he,
"I guess I'll leave the skiff at home, for fear that folks should see;   10
I read it in the story-book, that, for to kiss his dear,
Leander swam the Hellespont,[13]—and I will swim this here."

And he has leaped into the waves, and crossed the shining stream,
And he has clambered up the bank, all in the moonlight gleam;
Oh there were kisses sweet as dew, and words as soft as rain,—
But they have heard her father's step, and in he leaps again!

Out spoke the ancient fisherman,—"Oh, what was that, my daughter?"
" 'Twas nothing but a pebble, sir, I threw into the water."
"And what is that, pray tell me, love, that paddles off so fast?"
"It's nothing but a porpoise, sir, that's been a-swimming past."   20

Out spoke the ancient fisherman,—"Now bring me my harpoon!
I'll get into my fishing boat, and fix the fellow soon."
Down fell that pretty innocent, as falls a snow-white lamb,
Her hair dropped round her pallid cheeks, like seaweed on a clam.

Alas for those two loving ones! she waked not from her swound,
And he was taken with the cramp, and in the waves was drowned;
But Fate has metamorphosed them, in pity of their woe,
And now they keep an oyster-shop for mermaids down below.

OLIVER WENDELL HOLMES

Written After Swimming from Sestos to Abydos[14]

If, in the month of dark December,
　　Leander, who was nightly wont
(What maid will not the tale remember?)
　　To cross thy stream, broad Hellespont!

If, when the wintry tempest roar'd,
　　He sped to Hero, nothing loth,
And thus of old thy current pour'd,
　　Fair Venus! how I pity both!

For *me*, degenerate modern wretch,
　　Though in the genial month of May,　　　　　　10
My dripping limbs I faintly stretch,
　　And think I've done a feat to-day.

But since he cross'd the rapid tide,
　　According to the doubtful story,
To woo,—and—Lord knows what beside,
　　And swam for Love, as I for Glory;

'T were hard to say who fared the best:
　　Sad mortals! thus the Gods still plague you!
He lost his labour, I my jest;
　　For he was drown'd, and I've the ague.

GEORGE GORDON, LORD BYRON

From *Don Juan*
Canto the Second

XI

Juan embark'd—the ship got under way,
　　The wind was fair, the water passing rough:
A devil of a sea rolls in that bay,
　　As I, who've cross'd it oft, know well enough;
And, standing upon deck, the dashing spray
　　Flies in one's face, and makes it weather-tough:
And there he stood to take, and take again,
His first—perhaps his last—farewell of Spain.

XII

I can't but say it is an awkward sight
    To see one's native land receding through
The growing waters; it unmans one quite,
    Especially when life is rather new:
I recollect Great Britain's coast looks white,
    But almost every other country's blue,
When gazing on them, mystified by distance,
We enter on our nautical existence.

XIII

So Juan stood, bewilder'd on the deck:
    The wind sung, cordage strain'd, and sailors swore,
And the ship creak'd, the town became a speck,
    From which away so fair and fast they bore.
The best of remedies is a beef-steak
    Against sea-sickness: try it, sir, before
You sneer, and I assure you this is true,
For I have found it answer—so may you.

. . . .

XIX

'And, oh! if e'er I should forget, I swear—
    But that's impossible, and cannot be—
Sooner shall this blue ocean melt to air,
    Sooner shall earth resolve itself to sea,
Than I resign thine image, oh, my fair!
    Or think of any thing excepting thee;
A mind diseased no remedy can physic
(Here the ship gave a lurch, and he grew sea-sick).

XX

'Sooner shall heaven kiss earth (here he fell sicker),
    Oh, Julia! what is every other wo?
(For God's sake let me have a glass of liquor;
    Pedro, Battista, help me down below.)
Julia, my love! (you rascal, Pedro, quicker)—
    Oh, Julia! (this curst vessel pitches so)—
Beloved Julia, hear me still beseeching!'
(Here he grew inarticulate with retching.)

XXI

He felt that chilling heaviness of heart,
   Or rather stomach, which, alas! attends,
Beyond the best apothecary's art,
   The loss of love, the treachery of friends,
Or death of those we dote on, when a part
   Of us dies with them as each fond hope ends:
No doubt he would have been much more pathetic,
But the sea acted as a strong emetic.

XXII

Love's a capricious power: I've known it hold
   Out through a fever caused by its own heat,
But be much puzzled by a cough and cold,
   And find a quinsy° very hard to treat;   sore throat
Against all noble maladies he's bold,
   But vulgar illnesses don't like to meet,
Nor that a sneeze should interrupt his sigh,
Nor inflammations redden his blind eye.

XXIII

But worst of all is nausea, or a pain
   About the lower region of the bowels;
Love, who heroically breathes a vein,
   Shrinks from the application of hot towels,
And purgatives are dangerous to his reign,
   Sea-sickness death: his love was perfect, how else
Could Juan's passion, while the billows roar,
Resist his stomach, ne'er at sea before?

. . . .

XXXIII

It may be easily supposed, while this
   Was going on, some people were unquiet,
That passengers would find it much amiss
   To lose their lives, as well as spoil their diet;
That even the able seaman, deeming his
   Days nearly o'er, might be disposed to riot,
As upon such occasions tars will ask
For grog, and sometimes drink rum from the cask.

164

XXXIV

There's nought, no doubt, so much the spirit calms
　　As rum and true religion: thus it was,
Some plunder'd, some drank spirits, some sung psalms,
　　The high wind made the treble, and as bass
The hoarse harsh waves kept time; fright cured the qualms
　　Of all the luckless landsmen's sea-sick maws:
Strange sounds of wailing, blasphemy, devotion,
Clamour'd in chorus to the roaring ocean.

XXXV

Perhaps more mischief had been done, but for
　　Our Juan, who, with sense beyond his years,
Got to the spirit-room, and stood before
　　It with a pair of pistols; and their fears,
As if Death were more dreadful by his door
　　Of fire than water, spite of oaths and tears,
Kept still aloof the crew, who, ere they sunk,
Thought it would be becoming to die drunk.
. . . .

XLIV

The ship was evidently settling now
　　Fast by the head; and, all distinction gone,
Some went to prayers again, and made a vow
　　Of candles to their saints—but there were none
To pay them with; and some look'd o'er the bow;
　　Some hoisted out the boats; and there was one
That begg'd Pedrillo for an absolution,
Who told him to be damn'd—in his confusion.

XLV

Some lash'd them in their hammocks; some put on
　　Their best clothes, as if going to a fair;
Some cursed the day on which they saw the sun,
　　And gnash'd their teeth, and, howling, tore their hair;
And others went on as they had begun,
　　Getting the boats out, being well aware
That a tight boat will live in a rough sea,
Unless with breakers close beneath her lee.
. . . .

LI

At half-past eight o'clock, booms, hencoops, spars,
   And all things, for a chance, had been cast loose,
That still could keep afloat the struggling tars,
   For yet they strove, although of no great use:
There was no light in heaven but a few stars,
   The boats put off o'ercrowded with their crews;
She gave a heel, and then a lurch to port,
And, going down head foremost—sunk, in short.

LII

Then rose from sea to sky the wild farewell—
   Then shriek'd the timid, and stood still the brave,
Then some leap'd overboard with dreadful yell,
   As eager to anticipate their grave;
And the sea yawn'd around her like a hell,
   And down she suck'd with her the whirling wave,
Like one who grapples with his enemy,
And strives to strangle him before he die.

LIII

And first one universal shriek there rush'd,
   Louder than the loud ocean, like a crash
Of echoing thunder; and then all was hush'd,
   Save the wild wind and the remorseless dash
Of billows; but at intervals there gush'd,
   Accompanied with a convulsive splash,
A solitary shriek, the bubbling cry
Of some strong swimmer in his agony.

LIV

The boats, as stated, had got off before,
   And in them crowded several of the crew;
And yet their present hope was hardly more
   Than what it had been, for so strong it blew
There was slight chance of reaching any shore;
   And then they were too many, though so few—
Nine in the cutter, thirty in the boat,
Were counted in them when they got afloat.

LV

All the rest perish'd; near two hundred souls
    Had left their bodies; and what's worse, alas!
When over Catholics the ocean rolls,
    They must wait several weeks before a mass
Takes off one peck of purgatorial coals,
    Because, till people know what's come to pass,
They won't lay out their money on the dead—
It costs three francs for every mass that's said.

. . . .

LXVI

'T is thus with people in an open boat,
    They live upon the love of life, and bear
More than can be believed, or even thought,
    And stand like rocks the tempest's wear and tear;
And hardship still has been the sailor's lot,
    Since Noah's ark went cruising here and there;
She had a curious crew as well as cargo,
Like the first old Greek privateer, the Argo.[15]

LXVII

But man is a carnivorous production,
    And must have meals, at least one meal a day;
He cannot live, like woodcocks, upon suction,
    But, like the shark and tiger, must have prey;
Although his anatomical construction
    Bears vegetables, in a grumbling way,
Your labouring people think beyond all question,
Beef, veal, and mutton, better for digestion.

LXVIII

And thus it was with this our hapless crew;
    For on the third day there came on a calm,
And though at first their strength it might renew,
    And lying on their weariness like balm,
Lull'd them like turtles sleeping on the blue
    Of ocean, when they woke they felt a qualm,
And fell all ravenously on their provision,
Instead of hoarding it with due precision.

LXIX

The consequence was easily foreseen—
    They ate up all they had, and drank their wine,
In spite of all remonstrances, and then
    On what, in fact, next day were they to dine?
They hoped the wind would rise, these foolish men!
    And carry them to shore; these hopes were fine,
But as they had but one oar, and that brittle,
It would have been more wise to save their victual.

LXX

The fourth day came, but not a breath of air,
    And Ocean slumber'd like an unwean'd child:
The fifth day, and their boat lay floating there,
    The sea and sky were blue, and clear, and mild—
With their one oar (I wish they had had a pair)
    What could they do? and hunger's rage grew wild:
So Juan's spaniel, spite of his entreating,
Was kill'd and portion'd out for present eating.

LXXI

On the sixth day they fed upon his hide,
    And Juan, who had still refused, because
The creature was his father's dog that died,
    Now feeling all the vulture in his jaws,
With some remorse received (though first denied)
    As a great favour one of the fore-paws,
Which he divided with Pedrillo, who
Devour'd it, longing for the other too.
. . . .

LXXV

The lots were made, and mark'd, and mix'd, and handed,
    In silent horror, and their distribution
Lull'd even the savage hunger which demanded,
    Like the Promethean vulture,[16] this pollution;
None in particular had sought or plann'd it,
    'T was nature gnaw'd them to this resolution,
By which none were permitted to be neuter—
And the lot fell on Juan's luckless tutor.

LXXVI

He but requested to be bled to death:
  The surgeon had his instruments, and bled
Pedrillo, and so gently ebb'd his breath,
  You hardly could perceive when he was dead.
He died as born, a Catholic in faith,
  Like most in the belief in which they're bred,
And first a little crucifix he kiss'd,
And then held out his jugular and wrist.

LXXVII

The surgeon, as there was no other fee,
  Had his first choice of morsels for his pains;
But being thirstiest at the moment, he
  Preferr'd a draught from the fast-flowing veins:
Part was divided, part thrown in the sea,
  And such things as the entrails and the brains
Regaled two sharks, who follow'd o'er the billow—
The sailors ate the rest of poor Pedrillo.

LXXVIII

The sailors ate him, all save three or four,
  Who were not quite so fond of animal food;
To these was added Juan, who, before
  Refusing his own spaniel, hardly could
Feel now his appetite increased much more;
  'T was not to be expected that he should,
Even in extremity of their disaster,
Dine with them on his pastor and his master.

LXXIX

'Twas better that he did not; for, in fact,
  The consequence was awful in the extreme;
For they, who were most ravenous in the act,
  Went raging mad—Lord! how they did blaspheme!
And foam and roll, with strange convulsions rack'd,
  Drinking salt-water like a mountain-stream,
Tearing, and grinning, howling, screeching, swearing,
And, with hyæna-laughter, died despairing.
. . . .

LXXXI

And next they thought upon the master's mate,
 As fattest; but he saved himself, because,
Besides being much averse from such a fate,
 There were some other reasons: the first was,
He had been rather indisposed of late;
 And that which chiefly proved his saving clause
Was a small present made to him at Cadiz,
By general subscription of the ladies.

LXXXII

Of poor Pedrillo something still remain'd,
 But was used sparingly,—some were afraid,
And others still their appetites constrain'd,
 Or but at times a little supper made;
All except Juan, who throughout abstain'd,
 Chewing a piece of bamboo and some lead:
At length they caught two boobies and a noddy,
And then they left off eating the dead body.

LXXXIII

And if Pedrillo's fate should shocking be,
 Remember Ugolino condescends
To eat the head of his arch-enemy
 The moment after he politely ends
His tale: if foes be food in hell, at sea
 'T is surely fair to dine upon our friends,
When shipwreck's short allowance grows too scanty,
Without being much more horrible than Dante.[17]

. . . .

XCVII

As morning broke, the light wind died away,
 When he who had the watch sung out and swore,
If 't was not land that rose with the sun's ray,
 He wish'd that land he never might see more;
And the rest rubb'd their eyes and saw a bay,
 Or thought they saw, and shaped their course for shore;
For shore it was, and gradually grew
Distinct, and high, and palpable to view.

. . . .

XCVIII

And then of these some part burst into tears,
  And others, looking with a stupid stare,
Could not yet separate their hopes from fears,
  And seem'd as if they had no further care;
While a few pray'd (the first time for some years)—
  And at the bottom of the boat three were
Asleep: they shook them by the hand and head,
And tried to awaken them, but found them dead.

. . . .

CI

Meantime the current, with a rising gale,
  Still set them onwards to the welcome shore,
Like Charon's bark of spectres,[18] dull and pale:
  Their living freight was now reduced to four,
And three dead, whom their strength could not avail
  To heave into the deep with those before,
Though the two sharks still follow'd them, and dash'd
The spray into their faces as they splash'd.

CII

Famine, despair, cold, thirst, and heat, had done
  Their work on them by turns, and thinn'd them to
Such things a mother had not known her son
  Amidst the skeletons of that gaunt crew;
By night chill'd, by day scorch'd, thus one by one
  They perish'd, until wither'd to these few,
But chiefly by a species of self-slaughter,
In washing down Pedrillo with salt water.

. . . .

CIV

The shore look'd wild, without a trace of man,
  And girt by formidable waves; but they
Were mad for land, and thus their course they ran,
  Though right ahead the roaring breakers lay:
A reef between them also now began
  To show its boiling surf and bounding spray,
But finding no place for their landing better,
They ran the boat for shore,—and overset her.

171

CV

But in his native stream, the Guadalquivir,[19]
   Juan to lave his youthful limbs was wont;
And having learnt to swim in that sweet river,
   Had often turn'd the art to some account:
A better swimmer you could scarce see ever,
   He could, perhaps, have pass'd the Hellespont,
As once (a feat on which ourselves we prided)
Leander, Mr. Ekenhead,[20] and I did.

CVI

So here, though faint, emaciated, and stark,
   He buoy'd his boyish limbs, and strove to ply
With the quick wave, and gain, ere it was dark,
   The beach which lay before him, high and dry:
The greatest danger here was from a shark,
   That carried off his neighbour by the thigh;
As for the other two, they could not swim,
So nobody arrived on shore but him.

               GEORGE GORDON, LORD BYRON

Little Billee

There were three sailors in Bristol City,
Who took a boat and went to sea.

But first with beef and captain's biscuit,
And pickled pork they loaded she.

There was guzzling Jack and gorging Jimmy,
And the youngest he was little Bil-*ly*.

Now very soon they were so greedy,
They didn't leave not one split pea.

Says guzzling Jack to gorging Jimmy,
I am confounded hung-*ery*.   10

Says gorging Jim to guzzling Jacky,
We have no wittles, so we must eat *we*.

Says guzzling Jack to gorging Jimmy,
O gorging Jim, what a fool you be.

There's little Bill as is young and tender,
We're old and tough—so let's eat *he*.

O Bill, we're going to kill and eat you,
So undo the collar of your chemie.

When Bill he heard this information,
He used his pocket-handkerchee.   20

O let me say my Catechism,
As my poor mammy taught to me.

Make haste, make haste, says guzzling Jacky,
Whilst Jim pulled out his snicker-snee.

So Bill went up the main top-gallant mast,
When down he fell on his bended knee.

He scarce had said his Catechism,
When up he jumps: 'There's land I see!

'There's Jerusalem and Madagascar,
And North and South Ameri-*key*.   30

'There's the British fleet a-riding at anchor,
With Admiral Napier, K.C.B.'

So when they came to the Admiral's vessel,
He hanged fat Jack, and flogged Jim-*my*.

But as for little Bill, he made him
The Captain of a Seventy-three.

WILLIAM MAKEPEACE THACKERAY

The Yarn of the *Nancy Bell*

'Twas on the shores that round our coast
    From Deal to Ramsgate span,
That I found alone on a piece of stone
    An elderly naval man.

His hair was weedy, his beard was long,
    And weedy and long was he,
And I heard this wight on the shore recite,
    In a singular minor key:

'Oh, I am a cook and a captain bold,
    And the mate of the *Nancy* brig,   10
And a bo'sun tight, and a midshipmite,
    And the crew of the captain's gig.'

And he shook his fists and he tore his hair,
    Till I really felt afraid,
For I couldn't help thinking the man had been drinking,
    And so I simply said:

'Oh, elderly man, it's little I know
   Of the duties of men of the sea,
But I'll eat my hand if I understand
   How you can possibly be   20

'At once a cook, and a captain bold,
   And the mate of the *Nancy* brig,
And a bo'sun tight, and a midshipmite,
   And the crew of the captain's gig.'

Then he gave a hitch to his trousers, which
   Is a trick all seamen larn,
And having got rid of a thumping quid,
   He spun this painful yarn:

' 'Twas in the good ship *Nancy Bell*
   That we sailed to the Indian sea,   30
And there on a reef we come to grief,
   Which has often occurred to me.

'And pretty nigh all o' the crew was drowned
   (There was seventy-seven o' soul),
And only ten of the *Nancy's* men
   Said "Here!" to the muster-roll.

'There was me and the cook and the captain bold,
   And the mate of the *Nancy* brig,
And the bo'sun tight, and a midshipmite,
   And the crew of the captain's gig.   40

'For a month we'd neither wittles nor drink,
   Till a-hungry we did feel,
So we drawed a lot, and accordin' shot
   The captain for our meal.

'The next lot fell to the *Nancy's* mate,
   And a delicate dish he made;
Then our appetite with the midshipmite
   We seven survivors stayed.

'And then we murdered the bo'sun tight,
   And he much resembled pig;   50
Then we wittled free, did the cook and me,
   On the crew of the captain's gig.

'Then only the cook and me was left,
   And the delicate question, "Which
Of us two goes to the kettle?" arose
   And we argued it out as sich.

'For I loved that cook as a brother, I did,
    And the cook he worshipped me;
But we'd both be blowed if we'd either be stowed
    In the other chap's hold, you see.   60

' "I'll be eat if you dines off me," says TOM,
    "Yes, that," says I, "you'll be,"—
"I'm boiled if I die, my friend," quoth I,
    And "Exactly so," quoth he.

'Says he, "Dear JAMES, to murder me
    Were a foolish thing to do,
For don't you see that you can't cook *me*,
    While I can—and will—cook *you*!"

'So he boils the water, and takes the salt
    And the pepper in portions true   70
(Which he never forgot), and some chopped shalot,
    And some sage and parsley too.

' "Come here," says he, with a proper pride,
    Which his smiling features tell,
" 'Twill soothing be if I let you see,
    How extremely nice you'll smell."

'And he stirred it round and round and round,
    And he sniffed at the foaming froth;
When I ups with his heels, and smothers his squeals
    In the scum of the boiling broth.   80

'And I eat that cook in a week or less,
    And—as I eating be
The last of his chops, why, I almost drops,
    For a wessel in sight I see!

'And I never grin, and I never smile,
    And I never larf nor play,
But I sit and croak, and a single joke
    I have—which is to say:

'Oh, I am a cook and a captain bold,
    And the mate of the *Nancy* brig,   90
And a bo'sun tight, *and* a midshipmite,
    And the crew of the captain's gig!'

                        W. S. GILBERT

A Sailor's Yarn

This is the tale that was told to me
    By a battered and shattered son of the sea,—
To me and my messmate, Silas Green,
    When I was a guileless young marine.

───────────

'T was the good ship Gyascutus,
    All in the China seas,
With the wind a-lee and the capstan free
    To catch the summer breeze.

'T was Captain Porgie on the deck,
    To his mate in the mizzen hatch,   10
While the boatswain bold, in the forward hold,
    Was winding his larboard watch.

"Oh, how does our good ship head to-night?
    How heads our gallant craft?"
"Oh, she heads to the E. S. W. by N.,
    And the binnacle lies abaft!"

"Oh, what does the quadrant indicate,
    And how does the sextant stand?"
"Oh, the sextant's down to the freezing point,
    And the quadrant's lost a hand!"   20

"Oh, and if the quadrant has lost a hand
    And the sextant falls so low,
It's our bodies and bones to Davy Jones
    This night are bound to go!

"Oh, fly aloft to the garboard strake!
    And reef the spanker boom;
Bend a studding-sail on the martingale,
    To give her weather room.

"O boatswain, down in the for'ard hold,
    What water do you find?"   30
"Four foot and a half by the royal gaff
    And rather more behind!"

"O sailors, collar your marline spikes
    and each belaying-pin;
Come, stir your stumps and spike the pumps,
    Or more will be coming in!"

They stirred their stumps, they spiked the pumps,
    They spliced the mizzen brace;

Aloft and alow they worked, but oh!
    The water gained apace.   40

They bored a hole above the keel
    To let the water out;
But, strange to say, to their dismay,
    The water in did spout.

Then up spoke the Cook of our gallant ship,
    And he was a lubber brave:
"I have several wives in various ports,
    And my life I'd orter save."

Then up spoke the Captain of Marines,
    Who dearly loved his prog:°   victuals   50
"It's awful to die, and it's worse to be dry,
    And I move we pipes to grog."

Oh, then 't was the noble second mate
    What filled them all with awe;
The second mate, as bad men hate,
    And cruel skippers jaw.

He took the anchor on his back
    And leaped into the main;
Through foam and spray he clove his way,
    And sunk and rose again!   60

Through foam and spray, a league away
    The anchor stout he bore;
Till, safe at last, he made it fast
    And warped the ship ashore!

'T ain't much of a job to talk about,
    But a ticklish thing to see,
And suth'in to do, if I say it, too,
    For that second mate was me!

Such was the tale that was told to me
By that modest and truthful son of the sea;   70
And I envy the life of a second mate,
Though captains curse him and sailors hate,
For he ain't like some of the swabs I've seen,
As would go and lie to a poor marine.

JAMES J. ROCHE

"Soldier an' Sailor Too"
(*The Royal Regiment of Marines*)

As I was spittin' into the Ditch[21] aboard o' the *Crocodile,*
I seed a man on a man-o'-war got up in the Reg'lars'[22] style.
'E was scrapin' the paint from off of 'er plates, an' I sez to 'im, " 'Oo
    are you?"
Sez 'e, "I'm a Jolly—'Er Majesty's Jolly—soldier an' sailor too!"
Now 'is work begins by Gawd knows when, and 'is work is never
    through;
'E isn't one o' the reg'lar Line, nor 'e isn't one of the crew.
'E's a kind of a giddy harumfrodite—soldier an' sailor too!"

An', after, I met 'im all over the world, a-doin' all kinds of things,
Like landin' 'isself with a Gatlin' gun to talk to them 'eathen kings;
'E sleeps in an 'ammick instead of a cot, an' 'e drills with the deck
    on a slew,   10
An' 'e sweats like a Jolly—'Er Majesty's Jolly—soldier an' sailor too!
For there isn't a job on the top o' the earth the beggar don't know, nor
    do—
You can leave 'im at night on a bald man's 'ead, to paddle 'is own
    canoe—
'E's a sort of a bloomin' cosmopolouse—soldier an' sailor too.

We've fought 'em in trooper, we've fought 'em in dock, and drunk with
    'em in betweens,
When they called us the seasick scull'ry-maids, an' we called 'em the
    Ass-Marines;
But, when we was down for a double fatigue, from Woolwich to
    Bernardmyo,
We sent for the Jollies—'Er Majesty's Jollies—soldier an' sailor too!
They think for 'emselves, an' they steal for 'emselves, and they never
    ask what's to do,
But they're camped an' fed an' they're up an' fed before our bugle's
    blew.   20
Ho! they ain't no limpin' procrastitutes—soldier an' sailor too.

You may say we are fond of an 'arness-cut, or 'ootin' in barrick-yards,
Or startin' a Board School mutiny along o' the Onion Guards;
But once in a while we can finish in style for the ends of the earth to
    view,
The same as the Jollies—'Er Majesty's Jollies—soldier an' sailor too!
They come of our lot, they was brothers to us; they was beggars we'd
    met an' knew;

Yes, barrin' an inch in the chest an' the arm, they was doubles o' me an'
    you;
For they weren't no special chrysanthemums—soldier an' sailor too!

To take your chance in the thick of a rush, with firing all about,
Is nothing so bad when you've cover to 'and, an' leave an' likin' to
    shout: 30
But to stand an' be still to the *Birken'ead* drill[23] is a damn' tough bullet
    to chew,
An' they done it, the Jollies—'Er Majesty's Jollies—soldier an' sailor too!
Their work was done when it 'adn't begun; they was younger nor me
    an' you;
Their choice it was plain between drownin' in 'eaps an' bein' mopped by
    the screw,
So they stood an' was still to the *Birken'ead* drill, soldier an' sailor too!

We're most of us liars, we're 'arf of us thieves, an' the rest are as rank
    as can be,
But once in a while we can finish in style (which I 'ope it won't 'appen
    to me).
But it makes you think better o' you an' your friends, an' the work you
    may 'ave to do,
When you think o' the sinkin' *Victorier's* Jollies—soldier an' sailor too!
Now there isn't no room for to say ye don't know—they 'ave proved
    it plain and true—   40
That, whether it's Widow, or whether it's ship, Victorier's work is to
    do,
An' they done it, the Jollies—'Er Majesty's Jollies—soldier an' sailor too!

RUDYARD KIPLING

Poseidon's Law

When the robust and Brass-bound Man commissioned first for sea
His fragile raft, Poseidon laughed, and "Mariner," said he,
"Behold, a Law immutable I lay on thee and thine,
That never shall ye act or tell a falsehood at my shrine.

"Let Zeus adjudge your landward kin whose votive meal and salt
At easy-cheated altars win oblivion for the fault,
But you the unhoodwinked wave shall test—the immediate gulf
    condemn—
Except ye owe the Fates a jest, be slow to jest with them.

"Ye shall not clear by Greekly speech, nor cozen from your path
The twinkling shoal, the leeward beach, or Hadria's white-lipped
    wrath;   10
Nor tempt with painted cloth for wood my fraud-avenging hosts;
Nor make at all, or all make good, your bulwarks and your boasts.

"Now and henceforward serve unshod, through wet and wakeful shifts,
A present and oppressive God, but take, to aid, my gifts—
The wide and windward-opening eye, the large and lavish hand,
The soul that cannot tell a lie—except upon the land!"

In dromond and in catafract—wet, wakeful, windward-eyed—
He kept Poseidon's Law intact (his ship and freight beside),
But, once discharged the dromond's hold, the bireme beached once
    more,
Splendaciously mendacious rolled the Brass-bound Man ashore. . . .   20

The thranite now and thalamite are pressures low and high,
And where three hundred blades bit white the twin-propellers ply.
The God that hailed, the keel that sailed, are changed beyond recall,
But the robust and Brass-bound Man he is not changed at all!

From Punt returned, from Phormio's Fleet, from Javan and Gadire,[24]
He strongly occupies the seat about the tavern fire,
And, moist with much Falernian or smoked Massilian juice,[25]
Revenges there the Brass-bound Man his long-enforcèd truce!

RUDYARD KIPLING

A Sea Dialogue
(November 10, 1864)

CABIN PASSENGER
Friend, you seem thoughtful. I not wonder much
That he who sails the ocean should be sad.
I am myself reflective. When I think
Of all this wallowing beast, the Sea, has sucked
Between his sharp thin lips, the wedgy waves,
What heaps of diamonds, rubies, emeralds, pearls;
What piles of shekels, talents, ducats, crowns,
What bales of Tyrian mantles, Indian shawls,
Of laces that have blanked the weavers' eyes,
Of silken tissues, wrought by worm and man,   10
The half-starved workman, and the well-fed worm;
What marbles, bronzes, pictures, parchments, books;
What many-lobuled, thought-engendering brains;
Lie with the gaping sea-shells in his maw,—

I, too, am silent; for all language seems
A mockery, and the speech of man is vain.
O mariner, we look upon the waves
And they rebuke our babbling. 'Peace!' they say,—
'Mortal, be still!' My noisy tongue is hushed,
And with my trembling finger on my lips   20
My soul exclaims in ecstasy—

MAN AT WHEEL
                          Belay!

CABIN PASSENGER
Ah yes! 'Delay,'—it calls, 'nor haste to break
The charm of stillness with an idle word!
O mariner, I love thee, for thy thought
Strides even with my own, nay, flies before.
Thou art a brother to the wind and wave;
Have they not music for thine ear as mine,
When the wild tempest makes thy ship his lyre,
Smiting a cavernous basso from the shrouds   30
And climbing up his gamut through the stays,
Through buntlines, bowlines, ratlines, till it shrills
An alto keener than the locust sings,
And all the great Æolian[26] orchestra
Storms out its mad sonata in the gale?
Is not the scene a wondrous and—

MAN AT WHEEL
                          Avast!

CABIN PASSENGER
Ah yes, a vast, a vast and wondrous scene!
I see thy soul is open as the day
That holds the sunshine in its azure bowl   40
To all the solemn glories of the deep.
Tell me, O mariner, dost thou never feel
The grandeur of thine office,—to control
The keel that cuts the ocean like a knife
And leaves a wake behind it like a seam
In the great shining garment of the world?

MAN AT WHEEL
Belay y'r jaw, y' swab! y' hoss-marine!
                    (To the Captain.)
Ay, ay, Sir! Stiddy, Sir! Sou'wes'-b'sou'!

                    OLIVER WENDELL HOLMES

181

The Ship of Rio

There was a ship of Rio
  Sailed out into the blue,
And nine and ninety monkeys
  Were all her jovial crew.
From bos'un to the cabin boy,
  From quarter to caboose,
There weren't a stitch of calico
  To breech 'em—tight or loose;
From spar to deck, from deck to keel,
  From barnacle to shroud,   10
There weren't one pair of reach-me-downs
  To all that jabbering crowd.
But wasn't it a gladsome sight,
  When roared the deep-sea gales,
To see them reef her fore and aft,
  A-swinging by their tails!
Oh, wasn't it a gladsome sight,
  When glassy calm did come,
To see them squatting tailor-wise
  Around a keg of rum!   20
Oh, wasn't it a gladsome sight,
  When in she sailed to land,
To see them all a-scampering skip
  For nuts across the sand!

WALTER DE LA MARE

The Jumblies

They went to sea in a sieve, they did;
  In a sieve they went to sea:
In spite of all their friends could say,
On a winter's morn, on a stormy day,
  In a sieve they went to sea.
And when the sieve turned round and round,
And everyone cried, "You'll be drowned!"
They called aloud, "Our sieve ain't big,

182

But we don't care a button; we don't care a fig—
   In a sieve we'll go to sea!"
      Far and few, far and few,
         Are the lands where the Jumblies live.
         Their heads are green, and their hands are blue;
         And they went to sea in a sieve.

They sailed away in a sieve, they did,
   In a sieve they sailed so fast,
With only a beautiful pea-green veil
Tied with a ribbon, by way of a sail,
   To a small tobacco-pipe mast.
And everyone said who saw them go,
"Oh! won't they be soon upset, you know,
For the sky is dark, and the voyage is long;
And, happen what may, it's extremely wrong
   In a sieve to sail so fast."

The water it soon came in, it did;
   The water it soon came in.
So, to keep them dry, they wrapped their feet
In a pinky paper all folded neat;
   And they fastened it down with a pin.
And they passed the night in a crockery-jar;
And each of them said, "How wise we are!
Though the sky be dark, and the voyage be long,
Yet we never can think we were rash or wrong,
   While round in our sieve we spin."

And all night long they sailed away;
   And, when the sun went down,
They whistled and warbled a moony song
To the echoing sound of a coppery gong,
   In the shade of the mountains brown,
"O Timballoo! how happy we are
When we live in a sieve and a crockery-jar!
And all night long, in the moonlight pale,
We sail away with a pea-green sail
   In the shade of the mountains brown."

They sailed to the Western Sea, they did—
   To a land all covered with trees;
And they bought an owl, and a useful cart,
And a pound of rice, and a cranberry tart,
   And a hive of silvery bees;
And they bought a pig, and some green jackdaws,

10

20

30

40

50

And a lovely monkey with lollipop paws,
And seventeen bags of edelweiss tea,
And forty bottles of ring-bo-ree,
  And no end of Stilton cheese.

And in twenty years they all came back—
  In twenty years or more;
And everyone said, "How tall they've grown!
For they've been to the Lakes, and the Torrible Zone,
  And the hills of the Chankly Bore."
And they drank their health, and gave them a feast   60
Of dumplings made of beautiful yeast;
And everyone said, "If we only live,
We, too, will go to sea in a sieve,
  To the hills of the Chankly Bore."
    Far and few, far and few,
      Are the lands where the Jumblies live.
    Their heads are green, and their hands are blue;
      And they went to sea in a sieve.

EDWARD LEAR

A Sea Dirge

There are certain things—as, a spider, a ghost,
  The income-tax, gout, an umbrella for three—
That I hate, but the thing that I hate the most
  Is a thing they call the Sea.

Pour some salt water over the floor—
  Ugly I'm sure you'll allow it to be:
Suppose it extended a mile or more,
  That's very like the Sea.

Beat a dog till it howls outright—   10
  Cruel, but all very well for a spree:
Suppose that he did so day and night,
  That would be like the Sea.

I had a vision of nursery-maids;
  Tens of thousands passed by me—
All leading children with wooden spades,
  And this was by the Sea.

Who invented those spades of wood?
  Who was it cut them out of the tree?
None, I think, but an idiot could—   20
  Or one that loved the Sea.

It is pleasant and dreamy, no doubt, to float
    With 'thoughts as boundless, and souls as free':
But, suppose you are very unwell in the boat,
    How do you like the Sea?

'But it makes the intellect clear and keen'—
    Prove it! Prove it! How can that be?
'Why, what does "B sharp" (in music) mean,
    If not "the natural C"?'

What! Keen? With such questions as 'When's high tide?'   30
    'Is shelling shrimps an improvement to tea?'
'Were donkeys intended for man to ride?'
    Such are our thoughts by the Sea.

There is an insect that people avoid
    (Whence is derived the verb 'to flee').
Where have you been by it most annoyed?
    In lodgings by the Sea.

If you like your coffee with sand for dregs,
    A decided hint of salt in your tea,
And a fish taste in the very eggs—   40
    By all means choose the Sea.

And if, with these dainties to drink and eat,
    You prefer not a vestige of grass or tree,
And a chronic state of wet in your feet,
    Then—I recommend the Sea.

For *I* have friends who dwell by the coast—
    Pleasant friends they are to me!
It is when I am with them I wonder most
    That anyone likes the Sea.

They take me a walk: though tired and stiff,   50
    To climb the heights I madly agree;
And, after a tumble or so from the cliff,
    They kindly suggest the Sea.

I try the rocks, and I think it cool
    That they laugh with such an excess of glee,
As I heavily slip into every pool
    That skirts the cold cold Sea.

Once I met a friend in the street,
    With wife, and nurse, and children three:
Never again such a sight may I meet   60
    As that party from the Sea.

Their cheeks were hollow, their steps were slow,
    Convicted felons they seemed to be:
'Are you going to prison, dear friend?' 'Oh, no!
    We're returning from the Sea!'

LEWIS CARROLL

The Sea-Gull

Hark to the whimper of the sea-gull;
He weeps because he's not an ea-gull.
Suppose you were, you silly sea-gull,
Could you explain it to your she-gull?

OGDEN NASH

The Octopus

Tell me, O Octopus, I begs,
Is those things arms, or is they legs?
I marvel at thee, Octopus;
If I were thou, I'd call me Us.

OGDEN NASH

A Channel Passage

The damned ship lurched and slithered. Quiet and quick
    My cold gorge rose; the long sea rolled; I knew
I must think hard of something, or be sick;
    And could think hard of only one thing—*you!*
You, you alone could hold my fancy ever!
    And with you memories come, sharp pain, and dole.
Now there's a choice—heartache or tortured liver!
    A sea-sick body, or a you-sick soul!

Do I forget you? Retchings twist and tie me,
    Old meat, good meals, brown gobbets, up I throw.
Do I remember? Acrid return and slimy,
    The sobs and slobber of a last years woe.
And still the sick ship rolls. 'Tis hard, I tell ye,
To choose 'twixt love and nausea, heart and belly.

RUPERT BROOKE

Song of the Master and Boatswain[27]

At Dirty Dick's and Sloppy Joe's
　We drank our liquor straight,
Some went upstairs with Margery,
　And some, alas, with Kate;
And two by two like cat and mouse
The homeless played at keeping house.

There Wealthy Meg, the Sailor's Friend,
　And Marion, cow-eyed,
Opened their arms to me but I
　Refused to step inside;
I was not looking for a cage
In which to mope in my old age.

The nightingales are sobbing in
　The orchards of our mothers,
And hearts that we broke long ago
　Have long been breaking others;
Tears are round, the sea is deep:
Roll them overboard and sleep.

W. H. AUDEN

Sea-Chill

When Mrs. John Masefield and her husband, the author of "I Must Go Down to the Seas Again," arrived here on a liner, she said to a reporter, "It was too uppy-downy, and Mr. Masefield was ill."—News item.

I must go down to the seas again, where the billows romp and reel,[28]
So all I ask is a large ship that rides on an even keel,
And a mild breeze and a broad deck with a slight list to leeward,
And a clean chair in a snug nook and a nice, kind steward.

I must go down to the seas again, the sport of wind and tide,
As the gray wave and the green wave play leapfrog over the side.
And all I want is a glassy calm with a bone-dry scupper,
A good book and a warm rug and a light, plain supper.

I must go down to the seas again, though there I'm a total loss,
And can't say which is worst, the pitch, the plunge, the roll, the toss.
But all I ask is a safe retreat in a bar well tended,
And a soft berth and a smooth course till the long trip's ended.

ARTHUR GUITERMAN

Legends of the Sea

LEGENDS OF THE SEA ABOUND, yet most of them are reflections of legends of the land. Any legend, from folktale to epic story of heroes and gods, is built upon a set of beliefs held at the time of the legend's making; thus, belief in the Olympian gods and goddesses produced tales in which those beings appear and act, and the same is true for belief in lesser supernatural beings—demons and ghosts. As those beliefs led to related legends and tales on land so did they produce corresponding tales about the sea, tales that are reflected in the poems of the sea. The Greek and Roman pantheons consisted not only of gods of the earth and sky, forest nymphs, and other creatures, but also of a god of the sea, of naiads, and of sirens, and other denizens of the oceans; elves, fairies, giants, and trolls have as their sea-bred counterparts mermaids, mermen, silkies, and great sea monsters; beliefs in demon tempters and human spirits that inhabit the bodies of animals lead to the existence of such beings on both land and sea; if ghosts can wander the land, they can also wander the seas, ageless and deathless in their indestructible ships. In this way are the legends of the sea populated with creatures.

Themes for sea legends are also borrowed from the land and include many easily recognizable folk motifs: the demon tempter of *The Daemon Lover,* the inhuman father of *The Great Silkie of Sule Skerrie,* the destruction of the city in Edgar Allan Poe's *The City in the Sea,* the doomed love of mortal woman and supernatural being of Matthew Arnold's *The Forsaken Merman,* the portrait of sea birds inhabited by mariners' spirits of John Masefield's *Sea-Change,* and the picture of heaven in Rudyard Kipling's *The Last Chantey.* By far the most prevalent theme in the legends of the sea, however, is that of the wanderer.

Tales of wanderers whose meandering existence is dictated by a supernatural force are as old as the story of Adam and Eve and their expulsion from the Garden of Eden. The wanderer himself is often immortal and his wanderings are usually the result of his having offended a higher power. This is the theme of many sea poems: of Homer's *Odyssey,* where Odysseus offends Poseidon and therefore must wander the Mediterranean in his attempt to reach home; Samuel Taylor Coleridge's *The Rime of the Ancient Mariner,* where the mariner's crime against innocence and nature, the unwarranted killing of an albatross, causes his harrowing supernatural experiences at sea and a curse that makes him wander the earth, telling his story to certain men; and of all the poems about ghost ships—the soulless immortality of captain and ship in all versions of *The Flying Dutchman,* the endlessly repeated wreck and burning of the *Palatine* in John Greenleaf Whittier's poem, and the return with each fog of a lost hulk and the lost children aboard her in Bret Harte's *A Greyport Legend.* The prevalence of wanderers in sea poetry may result from the constant motion of the sea itself, always changing yet always the same; or it may have roots in the nature of seafaring life, where ships are away from their home ports for years at a time with little communication, where men and ships simply disappear with no sign or explanation, and where abandoned ships and boats survive to drift and be seen by passing sailors. Whatever the reason, the idea of the deathless wanderer of the sea is one that has captured the imaginations of poet and sailor alike for centuries.

From *The Odyssey*[1]
Book V
Lines 405–434

This spoke, a huge wave tooke him by the head
And hurld him o're-boord: ship and all it laid
Inverted quite amidst the waves, but he
Farre off from her sprawld, strowd about the sea,
His Sterne still holding, broken off; his Mast
Burst in the midst, so horrible a blast   410
Of mixt winds strooke it. Sailes and saile-yards fell
Amongst the billowes, and himselfe did dwell
A long time under water, nor could get
In haste his head out—wave with wave so met
In his depression, and his garments too
(Given by Calypso)[2] gave him much to do,
Hindring his swimming; yet he left not so
His drenched vessell, for the overthrow
Of her nor him, but gat at length againe
(Wrestling with Neptune) hold of her, and then   420
Sate in her Bulke, insulting over Death—
Which (with the salt streame prest to stop his breath)
He scap't and gave the sea againe to give
To other men. His ship so striv'd to live,

Floting at randon, cufft from wave to wave,
As you have seene the Northwind when he drave
In Autumne heapes of thorne-fed Grashoppers
Hither and thither; one heape this way beares,
Another that, and makes them often meete
In his confusde gales; so Ulysses' fleete   430
The winds hurl'd up and downe: now Boreas
Tost it to Notus, Notus gave it passe
To Eurus; Eurus Zephyr³ made pursue
The horrid Tennis.

Lines 504–511

At length escaping. Two nights yet, and daies,
He spent in wrestling with the sable seas,
In which space often did his heart propose
Death to his eyes. But when Aurora⁴ rose
And threw the third light from her orient haire,
The winds grew calme and cleare was all the aire,
Not one breath stirring. Then he might descrie
(Raisd by the high seas) cleare, the land was nie.

Lines 530–607

He heard a sound beate from the sea-bred rocks
Against which gave a huge sea horrid shocks,
That belcht upon the firme land weeds and fome,
With which were all things hid there—where no roome
Of fit capacitie was for any port,
Nor (from the sea) for any man's resort,
The shores, the rocks, and cliffes so prominent were.
'O,' said Ulysses then, 'now Jupiter
Hath given me sight of an unhop't for shore,
(Though I have wrought these seas so long, so sore)
Of rest yet no place shewes the slendrest prints,   540
The rugged shore so bristl'd is with flints,
Against which every way the waves so flocke,
And all the shore shewes as one eminent rocke—
So neare which tis so deepe, that not a sand
Is there for any tired foote to stand:
Nor flie his death-fast-following miseries,
Lest, if he land, upon him fore-right flies
A churlish wave to crush him gainst a Cliffe,
Worse than vaine rendring all his landing strife.

And should I swim to seeke a haven elsewhere,   550
Or land lesse wave-beate, I may justly feare
I shall be taken with a gale againe
And cast a huge way off into the Maine;
And there the great Earth-shaker (having seene
My so neare landing, and againe his spleene
Forcing me to him) will some Whale send out
(Of which a horrid number here about
His Amphitrite[5] breeds) to swallow me.
I well have prov'd with what malignitie
He treds my steps.' While this discourse he held,   560
A curst Surge gainst a cutting rocke impeld
His naked bodie, which it gasht and tore,
And had his bones broke, if but one sea more
Had cast him on it. But she prompted him
That never faild, and bad him no more swim
Still off and on, but boldly force the shore
And hug the rocke that him so rudely tore.
Which he with both hands sigh'd and claspt till past
The billowes' rage was; which scap't backe, so fast
The rocke repulst it, that it reft his hold,   570
Sucking him from it, and farre backe he rould.
And as the Polypus that (forc't from home
Amidst the soft sea, and neare rough land come
For shelter gainst the stormes that beate on her
At open sea, as she abroad doth erre)
A deale of gravill and sharpe little stones
Needfully gathers in her hollow bones:
So he forc't hither (by the sharper ill
Shunning the smoother), where he best hop't, still
The worst succeeded: for the cruell friend,   580
To which he clingd for succour, off did rend
From his broad hands the soken flesh so sore
That off he fell and could sustaine no more.
Quite under water fell he, and, past Fate,
Haplesse Ulysses there had lost the state
He held in life, if (still the grey-eyd Maid[6]
His wisedome prompting) he had not assaid
Another course and ceast t'attempt that shore,
Swimming, and casting round his eye, t'explore
Some other shelter. Then the mouth he found   590
Of faire Callicoe's flood, whose shores were crownd
With most apt succors—rocks so smooth they seemd
Polisht of purpose, land that quite redeemd

With breathlesse coverts th'other's blasted shores.
The flood he knew, and thus in heart implores:
'King of this River, heare! Whatever name
Makes thee invokt, to thee I humbly frame
My flight from Neptune's furies. Reverend is
To all the ever-living Deities
What erring man soever seekes their aid.
To thy both flood and knees a man dismaid   600
With varied sufferance sues. Yeeld then some rest
To him that is thy suppliant profest.'
    This (though but spoke in thought) the Godhead heard,
Her Current strait staid, and her thicke waves cleard
Before him, smooth'd her waters, and just where
He praid, halfe drownd, entirely sav'd him there.

Book XII
Lines 265–326

    'Then tooke they seate, and forth our passage strooke—
The fomie Sea beneath their labour shooke—
Rowd on in reach of an erected voice;
The Sirens[7] soone tooke note without our noice,
Tun'd those sweete accents that made charmes so strong
And these learn'd numbers made the Sirens' song: 270
   ' *"Come here, thou, worthy of a world of praise,*
That dost so high the Grecian glory raise.
Ulysses! stay thy ship, and that song heare
That none past ever but it bent his eare,
But left him ravishd and instructed more
By us than any ever heard before.
For we know all things whatsoever were
In wide Troy labour'd, whatsoever there
The Grecians and the Troyans both sustain'd
By those high issues that the Gods ordain'd: 280
And whatsoever all the earth can show
T'informe a knowledge of desert, we know."
   'This they gave accent in the sweetest straine
That ever open'd an enamour'd vaine—
When my constrain'd heart needs would have mine eare
Yet more delighted, force way forth, and heare.
To which end I commanded with all signe
Sterne lookes could make (for not a joynt of mine
Had powre to stirre) my friends to rise, and give
My limbs free way. They freely striv'd to drive   290

192

Their ship still on. When (farre from will to lose)
Eurylochus and Perimedes rose
To wrap me surer, and opprest me more
With many a halser than had use before.
When, rowing on without the reach of sound,
My friends unstopt their eares and me unbound,
And that Ile quite we quitted. But againe
Fresh feares emploid us. I beheld a maine
Of mighty billows, and a smoke ascend,
A horrid murmure hearing. Every friend   300
Astonisht sat: from every hand his oare
Fell quite forsaken: with the dismall Rore,
Where all things there made Echoes, stone still stood
Our ship it selfe, because the ghastly flood
Tooke all men's motions from her in their owne:
I through the ship went, labouring up and downe
My friends' recoverd spirits. One by one
I gave good words, and said that well were knowne
These ills to them before: I told them all;
And that these could not prove more capitall   310
Than those the Cyclop⁸ blockt us up in, yet
My vertue, wit, and heaven-helpt Counsailes set
Their freedomes open. I could not beleeve
But they rememberd it, and wisht them give
My equall care and meanes now equall trust:
The strength they had for stirring up they must
Rouze and extend, to trie if Jove had laid
His powres in theirs up, and would adde his aid
To scape even that death. In particular then
I told our Pylot that past other men   320
He most must beare firme spirits, since he swaid
The Continent that all our spirits convaid
In his whole guide of her. He saw there boile
The fierie whirlpooles that to all our spoile
Inclosde a Rocke, without which he must stere,
Or all our ruines stood concluded there.

Lines 570–636

'The Iland left so farre that land no where
But onely sea and skie had powre t'appeare,
Jove fixt a cloud above our ship, so blacke

That all the sea it darkned. Yet from wracke
She ranne a good free time, till from the West
Came Zephyr ruffling forth, and put his breast
Out in a singing tempest so most vast
It burst the Gables that made sure our Mast;
Our Masts came tumbling downe, our tackle downe
Rusht to the Pump, and by our Pylot's crowne
The maine Mast past his fall, pasht all his Skull—   580
And all this wracke but one flaw made at full.
Off from the Sterne the Sternesman diving fell,
And from his sinews flew his Soule to hell.
Together, all this time Jove's Thunder chid,
And through and through the ship his lightning glid
Till it embrac't her round; her bulke was filld
With nasty sulphur, and her men were killd,
Tumbl'd to Sea, like Sea-mews swumme about,
And there the date of their returne was out.
    'I tost from side to side still, till all broke   590
Her Ribs were with the storme, and she did choke
With let-in Surges, for the Mast, torne downe,
Tore her up pecemeale, and for me to drowne
Left little undissolv'd. But to the Mast
There was a lether Thong left, which I cast
About it and the keele, and so sat tost
With banefull weather till the West had lost
His stormy tyranny. And then arose
The South, that bred me more abhorred woes—
For backe againe his blasts expelld me quite   600
On ravenous Charybdis.⁹ All that Night
I totter'd up and downe, till Light and I
At Scylla's Rocke¹⁰ encounterd, and the nie
Dreadfull Charybdis. As I drave on these,
I saw Charybdis supping up the seas,
And had gone up together if the tree
That bore the wilde figs had not rescu'd me—
To which I leapt and left my keele, and, hie
Clambring upon it, did as close imply
My brest about it as a Reremouse could.   610
Yet might my feete on no stub fasten hold
To ease my hands, the roots were crept so low
Beneath the earth, and so aloft did grow
The far-spred armes that (though good height I gat)
I could not reach them. To the maine Bole flat
I therefore still must cling, till up againe

194

She belcht my Mast, and after that amaine
My keele came tumbling. So at length it chanc't
To me as to a Judge, that, long advanc't
To judge a sort of hote yong fellowes' jarres,   620
At length time frees him from their civill warres,
When glad he riseth, and to dinner goes:
So time at length release with joyes my woes,
And from Charybdis' mouth appear'd my keele.
To which (my hand now loosd, and now my heele)
I altogether with a huge noise dropt,
Just in her midst fell, where the Mast was propt,
And there rowd off, with owers of my hands.
God and Man's Father would not from her sands
Let Scylla see me, for I then had died   630
That bitter death that my poore friends supplied.
   'Nine Daies at Sea I hover'd: the tenth Night
In th'Ile Ogygia, where abode the bright
And right renoum'd Calypso, I was cast
By powre of Deitie—where I liv'd embrac't
With Love and feasts.

HOMER

The Daemon Lover

"O where have ye been, my dearest dear,
   These seven long years and more?"
"I am come to seek my former vows,
   That ye promised me before."

"Away with your former vows," she says,
   "Or else ye will breed strife;
Away with your former vows," she says,
   "For I am become a wife.

I am married to a ship-carpenter,
   A ship-carpenter he's bound;   10
I would not he knew my mind this night,
   For twice five hundred pound."

   ....   *(Stanza lost)*

She has put her foot on good ship-board,
   And on ship-board she's gone,
And the veil that hung over her face
   Was all with gold begone.

She had not sailed a league, a league,
  A league but barely two,
Till she did mind on the husband she left,
  And her wee young son also.   20

"O, hold your tongue, my dearest dear,
  Let all your follies abee;
I'll show where the white lilies grow,
  On the banks of Italie."

She had not sailed a league, a league,
  A league but barely three,
Till grim, grim grew his countenance,
  And gurly grew the sea.

"O, hold your tongue, my dearest dear,
  Let all your follies abee;   30
I'll show where the white lilies grow,
  In the bottom of the sea!"

He's taken her by the milk-white hand,
  And he's thrown her in the main;
And full five-and-twenty hundred ships
  Sank all on the coast of Spain.

ANONYMOUS

The Great Silkie° of Sule Skerrie   seal

An earthly nourrice° sit and sings,   nurse
And aye she sings, "Bye, lily wean,
Little ken I my bairnis° father,   child's
Far less the land that he stops in."

Then one arose at her bed-foot,
And a grumly guest I'm sure was he;
"Here am I, thy barnis' father,
Although that I be not comelie.

I am a man, upon the land,
And I am a silkie in the sea;   10
And when I'm far and far frae land,
My dwelling is in Sule Skerrie."

"It was na weel," quoth the maiden fair,
"It was na weel, indeed," quoth she,
"That the Great Silkie of Sule Skerrie
Should hae come and aught a bairn to me."

Now he has ta'en a purse of gold,
And he has put in upon her knee,
Saying, "Gie to me my little young son,   20
And take thee up thy nourrice-fee.

It shall come to pass on a summer's day,
When the sun shines hot on every stane,
That I will take my little young son,
And teach him for to swim the faem.

And thou shalt marry a proud gunner,
And a proud gunner I'm sure he'll be,
And the very first shot that e'er he shoots,
He'll shoot both my young son and me."

ANONYMOUS

From *Richard III*
Act I, Scene IV
Lines 16–41

        ... As we paced along
Upon the giddy footing of the hatches,
Methought that Gloucester stumbled, and in falling
Struck me, that thought to stay him, overboard,
Into the tumbling billows of the main.   20
Lord, Lord! Methought what pain it was to drown!
What dreadful noise of waters in mine ears!
What ugly sights of death within mine eyes!
Methought I saw a thousand fearful wrecks,
Ten thousand men that fishes gnawed upon,
Wedges of gold, great anchors, heaps of pearl,
Inestimable stones, unvalued jewels,
All scattered in the bottom of the sea.
Some lay in dead men's skulls, and in those holes
Where eyes did once inhabit there were crept,   30
As 'twere in scorn of eyes, reflecting gems,
Which wooed the slimy bottom of the deep
And mocked the dead bones that lay scattered by.

            Had you such leisure in the time of death
To gaze upon the secrets of the deep?
            Methought I had, and often did I strive
To yield the ghost. But still the envious flood
Kept in my soul, and would not let it forth
To seek the empty, vast, and wandering air,
But smothered it within my panting bulk,   40
Which almost burst to belch it in the sea.

WILLIAM SHAKESPEARE

From *The Tempest*
Act I, Scene II
Lines 397–403

Full fathom five thy father lies,
    Of his bones are coral made,
Those are pearls that were his eyes.
    Nothing of him that doth fade
But doth suffer a sea change
Into something rich and strange.
Sea nymphs hourly ring his knell.

WILLIAM SHAKESPEARE

The Rime of the Ancient Mariner

ARGUMENT

How a Ship having passed the Line was driven by storms to the cold
Country towards the South Pole; and how from thence she made her
course to the tropical Latitude of the Great Pacific Ocean; and of the
strange things that befell; and in what manner the Ancyent Marinere
came back to his own Country.

PART I

An ancient Mariner
meeteth three Gallants
bidden to a wedding-
feast, and detaineth one.

It is an ancient Mariner,
And he stoppeth one of three.
'By thy long grey beard and glittering eye,
Now wherefore stopp'st thou me?

The Bridegroom's doors are opened wide,
And I am next of kin;
The guests are met, the feast is set:
May'st hear the merry din.'

198

He holds him with his skinny hand,
'There was a ship,' quoth he.
'Hold off! unhand me, grey-beard loon!'
Eftsoons his hand dropt he.

He holds him with his glittering eye—
The Wedding-Guest stood still,
And listens like a three years' child:
The Mariner hath his will.

The Wedding-Guest sat on a stone:
He cannot choose but hear;
And thus spake on that ancient man,
The bright-eyed Mariner.

'The ship was cheered, the harbour cleared,
Merrily did we drop
Below the kirk, below the hill,
Below the lighthouse top.

The Sun came up upon the left,
Out of the sea came he!
And he shone bright, and on the right
Went down into the sea.

Higher and higher every day,
Till over the mast at noon—'
The Wedding-Guest here beat his breast,
For he heard the loud bassoon.

The bride hath paced into the hall,
Red as a rose is she;
Nodding their heads before her goes
The merry minstrelsy.

The Wedding-Guest he beat his breast,
Yet he cannot choose but hear;
And thus spake on that ancient man,
The bright-eyed Mariner.

'And now the STORM-BLAST came, and he
Was tyrannous and strong:
He struck with his o'ertaking wings,
And chased us south along.

With sloping masts and dipping prow,
As who pursued with yell and blow
Still treads the shadow of his foe,
And forward bends his head,
The ship drove fast, loud roared the blast,
And southward aye we fled.

10

20

30

40

50

199

And now there came both mist and snow,
And it grew wondrous cold:
And ice, mast-high, came floating by,
As green as emerald.

The land of ice, and of fearful sounds where no living thing was to be seen.

And through the drifts the snowy clifts
Did send a dismal sheen:
Nor shapes of men nor beasts we ken—
The ice was all between.

The ice was here, the ice was there,
The ice was all around: 60
It cracked and growled, and roared and howled,
Like noises in a swound!

Till a great sea-bird, called the Albatross, came through the snow-fog, and was received with great joy and hospitality.

At length did cross an Albatross,
Thorough the fog it came;
As if it had been a Christian soul,
We hailed it in God's name.

It ate the food it ne'er had eat,
And round and round it flew.
The ice did split with a thunder-fit;
The helmsman steered us through!   70

And lo! the Albatross proveth a bird of good omen, and followeth the ship as it returned northward through fog and floating ice.

And a good south wind sprung up behind;
The Albatross did follow,
And every day, for food or play,
Came to the mariner's hollo!

In mist or cloud, on mast or shroud,
It perched for vespers nine;
Whiles all the night, through fog-smoke white,
Glimmered the white Moon-shine.'

The ancient Mariner inhospitably killeth the pious bird of good omen.

'God save thee, ancient Mariner!
From the fiends, that plague thee thus!—   80
Why look'st thou so?'—With my cross-bow
I shot the ALBATROSS.

PART II

The Sun now rose upon the right:
Out of the sea came he,
Still hid in mist, and on the left
Went down into the sea.

200

And the good south wind still blew behind,
But no sweet bird did follow,
Nor any day for food or play
Came to the mariners' hollo!   90

His shipmates cry out against the ancient Mariner, for killing the bird of good luck.

And I had done a hellish thing,
And it would work 'em woe:
For all averred, I had killed the bird
That made the breeze to blow.
Ah wretch! said they, the bird to slay,
That made the breeze to blow!

But when the fog cleared off, they justify the same, and thus make themselves accomplices in the crime.

Nor dim nor red, like God's own head,
The glorious Sun uprist:
Then all averred, I had killed the bird
That brought the fog and mist.   100
'Twas right, said they, such birds to slay,
That bring the fog and mist.

The fair breeze continues; the ship enters the Pacific Ocean, and sails northward, even till it reaches the Line.

The fair breeze blew, the white foam flew,
The furrow followed free;
We were the first that ever burst
Into that silent sea.

Down dropt the breeze, the sails dropt down,
'Twas sad as sad could be;
The ship hath been suddenly becalmed. And we did speak only to break
The silence of the sea!   110

All in a hot and copper sky,
The bloody Sun, at noon,
Right up above the mast did stand,
No bigger than the Moon.

Day after day, day after day,
We stuck, nor breath nor motion;
As idle as a painted ship
Upon a painted ocean.

And the Albatross begins to be avenged. Water, water, every where,
And all the boards did shrink;   120
Water, water, every where,
Nor any drop to drink.

The very deep did rot: O Christ!
That ever this should be!
Yea, slimy things did crawl with legs
Upon the slimy sea.

About, about, in reel and rout
The death-fires danced at night;
The water, like a witch's oils,
Burnt green, and blue and white.   130

And some in dreams assuréd were
Of the Spirit that plagued us so;
Nine fathom deep he had followed us
From the land of mist and snow.

And every tongue, through utter drought,
Was withered at the root;
We could not speak, no more than if
We had been choked with soot.

Ah! well a-day! what evil looks
Had I from old and young!   140
Instead of the cross, the Albatross
About my neck was hung.

PART III

There passed a weary time. Each throat
Was parched, and glazed each eye.
A weary time! a weary time!
How glazed each weary eye,
When looking westward, I beheld
A something in the sky.

At first it seemed a little speck,
And then it seemed a mist;   150
It moved and moved, and took at last
A certain shape, I wist.

A speck, a mist, a shape, I wist!
And still it neared and neared:
As if it dodged a water-sprite,
It plunged and tacked and veered.

With throats unslaked, with black lips baked,
We could nor laugh nor wail;
Through utter drought all dumb we stood!
I bit my arm, I sucked the blood,   160
And cried, A sail! a sail!

With throats unslaked, with black lips baked,
Agape they heard me call:
Gramercy! they for joy did grin,
And all at once their breath drew in,
As they were drinking all.

A flash of joy;

See! see! (I cried) she tacks no more!
Hither to work us weal;
Without a breeze, without a tide,
She steadies with upright keel!   170

And horror follows. For can it be a ship that comes onward without wind or tide?

The western wave was all a-flame.
The day was well nigh done!
Almost upon the western wave
Rested the broad bright Sun;
When that strange shape drove suddenly
Betwixt us and the Sun.

And straight the Sun was flecked with bars,
(Heaven's Mother send us grace!)
As if through a dungeon-grate he peered
With broad and burning face.   180

It seemeth him but the skeleton of a ship.

Alas! (thought I, and my heart beat loud)
How fast she nears and nears!
Are those *her* sails that glance in the Sun,
Like restless gossameres?

And its ribs are seen as bars on the face of the setting Sun.

Are those *her* ribs through which the Sun
Did peer, as through a grate?
And is that Woman all her crew?
Is that a DEATH? and are there two?
Is DEATH that woman's mate?

The Spectre-Woman and her Death-mate, and no other on board the skeleton ship.

Her lips were red, *her* looks were free,   190
Her locks were yellow as gold:
Her skin was as white as leprosy,
The Night-mare LIFE-IN-DEATH was she,
Who thicks man's blood with cold.

Like vessel, like crew!

Death and Life-in-Death have diced for the ship's crew and she (the latter) winneth the ancient Mariner.

The naked hulk alongside came,
And the twain were casting dice;
'The game is done! I've won! I've won!'
Quoth she, and whistles thrice.

The Sun's rim dips; the stars rush out:
At one stride comes the dark;   200
With far-heard whisper, o'er the sea,
Off shot the spectre-bark.

No twilight within the courts of the Sun.

203

We listened and looked sideways up!
Fear at my heart, as at a cup,
My life-blood seemed to sip!
The stars were dim, and thick the night,
The steersman's face by his lamp gleamed white;
From the sails the dew did drip—

Till clomb above the eastern bar
The hornéd Moon, with one bright star   210
Within the nether tip.

One after one, by the star-dogged Moon,
Too quick for groan or sigh,
Each turned his face with a ghastly pang,
And cursed me with his eye.

Four times fifty living men,
(And I heard nor sigh nor groan)
With heavy thump, a lifeless lump,
They dropped down one by one.

The souls did from their bodies fly,—   220
They fled to bliss or woe!
And every soul, it passed me by,
Like the whizz of my crossbow!

PART IV

'I fear thee, ancient Mariner!
I fear thy skinny hand!
And thou art long, and lank, and brown,
As is the ribbed sea-sand.

I fear thee and thy glittering eye,
And thy skinny hand, so brown.'—

Fear not, fear not, thou Wedding-Guest!   230
This body dropt not down.

Alone, alone, all, all alone,
Alone on a wide wide sea!
And nevery a saint took pity on
My soul in agony.

The many men, so beautiful!
And they all dead did lie:
And a thousand thousand slimy things
Lived on; and so did I.

And envieth that *they* should live, and so many lie dead.

I looked upon the rotting sea,   240
And drew my eyes away;
I looked upon the rotting deck,
And there the dead men lay.

I looked to heaven, and tried to pray;
But ere ever a prayer had gusht,
A wicked whisper came, and made
My heart as dry as dust.

I closed my lids, and kept them close,
And the balls like pulses beat;
For the sky and the sea, and the sea and the sky   250
Lay like a load on my weary eye,
And the dead were at my feet.

But the curse liveth for him in the eye of the dead men.

The cold sweat melted from their limbs,
Nor rot nor reek did they:
The look with which they looked on me
Had never passed away.

An orphan's curse would drag to hell
A spirit from on high;
But oh! more horrible than that
Is the curse in a dead man's eye!   260
Seven days, seven nights, I saw that curse,
And yet I could not die.

In his loneliness and fixedness he yearneth towards the journeying Moon, and the stars that still sojourn, yet still move onward; and every where the blue sky belongs to them, and is their appointed rest, and their native country and their own natural homes, which they enter unannounced as lords that are certainly expected and yet there is a silent joy at their arrival.

The moving Moon went up the sky,
And no where did abide:
Softly she was going up,
And a star or two beside—

Her beams bemocked the sultry main,
Like April hoar-frost spread;
But where the ship's huge shadow lay,
The charméd water burnt alway   270
A still and awful red.

By the light of the Moon he beholdeth God's creatures of the great calm.

Beyond the shadow of the ship,
I watched the water-snakes:
They moved in tracks of shining white,
And when they reared, the elfish light
Fell off in hoary flakes.

Within the shadow of the ship
I watched their rich attire:
Blue, glossy green, and velvet black,
They coiled and swam; and every track   280
Was a flash of golden fire.

O happy living things! no tongue
Their beauty might declare:
A spring of love gushed from my heart,

And I blessed them unaware:
Sure my kind saint took pity on me,
And I blessed them unaware.

The self-same moment I could pray;
And from my neck so free
The Albatross fell off, and sank   290
Like lead into the sea.

PART V

Oh sleep! it is a gentle thing,
Beloved from pole to pole!
To Mary Queen the praise be given!
She sent the gentle sleep from Heaven,
That slid into my soul.

The silly buckets on the deck,
That had so long remained,
I dreamt that they were filled with dew;
And when I awoke, it rained.   300

My lips were wet, my throat was cold,
My garments all were dank;
Sure I had drunken in my dreams,
And still my body drank.

I moved, and could not feel my limbs:
I was so light—almost
I thought that I had died in sleep,
And was a blessèd ghost.

And soon I heard a roaring wind:
It did not come anear;   310
But with its sound it shook the sails,
That were so thin and sere.

The upper air burst into life!
And a hundred fire-flags sheen,
To and fro they were hurried about!
And to and fro, and in and out,
The wan stars danced between.

And the coming wind did roar more loud,
And the sails did sigh like sedge;
And the rain poured down from one black cloud;
The Moon was at its edge.   321

The thick black cloud was cleft, and still
The Moon was at its side:
Like waters shot from some high crag,
The lightning fell with never a jag,
A river steep and wide.

The bodies of the ship's crew are inspired and the ship moves on;
The loud wind never reached the ship,
Yet now the ship moved on!
Beneath the lightning and the Moon
The dead men gave a groan.   330

They groaned, they stirred, they all uprose,
Nor spake, nor moved their eyes;
It had been strange, even in a dream,
To have seen those dead men rise.

The helmsman steered, the ship moved on;
Yet never a breeze up-blew;
The mariners all 'gan work the ropes,
Where they were wont to do;
They raised their limbs like lifeless tools—
We were a ghastly crew.   340

The body of my brother's son
Stood by me, knee to knee:
The body and I pulled at one rope,
But he said nought to me.

But not by the souls of the men, nor by dæmons of earth or middle air, but by a blessed troop of angelic spirits, sent down by the invocation of the guardian saint.
'I fear thee, ancient Mariner!'
Be calm, thou Wedding-Guest!
'Twas not those souls that fled in pain,
Which to their corses came again,
But a troop of spirits blest:

For when it dawned—they dropped their arms,
And clustered round the mast;   351
Sweet sounds rose slowly through their mouths,
And from their bodies passed.

Around, around, flew each sweet sound,
Then darted to the Sun;
Slowly the sounds came back again,
Now mixed, now one by one.

Sometimes a-dropping from the sky
I heard the sky-lark sing;
Sometimes all little birds that are, 360
How they seemed to fill the sea and air
With their sweet jargoning!

And now 'twas like all instruments,
Now like a lonely flute;
And now it is an angel's song,
That makes the heavens be mute.

It ceased; yet still the sails made on
A pleasant noise till noon,
A noise like of a hidden brook
In the leafy month of June, 370
That to the sleeping woods all night
Singeth a quiet tune.

Till noon we quietly sailed on,
Yet never a breeze did breathe:
Slowly and smoothly went the ship,
Moved onward from beneath.

Under the keel nine fathom deep,
From the land of mist and snow,
The spirit slid: and it was he
That made the ship to go. 380
The sails at noon left off their tune,
And the ship stood still also.

The Sun, right up above the mast,
Had fixed her to the ocean:
But in a minute she 'gan stir,
With a short uneasy motion—
Backwards and forwards half her length
With a short uneasy motion.

Then like a pawing horse let go,
She made a sudden bound: 390
It flung the blood into my head,
And I fell down in a swound.

The Polar Spirit's fellow-dæmons, the invisible inhabitants of the element, take part in his wrong; and two of them relate, one to the other, that penance long and heavy for the ancient Mariner hath been accorded to the Polar Spirit, who returneth southward.

How long in that same fit I lay,
I have not to declare;
But ere my living life returned,
I heard and in my soul discerned
Two voices in the air.

'Is it he?' quoth one, 'Is this the man?
By him who died on cross,
With his cruel bow he laid full low   400
The harmless Albatross.

The spirit who bideth by himself
In the land of mist and snow,
He loved the bird that loved the man
Who shot him with his bow.'

The other was a softer voice,
As soft as honey-dew:
Quoth he, 'The man hath penance done,
And penance more will do.'

PART VI

FIRST VOICE

'But tell me, tell me! speak again,   410
Thy soft response renewing—
What makes that ship drive on so fast?
What is the ocean doing?'

SECOND VOICE

'Still as a slave before his lord,
The ocean hath no blast;
His great bright eye most silently
Up to the Moon is cast—

If he may know which way to go;
For she guides him smooth or grim.
See, brother, see! how graciously   420
She looketh down on him.'

FIRST VOICE

The Mariner hath been cast into a trance; for the angelic power causeth the vessel to drive northward faster than human life could endure.

'But why drives on that ship so fast,
Without or wave or wind?'

SECOND VOICE

'The air is cut away before,
And closes from behind.

209

Fly, brother, fly! more high, more high!
Or we shall be belated:
For slow and slow that ship will go,
When the Mariner's trance is abated.'

The supernatural motion
is retarded; the Mariner
awakes, and his penance
begins anew.

I woke, and we were sailing on   430
As in a gentle weather:
'Twas night, calm night, the moon was high;
The dead men stood together.

All stood together on the deck,
For a charnel-dungeon fitter:
All fixed on me their stony eyes,
That in the Moon did glitter.

The pang, the curse, with which they died,
Had never passed away:
I could not draw my eyes from theirs,   440
Nor turn them up to pray.

The curse is finally ex-
piated.

And now this spell was snapt: once more
I viewed the ocean green,
And looked far forth, yet little saw
Of what had else been seen—

Like one, that on a lonesome road
Doth walk in fear and dread,
And having once turned round walks on,
And turns no more his head;
Because he knows, a frightful fiend   450
Doth close behind him tread.

But soon there breathed a wind on me,
Nor sound nor motion made:
Its path was not upon the sea,
In ripple or in shade.

It raised my hair, it fanned my cheek
Like a meadow-gale of spring—
It mingled strangely with my fears,
Yet it felt like a welcoming.

Swiftly, swiftly flew the ship,   460
Yet she sailed softly too:
Sweetly, sweetly blew the breeze—
On me alone it blew.

And the ancient Mariner
beholdeth his native
country.

Oh! dream of joy! is this indeed
The light-house top I see?
Is this the hill? is this the kirk?
Is this mine own countree?

210

We drifted o'er the harbour-bar,
And I with sobs did pray—
O let me be awake, my God!   470
Or let me sleep alway.

The harbour-bay was clear as glass,
So smoothly it was strewn!
And on the bay the moonlight lay,
And the shadow of the Moon.

The rock shone bright, the kirk no less,
That stands above the rock:
The moonlight steeped in silentness
The steady weathercock.

And the bay was white with silent light,   480
Till rising from the same,
The angelic spirits leave Full many shapes, that shadows were,
the dead bodies, In crimson colours came.
And appear in their own
forms of light.
A little distance from the prow
Those crimson shadows were:
I turned my eyes upon the deck—
Oh, Christ! what saw I there!

Each corse lay flat, lifeless and flat,
And, by the holy rood!
A man all light, a seraph-man,   490
On every corse there stood.

This seraph-band, each waved his hand:
It was a heavenly sight!
They stood as signals to the land,
Each one a lovely light;

This seraph-band, each waved his hand,
No voice did they impart—
No voice; but oh! the silence sank
Like music on my heart.

But soon I heard the dash of oars,   500
I heard the Pilot's cheer;
My head was turned perforce away
And I saw a boat appear.

The Pilot and the Pilot's boy,
I heard them coming fast:
Dear Lord in Heaven! it was a joy
The dead men could not blast.

211

I saw a third—I heard his voice:
It is the Hermit good!
He singeth loud his godly hymns   510
That he makes in the wood.
He'll shrieve my soul, he'll wash away
The Albatross's blood.

PART VII

This Hermit good lives in that wood
Which slopes down to the sea.
How loudly his sweet voice he rears!
He loves to talk with marineres
That come from a far countree.

He kneels at morn, and noon, and eve—
He hath a cushion plump: 520
It is the moss that wholly hides
The rotted old oak-stump.

The skiff-boat neared: I heard them talk,
'Why, this is strange, I trow!
Where are those lights so many and fair,
That signal made but now?'

'Strange, by my faith!' the Hermit said—
'And they answered not our cheer!
The planks looked warped! and see those sails,
How thin they are and sere!   530
I never saw aught like to them,
Unless perchance it were

Brown skeletons of leaves that lag
My forest-brook along;
When the ivy-tod is heavy with snow,
And the owlet whoops to the wolf below,
That eats the she-wolf's young.'

'Dear Lord! it hath a fiendish look—
(The Pilot made reply)
I am a-feared'—'Push on, push on!'   540
Said the Hermit cheerily.

The boat came closer to the ship,
But I nor spake nor stirred;
The boat came close beneath the ship,
And straight a sound was heard.

The ship suddenly sink-
eth.

Under the water it rumbled on,
Still louder and more dread:
It reached the ship, it split the bay;
The ship went down like lead.

The ancient Mariner is
saved in the Pilot's boat.

Stunned by that loud and dreadful sound,   550
Which sky and ocean smote,
Like one that hath been seven days drowned
My body lay afloat;
But swift as dreams, myself I found
Within the Pilot's boat.

Upon the whirl, where sank the ship,
The boat spun round and round;
And all was still, save that the hill
Was telling of the sound.

I moved my lips—the Pilot shrieked   560
And fell down in a fit;
The holy Hermit raised his eyes,
And prayed where he did sit.

I took the oars: the Pilot's boy,
Who now doth crazy go,
Laughed loud and long, and all the while
His eyes went to and fro.
'Ha! ha!' quoth he, 'full plain I see,
The Devil knows how to row.'

And now, all in my own countree,   570
I stood on the firm land!
The Hermit stepped forth from the boat,
And scarcely he could stand.

The ancient Mariner ear-
nestly entreateth the
Hermit to shrieve him;
and the penance of life
falls on him.

'O shrieve me, shrieve me, holy man!'
The Hermit crossed his brow.
'Say quick,' quoth he, 'I bid thee say—
What manner of man art thou?'

Forthwith this frame of mine was wrenched
With a woful agony,
Which forced me to begin my tale;   580
And then it left me free.

And ever and anon
through out his future
life an agony constrain-
eth him to travel from
land to land;

Since then, at an uncertain hour,
That agony returns:
And till my ghastly tale is told,
This heart within me burns.

I pass, like night, from land to land;
I have strange power of speech;
That moment that his face I see,
I know the man that must hear me:
To him my tale I teach.   590

What loud uproar bursts from that door!
The wedding-guests are there:
But in the garden-bower the bride
And bride-maids singing are:
And hark the little vesper bell,
Which biddeth me to prayer!

O Wedding-Guest! this soul hath been
Alone on a wide wide sea:
So lonely 'twas, that God himself
Scarce seeméd there to be.   600

O sweeter than the marriage-feast,
'Tis sweeter far to me,
To walk together to the kirk
With a goodly company!—

To walk together to the kirk,
And all together pray,
While each to his great Father bends,
Old men, and babes, and loving friends
And youths and maidens gay!

And to teach, by his own example, love and reverence to all things that God made and loveth.

Farewell, farewell! but this I tell   610
To thee, thou Wedding-Guest!
He prayeth well, who loveth well
Both man and bird and beast.

He prayeth best, who loveth best
All things both great and small;
For the dear God who loveth us,
He made and loveth all.

The Mariner, whose eye is bright,
Whose beard with age is hoar,
Is gone: and now the Wedding-Guest   620
Turned from the bridegroom's door.

He went like one that hath been stunned,
And is of sense forlorn:
A sadder and a wiser man,
He rose the morrow morn.

SAMUEL TAYLOR COLERIDGE

214

The *Palatine*

Leagues north, as fly the gull and auk,
Point Judith[11] watches with eye of hawk;
Leagues south, thy beacon flames, Montauk![12]

Lonely and wind-shorn, wood-forsaken,
With never a tree for Spring to waken,
For tryst of lovers or farewells taken,

Circled by waters that never freeze,
Beaten by billow and swept by breeze,
Lieth the island of Manisees,[13]

Set at the mouth of the Sound to hold   10
The coast lights up on its turret old,
Yellow with moss and sea-fog mould.

Dreary the land when gust and sleet
At its doors and windows howl and beat,
And Winter laughs at its fires of peat!

But in summer time, when pool and pond,
Held in the laps of valleys fond,
Are blue as the glimpses of sea beyond;

When the hills are sweet with the brier-rose,
And, hid in the warm, soft dells, unclose   20
Flowers the mainland rarely knows;

When boats to their morning fishing go,
And, held to the wind and slanting low,
Whitening and darkening the small sails show,—

Then is that lonely island fair;
And the pale health-seeker findeth there
The wine of life in its pleasant air.

No greener valleys the sun invite,
On smoother beaches no sea-birds light,
No blue waves shatter to foam more white!   30

There, circling ever their narrow range,
Quaint tradition and legend strange
Live on unchallenged, and know no change.

Old wives spinning their webs of tow,
Or rocking weirdly to and fro
In and out of the peat's dull glow,

And old men mending their nets of twine,
Talk together of dream and sign,
Talk of the lost ship *Palatine*,—

The ship that, a hundred years before,
Freighted deep with its goodly store,
In the gales of the equinox went ashore.

The eager islanders one by one
Counted the shots of her signal gun,
And heard the crash when she drove right on!

Into the teeth of death she sped:
(May God forgive the hands that fed
The false lights over the rocky Head!)

O men and brothers! what sights were there!
White up-turned faces, hands stretched in prayer!
Where waves had pity, could ye not spare?

Down swooped the wreckers, like birds of prey
Tearing the heart of the ship away,
And the dead had never a word to say.

And then, with ghastly shimmer and shine
Over the rocks and the seething brine,
They burned the wreck of the *Palatine*.

In their cruel hearts, as they homeward sped,
"The sea and the rocks are dumb," they said:
"There'll be no reckoning with the dead."

But the year went round, and when once more
Along their foam-white curves of shore
They heard the line-storm rave and roar,

Behold! again, with shimmer and shine,
Over the rocks and the seething brine,
The flaming wreck of the *Palatine*!

So, haply in fitter words than these,
Mending their nets on their patient knees
They tell the legend of Manisees.

Nor looks nor tones a doubt betray;
"It is known to us all," they quietly say;
"We too have seen it in our day."

Is there, then, no death for a word once spoken?
Was never a deed but left its token
Written on tables never broken?

40

50

60

70

Do the elements subtle reflections give?
Do pictures of all the ages live
On Nature's infinite negative,

Which, half in sport, in malice half,
She shows at times, with shudder or laugh,   80
Phantom and shadow in photograph?

For still, on many a moonless night,
From Kingston Head and from Montauk light
The spectre kindles and burns in sight.

Now low and dim, now clear and higher,
Leaps up the terrible Ghost of Fire,
Then, slowly sinking, the flames expire.

And the wise Sound skippers, though skies be fine,
Reef their sails when they see the sign
Of the blazing wreck of the *Palatine!*

JOHN GREENLEAF WHITTIER

The Flying Dutchman

Unyielding in the pride of his defiance,
   Afloat with none to serve or to command,
Lord of himself at last, and all by Science,
   He seeks the Vanished Land.

Alone, by the one light of his one thought,
   He steers to find the shore from which we came,
Fearless of in what coil he may be caught
   On seas that have no name.

Into the night he sails; and after night
   There is a dawning, though there be no sun;   10
Wherefore, with nothing but himself in sight,
   Unsighted, he sails on.

At last there is a lifting of the cloud
   Between the flood before him and the sky;
And then—though he may curse the Power aloud
   That has no power to die—

He steers himself away from what is haunted
   By the old ghost of what has been before,—
Abandoning, as always, and undaunted,
   One fog-walled island more.

EDWIN ARLINGTON ROBINSON

A Greyport Legend

They ran through the streets of the seaport town,
They peered from the decks of the ships that lay;
The cold sea-fog that came whitening down
Was never as cold or white as they.
    "Ho, Starbuck and Pinckney and Tenterden!
    Run for your shallops, gather your men,
        Scatter your boats on the lower bay."

Good cause for fear! In the thick mid-day
The hulk that lay by the rotting pier,
Filled with the children in happy play,   10
Parted its moorings and drifted clear,
    Drifted clear beyond reach or call,—
    Thirteen children they were in all,—
        All adrift in the lower bay!

Said a hard-faced skipper, "God help us all!
She will not float till the turning tide!"
Said his wife, "My darling will hear *my* call,
Whether in sea or heaven she bide;"
    And she lifted a quavering voice and high,
    Wild and strange as a sea-bird's cry,   20
        Till they shuddered and wondered at her side.

The fog drove down on each laboring crew,
Veiled each from each and the sky and shore:
There was not a sound but the breath they drew,
And the lap of water and creak of oar;
    And they felt the breath of the downs, fresh blown
    O'er leagues of clover and cold gray stone,
        But not from the lips that had gone before.

They came no more. But they tell the tale
That, when fogs are thick on the harbor reef,   30
The mackerel fishers shorten sail—
For the signal they know will bring relief;
    For the voices of children, still at play
    In a phantom hulk that drifts alway
        Through channels whose waters never fail.

It is but a foolish shipman's tale,
A theme for a poet's idle page;
But still, when the mists of Doubt prevail,
And we lie becalmed by the shores of Age,
  We hear from the misty troubled shore   40
  The voice of the children gone before,
  Drawing the soul to its anchorage.

BRET HARTE

The Ballad of Dead Men's Bay

The sea swings owre the slants of sand,
  All white with winds that drive;
The sea swirls up to the still dim strand,
  Where nae man comes alive.

At the grey soft edge of the fruitless surf
  A light flame sinks and springs;
At the grey soft rim of the flowerless turf
  A low flame leaps and clings.

What light is this on a sunless shore,
  What gleam on a starless sea?   10
Was it earth's or hell's waste womb that bore
  Such births as should not be?

As lithe snakes turning, as bright stars burning,
  They bicker and beckon and call;
As wild waves churning, as wild winds yearning,
  They flicker and climb and fall.

A soft strange cry from the landward rings—
  "What ails the sea to shine?"
A keen sweet note from the spray's rim springs—
  "What fires are these of thine?"   20

A soul am I that was born on earth
  For ae day's waesome span:
Death bound me fast on the bourn of birth
  Ere I were christened man.

"A light by night, I fleet and fare
  Till the day of wrath and woe;
On the hems of earth and the skirts of air
  Winds hurl me to and fro."

"O well is thee, though the weird be strange
    That bids thee flit and flee;
For hope is child of the womb of change,
    And hope keeps watch with thee.

"When the years are gone, and the time is come,
    God's grace may give thee grace;
And thy soul may sing, though thy soul were dumb,
    And shine before God's face.

"But I, that lighten and revel and roll
    With the foam of the plunging sea,
No sign is mine of a breathing soul
    That God should pity me.

"Nor death, nor heaven, nor hell, nor birth
    Hath part in me nor mine:
Strong lords are these of the living earth
    And loveless lords of thine.

"But I that know nor lord nor life
    More sure than storm or spray,
Whose breath is made of sport and strife,
    Whereon shall I find stay?"

"And wouldst thou change thy doom with me,
    Full fain with thee would I:
For the life that lightens and lifts the sea
    Is more than earth or sky.

"And what if the day of doubt and doom
    Shall save nor smite not me?
I would not rise from the slain world's tomb
    If there be no more sea.

"Take he my soul that gave my soul,
    And give it thee to keep;
And me, while seas and stars shall roll
    Thy life that falls on sleep."

That word went up through the mirk mid sky,
    And even to God's own ear:
And the Lord was ware of the keen twin cry,
    And wroth was he to hear.

He 's tane the soul of the unsained child
    That fled to death from birth;
He 's tane the light of the wan sea wild,
    And bid it burn on earth.

He 's given the ghaist of the babe new-born
    The gift of the water-sprite,
To ride on revel from morn to morn
    And roll from night to night.

70

He 's given the sprite of the wild wan sea
    The gift of the new-born man,
A soul for ever to bide and be
    When the years have filled their span.

When a year was gone and a year was come,
    O loud and loud cried they—
"For the lee-lang year thou hast held us dumb
    Take now thy gifts away!"

80

O loud and lang they cried on him,
    And sair and sair they prayed:
"Is the face of thy grace as the night's face grim
    For those thy wrath has made?"

A cry more bitter than tears of men
    From the rim of the dim grey sea;—
"Give me my living soul again,
    The soul thou gavest me,
The doom and the dole of kindly men,
    To bide my weird and be!"

90

A cry more keen from the wild low land
    Than the wail of waves that roll;—
"Take back the gift of a loveless hand,
    Thy gift of doom and dole,
The weird of men that bide on land;
    Take from me, take my soul!"

The hands that smite are the hands that spare;
    They build and break the tomb;
They turn to darkness and dust and air
    The fruits of the waste earth's womb;
But never the gift of a granted prayer,
    The dole of a spoken doom.

100

Winds may change at a word unheard,
    But none may change the tides:
The prayer once heard is as God's own word;
    The doom once dealt abides.

And ever a cry goes up by day,
  And ever a wail by night;
And nae ship comes by the weary bay
But her shipmen hear them wail and pray,   110
  And see with earthly sight
The twofold flames of the twin lights play
Where the sea-banks green and the sea-floods grey
Are proud of peril and fain of prey,
And the sand quakes ever; and ill fare they
  That look upon that light.

ALGERNON CHARLES SWINBURNE

Ulysses

It little profits that an idle king,
By this still hearth, among these barren crags,
Matched with an aged wife, I mete and dole
Unequal laws unto a savage race,
That hoard, and sleep, and feed, and know not me.

  I cannot rest from travel; I will drink
Life to the lees. All times I have enjoyed
Greatly, have suffered greatly, both with those
That loved me, and alone; on shore, and when
Through scudding drifts the rainy Hyades   10
Vexed the dim sea. I am become a name;
For always roaming with a hungry heart
Much have I seen and known—cities of men
And manners, climates, councils, governments,
Myself not least, but honoured of them all—
And drunk delight of battle with my peers,
Far on the ringing plains of windy Troy.
I am a part of all that I have met;
Yet all experience is an arch wherethrough
Gleams that untraveled world whose margin fades   20
Forever and forever when I move.
How dull it is to pause, to make an end,
To rust unburnished, not to shine in use!
As though to breathe were life! Life piled on life
Were all too little, and of one to me
Little remains; but every hour is saved
From that eternal silence, something more,

A bringer of new things; and vile it were
For some three suns to store and hoard myself,
And this gray spirit yearning in desire   30
To follow knowledge like a sinking star,
Beyond the utmost bound of human thought.

This is my son, mine own Telemachus,
To whom I leave the sceptre and the isle—
Well-loved of me, discerning to fulfill
This labour, by slow prudence to make mild
A rugged people, and through soft degrees
Subdue them to the useful and the good.
Most blameless is he, centered in the sphere
Of common duties, decent not to fail   40
In offices of tenderness, and pay
Meet adoration to my household gods,
When I am gone. He works his work, I mine.

There lies the port; the vessel puffs her sail;
There gloom the dark, broad seas. My mariners,
Souls that have toiled, and wrought, and thought with me—
That ever with a frolic welcome took
The thunder and the sunshine, and opposed
Free hearts, free foreheads—you and I are old;
Old age hath yet his honour and his toil.   50
Death closes all; but something ere the end,
Some work of noble note, may yet be done,
Not unbecoming men that strove with Gods.
The lights begin to twinkle from the rocks;
The long day wanes; the slow moon climbs; the deep
Moans round with many voices. Come, my friends,
'Tis not too late to seek a newer world.
Push off, and sitting well in order smite
The sounding furrows; for my purpose holds
To sail beyond the sunset, and the baths   60
Of all the western stars, until I die.
It may be that the gulfs will wash us down;
It may be we shall touch the Happy Isles,[14]
And see the great Achilles, whom we knew.
Though much is taken, much abides; and though
We are not now that strength which in old days
Moved earth and heaven, that which we are, we are—
One equal temper of heroic hearts,
Made weak by time and fate, but strong in will
To strive, to seek, to find, and not to yield.

ALFRED, LORD TENNYSON

The Sailor Boy

He rose at dawn and, fired with hope,
    Shot o'er the seething harbour-bar,
And reach'd the ship and caught the rope,
    And whistled to the morning star.

And while he whistled long and loud
    He heard a fierce mermaiden cry,
'O boy, tho' thou art young and proud,
    I see the place where thou wilt lie.

'The sands and yeasty surges mix
    In caves about the dreary bay,   10
And on thy ribs the limpet sticks,
    And in thy heart the scrawl shall play.'

'Fool,' he answer'd, 'death is sure
    To those that stay and those that roam,
But I will nevermore endure
    To sit with empty hands at home.

'My mother clings about my neck,
    My sisters crying, "Stay for shame;"
My father raves of death and wreck,—
    They are all to blame, they are all to blame.   20

'God help me! save I take my part
    Of danger on the roaring sea,
A devil rises in my heart,
    Far worse than any death to me.'

ALFRED, LORD TENNYSON

The City in the Sea

Lo! Death has reared himself a throne
In a strange city lying alone
Far down within the dim West,
Where the good and the bad and the worst and the best
Have gone to their eternal rest.
There shrines and palaces and towers
(Time-eaten towers that tremble not!)
Resemble nothing that is ours.
Around, by lifting winds forgot,
Resignedly beneath the sky   10
The melancholy waters lie.

No rays from the holy heaven come down
On the long night-time of that town;
But light from out the lurid sea
Streams up the turrets silently—
Gleams up the pinnacles far and free—
Up domes—up spires—up kingly halls—
Up fanes—up Babylon-like walls—
Up shadowy long-forgotten bowers
Of sculptured ivy and stone flowers—   20
Up many and many a marvellous shrine
Whose wreathéd friezes intertwine
The viol, the violet, and the vine.
Resignedly beneath the sky
The melancholy waters lie.
So blend the turrets and shadows there
That all seem pendulous in air,
While from a proud tower in the town
Death looks gigantically down.

There open fanes and gaping graves   30
Yawn level with the luminous waves;
But not the riches there that lie
In each idol's diamond eye—
Not the gayly-jewelled dead
Tempt the waters from their bed;
For no ripples curl, alas!
Along that wilderness of glass—
No swellings tell that winds may be
Upon some far-off happier sea—

No heavings hint that winds have been 40
On seas less hideously serene.

But lo, a stir is in the air!
The wave—there is a movement there!
As if the towers had thrust aside,
In slightly sinking, the dull tide—
As if their tops had feebly given
A void within the filmy Heaven.
The waves have now a redder glow—
The hours are breathing faint and low—
And when, amid no earthly moans, 50
Down, down that town shall settle hence,
Hell, rising from a thousand thrones,
Shall do it reverence.

EDGAR ALLAN POE

The Forsaken Merman

Come, dear children, let us away;
Down and away below!
Now my brothers call from the bay,
Now the great winds shoreward blow,
Now the salt tides seaward flow;
Now the wild white horses play,
Champ and chafe and toss in the spray.
Children dear, let us away!
This way, this way!

Call her once before you go— 10
Call once yet!
In a voice that she will know:
'Margaret! Margaret!'
Children's voices should be dear
(Call once more) to a mother's ear;
Children's voices, wild with pain—
Surely she will come again!
Call her once and come away;
This way, this way!
'Mother dear, we cannot stay! 20
The wild white horses foam and fret.'
Margaret! Margaret!

Come, dear children, come away down;
Call no more!
One last look at the white-wall'd town,
And the little grey church on the windy shore,
Then come down!
She will not come though you call all day;
Come away, come away!

Children dear, was it yesterday   30
We heard the sweet bells over the bay?
In the caverns where we lay,
Through the surf and through the swell,
The far-off sound of a silver bell?
Sand-strewn caverns, cool and deep,
Where the winds are all asleep;
Where the spent lights quiver and gleam,
Where the salt weed sways in the stream,
Where the sea-beasts, ranged all round,
Feed in the ooze of their pasture-ground;   40
Where the sea-snakes coil and twine,
Dry their mail and bask in the brine;
Where great whales come sailing by,
Sail and sail, with unshut eye,
Round the world for ever and aye?
When did music come this way?
Children dear, was it yesterday?

Children dear, was it yesterday
(Call yet once) that she went away?
Once she sate with you and me,   50
On a red gold throne in the heart of the sea,
And the youngest sate on her knee.
She comb'd its bright hair, and she tended it well,
When down swung the sound of a far-off bell.
She sigh'd, she look'd up through the clear green sea;
She said: 'I must go, for my kinsfolk pray
In the little grey church on the shore to-day.
'Twill be Easter-time in the world—ah me!
And I lose my poor soul, Merman! here with thee.'
I said: 'Go up, dear heart, through the waves;   60
Say thy prayer, and come back to the kind sea-caves!'
She smiled, she went up through the surf in the bay.
Children dear, was it yesterday?

Children dear, were we long alone?
'The sea grows stormy, the little ones moan;
Long prayers,' I said, 'in the world they say;
Come!' I said; and we rose through the surf in the bay.
We went up the beach, by the sandy down
  Where the sea-stocks bloom, to the white-wall'd town;
Through the narrow paved streets, where all was still,   70
To the little grey church on the windy hill.
From the church came a murmur of folk at their prayers,
But we stood without in the cold blowing airs.
We climb'd on the graves, on the stones worn with rains,
And we gazed up the aisle through the small leaded panes.
She sate by the pillar; we saw her clear:
'Margaret, hist! come quick, we are here!
Dear heart,' I said, 'we are long alone;
The sea grows stormy, the little ones moan.'
But, ah, she gave me never a look,   80
For her eyes were seal'd to the holy book!
Loud prays the priest; shut stands the door.
Come away, children, call no more!
Come away, come down, call no more!

  Down, down, down!
Down to the depths of the sea!
She sits at her wheel in the humming town,
Singing most joyfully.
Hark what she sings: 'O joy, O joy,
For the humming street, and the child with its toy!   90
For the priest, and the bell, and the holy well;
For the wheel where I spun,
And the blessed light of the sun!'
And so she sings her fill,
Singing most joyfully,
Till the spindle drops from her hand,
And the whizzing wheel stands still.
She steals to the window, and looks at the sand,
And over the sand at the sea;
And her eyes are set in a stare;   100
And anon there breaks a sigh,
And anon there drops a tear,
From a sorrow-clouded eye,
And a heart sorrow-laden,
A long, long sigh;
For the cold strange eyes of a little Mermaiden
And the gleam of her golden hair.

Come away, away children;
Come children, come down!
The hoarse wind blows coldly;
Lights shine in the town.
She will start from her slumber
When gusts shake the door;
She will hear the winds howling,
Will hear the waves roar.
We shall see, while above us
The waves roar and whirl,
A ceiling of amber,
A pavement of pearl.
Singing: 'Here came a mortal,
But faithless was she!
And alone dwell for ever
The kings of the sea.'

But, children, at midnight,
When soft the winds blow,
When clear falls the moonlight,
When spring-tides are low;
When sweet airs come seaward
From heaths starr'd with broom,
And high rocks throw mildly
On the blanch'd sands a gloom;
Up the still, glistening beaches,
Up the creeks we will hie,
Over banks of bright seaweed
The ebb-tide leaves dry.
We will gaze, from the sand-hills,
At the white, sleeping town;
At the church on the hill-side—
And then come back down.
Singing: 'There dwells a loved one,
But cruel is she!
She left lonely for ever
The kings of the sea.'

MATTHEW ARNOLD

110

The Ocean Said to Me Once

The ocean said to me once,
"Look!
"Yonder on the shore
"Is a woman, weeping.
"I have watched her.
"Go you and tell her this,—
"Her lover I have laid
"In cool green hall.
"There is wealth of golden sand
"And pillars, coral-red;
"Two white fish stand guard at his bier.

"Tell her this
"And more,—
"That the king of the seas
"Weeps too, old, helpless man.
"The bustling fates
"Heap his hands with corpses
"Until he stands like a child
"With surplus of toys."

STEPHEN CRANE

The Last Chantey

"And there was no more sea."

Thus said the Lord in the Vault above the Cherubim,
    Calling to the Angels and the Souls in their degree:
        "Lo! Earth has passed away
        On the smoke of Judgment Day.
    That Our word may be established shall We gather up the sea?"

Loud sang the souls of the jolly, jolly mariners:
    "Plague upon the hurricane that made us furl and flee!
        But the war is done between us,
        In the deep the Lord hath seen us—
    Our bones we'll leave the barracout',°   barracuda
            and God may sink the sea!"   10

Then said the soul of Judas that betrayèd Him:
    "Lord, hast Thou forgotten Thy covenant with me?
        How once a year I go
        To cool me on the floe?
    And Ye take my day of mercy if Ye take away the sea."

230

Then said the soul of the Angel of the Off-shore Wind:
  (He that bits the thunder when the bull-mouthed breakers flee):
    "I have watch and ward to keep
    O'er Thy wonders on the deep,
  And Ye take mine honour from me if Ye take away the sea!"   20

Loud sang the souls of the jolly, jolly mariners:
  "Nay, but we were angry, and a hasty folk are we.
    If we worked the ship together
    Till she foundered in foul weather,
  Are we babes that we should clamour for a vengeance on the sea?"

Then said the souls of the slaves that men threw overboard:
  "Kennelled in the picaroon a weary band were we;
    But Thy arm was strong to save,
    And it touched us on the wave,
  And we drowsed the long tides idle till Thy Trumpets tore the
      sea."   30

Then cried the soul of the stout Apostle Paul to God:
  "Once we frapped[15] a ship, and she laboured woundily.
    There were fourteen score of these,
    And they blessed Thee on their knees,
  When they learned Thy Grace and Glory under Malta by the sea!"

Loud sang the souls of the jolly, jolly mariners,
  Plucking at their harps, and they plucked unhandily:
    "Our thumbs are rough and tarred,
    And the tune is something hard—
  May we lift a Deepsea Chantey such as seamen use at sea?"   40

Then said the souls of the gentlemen-adventurers—
  Fettered wrist to bar all for red iniquity:
    "Ho, we revel in our chains
    O'er the sorrow that was Spain's!
  Heave or sink it, leave or drink it, we were masters of the sea!"

Up spake the soul of a grey Gothavn 'speckshioner—
  (He that led the flenching[16] in the fleets of fair Dundee):
    "Oh, the ice-blink white and near,
    And the bowhead breaching clear!
  Will Ye whelm them all for wantonness that wallow in the sea?" 50

Loud sang the souls of the jolly, jolly mariners,
  Crying: "Under Heaven, here is neither lead nor lee!
    Must we sing for evermore
    On the windless, glassy floor?
  Take back your golden fiddles and we'll beat to open sea!"

Then stooped the Lord, and He called the good sea up to Him,
  And 'stablishèd its borders unto all eternity,
    That such as have no pleasure
    For to praise the Lord by measure,
  They may enter into galleons and serve Him on the sea.   60

Sun, Wind, and Cloud shall fail not from the face of it,
  Stinging, ringing spindrift, nor the fulmar flying free;
    And the ships shall go abroad
    To the Glory of the Lord
  Who heard the silly sailor-folk and gave them back their sea!

RUDYARD KIPLING

Sea-Change

'Goneys an' gullies an' all o' the birds o' the sea
  They ain't no birds, not really,' said Billy the Dane.
'Not mollies, nor gullies, nor goneys at all,' said he,
  'But simply the sperrits of mariners livin' again.

'Them birds goin' fishin' is nothin' but souls o' the drowned,
  Souls o' the drowned an' the kicked as are never no more;
An' that there haughty old albatross cruisin' around,
  Belike he's Admiral Nelson or Admiral Noah.

'An' merry's the life they are living. They settle and dip,
  They fishes, they never stands watches, they waggle their wings;
When a ship comes by, they fly to look at the ship
  To see how the nowaday mariners manages things.

'When freezing aloft in a snorter, I tell you I wish—
  (Though maybe it ain't like a Christian)—I wish I could be
A haughty old copper-bound albatross dipping for fish
  And coming the proud over all o' the birds o' the sea.'

JOHN MASEFIELD

The Sea as Metaphor

FROM THE EARLIEST WRITINGS, men have used aspects of the physical world to imply, describe, or signify abstract ideas and concepts. Poetry itself is in large part founded on the technique of creating a picture of some part of the physical world that is meant to be compared with some other part of the world or with an abstract concept. This use of figurative language, of metaphor and simile, is the poet's stock-in-trade, and many entire poems are built upon a single comparison. The building of a poem on a single, extended metaphor is widely used in sea poetry, and that metaphor is, of course, some aspect of the sea. Each poet uses the sea a little differently in the construction of his poem, but generally takes as his theme one of four ideas—religion, philosophy, politics, or love.

Some poets have chosen the great and mysterious creatures that inhabit the sea to illuminate their religious themes, as have the anonymous author of *The Whale*, Henry W. Longfellow in *Seaweed*, and Oliver Wendell Holmes in *The Chambered Nautilus*; other poets use the sea itself, as do John Greenleaf Whittier in *Burning Drift-Wood*, Gerard Manley Hopkins in *Heaven-Haven*, and Matthew Arnold in *To Marguerite—Continued*. Most poets, however, have found a similarity between a sea voyage and man's life on earth; the ship that makes the voyage is likened either to the man himself—as in Cynewulf's *The Voyage of Life*, Stanza XL from Book I of Edmund Spenser's *The Faerie Queene*, Sir Thomas Wyatt's *My Galley*, Walt Whitman's *Joy, Shipmate, Joy!*, Robert Louis Stevenson's *Man Sails the Deep A While*, Alfred, Lord Tennyson's *Crossing the Bar*, John Masefield's *Port of Many Ships*, and D. H. Lawrence's *The Ship of Death*—or to the world itself, as in Sidney Lanier's *The Ship of Earth* and Stephen Crane's *God Fashioned the Ship of the World Carefully*.

The metaphor of life as a voyage lends itself, quite naturally, to philosophical as well as religious thought: Arthur Hugh Clough's *Qua Cursum Ventus*, Frederick Goddard Tuckerman's *Put Off Thy Bark from Shore*, Longfellow's *Ultima Thule* and *Ships That Pass in the Night*, William Dean Howells's *Hope*, and Robinson Jeffers's *Boats in a Fog*. The sea itself is a metaphor for a specific idea in Percy Bysshe Shelley's *Time*, Longfellow's

The Tide Rises, the Tide Falls, Ralph Waldo Emerson's *Sea-Shore,* Christina Rossetti's *Sleep at Sea,* Emily Dickinson's *I Started Early—Took My Dog,* Richard Eberhart's *Sea-Ruck,* T. S. Eliot's *Marina,* Robert Frost's *Once by the Pacific,* and Wallace Stevens's *The Idea of Order at Key West* and *Sea Surface Full of Clouds.*

Poets with political themes have found the ship as a nation, with her captain as the leader of that nation, to be a suitable metaphor: Longfellow wrote the now well-known line, "Thou, too, sail on, O Ship of State," in his *The Building of the Ship,* and Whitman's *O Captain! My Captain!* is an elegy on the death of Abraham Lincoln. In *Henry IV,* Shakespeare compares a king to a ship's boy and in *Henry VI,* in a metaphor now so well known that it is a cliché, he likens battle to the changes of the tide; William Carlos Williams, in *The Yachts,* portrays the wealthy and powerful as large, swift yachts that sail on heedless of the supplications of people adrift on the sea of life.

Still other poets have found in the sea metaphors for love and the relationship between men and women. Michael Drayton's *Like an Adventurous Sea-Farer Am I* compares the seafarer to a lover; Robert Graves's *Sail and Oar* uses the metaphor of a boat to look at the characteristics of each sex; E. E. Cummings likens his love to the sea in *as is the sea marvelous;* and, in *Sailor's Harbor,* Henry Reed finds his thoughts becalmed in his love's absence.

The sea is perhaps the most prevalent extended metaphor in poetry. Because of its role as mother of life, because of its frequently manifested power, and because of its self-evident mutability, the sea naturally stands as a metaphor for life, as both poet and sailor know.

From Job 41

Canst thou draw out leviathan with an hook? or his tongue with a cord which thou lettest down?

2 Canst thou put an hook into his nose? or bore his jaw through with a thorn?

3 Will he make many supplications unto thee? will he speak soft words unto thee?

4 Will he make a covenant with thee? wilt thou take him for a servant for ever?

5 Wilt thou play with him as with a bird? or wilt thou bind him for thy maidens?

6 Shall the companions make a banquet of him? shall they part him among the merchants?

7 Canst thou fill his skin with barbed irons? or his head with fish spears?

8 Lay thine hand upon him, remember the battle, do no more.

9 Behold, the hope of him is in vain: shall not one be cast down even at the sight of him?

10 None is so fierce that dare stir him up: who then is able to stand before me?

From *Physiologus*
Lines 75–150
The Whale[1]

Now I will fashion   the tale of a fish,
With wise wit singing   in measured strains
The song of the Great Whale.   Often unwittingly
Ocean-mariners   meet with this monster,
Fastitocalon,   fierce and menacing,
The Great Sea-Swimmer   of the ocean-streams.   80
   Like a rough rock   is the Whale's appearance,
Or as if there were swaying   by the shore of the sea
A great mass of sedge   in the midst of the sand dunes;
So it seems to sailors   they see an island,
And they firmly fasten   their high-prowed ships
With anchor-ropes   to the land that is no land,
Hobble their sea-steeds   at ocean's end,
Land bold on the island   and leave their barks
Moored at the water's edge   in the wave's embrace.
   There they encamp,   the sea-weary sailors,   90
Fearing no danger.   They kindle a fire;

235

High on the island   the hot flames blaze
And joy returns   to travel-worn hearts
Eager for rest.   Then, crafty in evil,
When the Whale feels the sailors   are fully set
And firmly lodged,   enjoying fair weather,
Suddenly with his prey   Ocean's Guest plunges
Down in the salt wave   seeking the depths,
In the hall of death   drowning sailors and ships.
    Such is the manner of demons,   the devils' way,   100
Luring from virtue,   inciting to lust,
By secret power   deceiving men's souls
That they may seek help   at the hands of their foes
And, fixed in sin,   find abode with the Fiend.
Sly and deceitful,   when the Devil perceives
Out of hell-torment   that each of mankind,
Of the race of men,   is bound with his ring,
Then with cunning craft   the Dark Destroyer
Takes proud and humble   who here on earth
Through sin did his will.   Seizing them suddenly   110
Shrouded in darkness,   estranged from good,
He seeks out hell,   the bottomless abyss
In the misty gloom;   even as the Great Whale
Who drowns the mariners,   sea-steeds and men.
    A second trait has he,   the proud Sea-Thrasher,
Even more marvelous: when hunger torments
And the fierce Water-Monster   is fain of food,
Then the Ocean-Warden   opens his mouth,
Unlocks his wide jaws,   and a winsome odor
Comes from his belly;   other kinds of fish   120
Are deceived thereby,   all eagerly swimming
To where the sweet fragrance   comes flowing forth.
In unwary schools   they enter within
Till the wide mouth is filled. Then swiftly the Whale
Over his sea-prey   snaps his grim jaws.
    So is it with him   in this transient time
Who takes heed to his life   too late and too little,
Letting vain delights   through their luring fragrance
Ensnare his soul   till he slips away,
Soiled with sin,   from the King of glory.   130
Before them the Devil   after death's journey
Throws open hell   for all who in folly
Fulfilled the lying   lusts of the flesh
Against the law.   But when the Wily One,
Expert in evil,   has brought into bonds

In the burning heat   those cleaving to him
Laden with sins,   who during their life-days
Did his bidding,   on them after death
His savage jaws   he snaps together,
The gates of hell.   Who gather there   140
Know no retreat,   no return out thence,
Any more than the fishes   swimming the sea
Can escape from the grip   of the Great Whale.
    Therefore by every means   (should every man
Serve the Lord God)   and strive against devils
By words and works,   that we may behold
The King of glory.   In this transient time
Let us seek for peace   and healing at His hands,
That we in grace may dwell   with Him so dear
And have His bliss   and blessedness for ever!

ANONYMOUS

From *Crist*
Lines 850–866
The Voyage of Life

Now is it most like   as if on ocean
Across cold water   we sail in our keels,
Over the wide sea   in our ocean-steeds,
Faring on in our flood-wood.   Fearful the stream,
The tumult of waters,   whereon we toss
In this feeble world.   Fierce are the surges
On the ocean-lanes.   Hard was our life
Before we made harbor   over the foaming seas.
Then help was vouchsafed   when God's Spirit-Son
Guided us to the harbor of salvation   and granted us grace
That we may understand   over the ship's side
Where to moor our sea-steeds,   our ocean-stallions,
Fast at anchor.   Let us fix our hope
Upon that haven   which the Lord of heaven,
In holiness on high,   has opened by His Ascension.

CYNEWULF

From *Henry IV, Part II*
Act III, Scene I
Lines 18–31

Wilt thou upon the high and giddy mast
Seal up the ship boy's eyes, and rock his brains
In cradle of the rude imperious surge
And in the visitation of the winds,
Who take the ruffian billows by the top,
Curling their monstrous heads and hanging them
With deafening clamor in the slippery clouds,
That, with the hurly,° death itself awakes?   noise
Canst thou, O partial Sleep, give thy repose
To the wet sea boy in an hour so rude,
And in the calmest and most stillest night,
With all appliances and means to boot,
Deny it to a king? Then happy low, lie down!
Uneasy lies the head that wears a crown.

WILLIAM SHAKESPEARE

From *Henry VI, Part III*
Act II, Scene V
Lines 5–13

Now sways it this way, like a mighty sea
Forced by the tide to combat with the wind.
Now sways it that way, like the selfsame sea
Forced to retire by fury of the wind.
Sometime the flood prevails, and then the wind,
Now one the better, then another best,
Both tugging to be victors, breast to breast,
Yet neither conqueror nor conquerèd:
So is the equal poise of this fell war.

WILLIAM SHAKESPEARE

From *The Faerie Queene*
Book I, Canto IX, Stanza XL

'He there does now enjoy eternall rest
And happy ease, which thou doest want and crave,
And further from it daily wanderest:
What if some little payne the passage have,
That makes frayle flesh to feare the bitter wave?
Is not short payne well borne, that bringes long ease,
And layes the soule to sleepe in quiet grave?
Sleepe after toyle, port after stormie seas,
Ease after warre, death after life does greatly please.'

EDMUND SPENSER

From *The Faerie Queene*
Book VI, Canto XII, Stanza I

Like as a ship, that through the ocean wyde
Directs her course unto one certaine cost.
Is met of many a counter winde and tyde,
With which her winged speed is let and crost,
And she her selfe in stormie surges tost;
Yet making many a borde, and many a bay,
Still winneth way, he hath her compasse lost;
Right so it fares with me in this long way,
Whose course is often stayd, yet never is astray.

EDMUND SPENSER

My Galley

My galley chargéd with forgetfulness
Thorough sharp seas, in winter nights doth pass
'Tween rock and rock; and eke° mine enemy, alas,   also
That is my lord, steereth with cruelness,
And every oar a thought in readiness,
As though that death were light in such a case.
An endless wind doth tear the sail apace
Of forcéd sighs and trusty fearfulness.
A rain of tears, a cloud of dark disdain,
Hath done the wearied cords great hinderance,
Wreathéd with error and eke with ignorance.
The stars be hid that led me to this pain,
Drownéd is reason that should me consort,
And I remain despairing of the port.

SIR THOMAS WYATT

Like an Adventurous Sea-Farer Am I

Like an adventurous Sea-farer am I,
Who hath some long and dang'rous Voyage beene,
And calld to tell of his Discovery,
How farre he sayld, what Countries he had seene:
Proceeding from the Port whence he put forth,
Shewes by his Compasse how his Course he steer'd
When East, when West, when South and when by North,
As how the Pole to ev'ry place was rear'd;
What Capes he doubled, of what Continent,
The Gulphes and Straits that strangely he had past,
Where most becalm'd, where with foule Weather spent,
And on what Rockes in perill to be cast.
    Thus in my Love Time calls me to relate
    My tedious Travells and oft-varying Fate.

MICHAEL DRAYTON

Time

Unfathomable Sea! whose waves are years,
  Ocean of Time, whose waters of deep woe
Are brackish with the salt of human tears!
    Thou shoreless flood, which in thy ebb and flow
  Claspest the limits of mortality,
  And sick of prey, yet howling on for more,
Vomitest thy wrecks on its inhospitable shore;
  Treacherous in calm, and terrible in storm,
      Who shall put forth on thee,
      Unfathomable Sea?

                    PERCY BYSSHE SHELLEY

Qua Cursum Ventus[2]

As ships, becalmed at eve, that lay
  With canvas drooping, side by side,
Two towers of sail at dawn of day
  Are scarce long leagues apart descried;

When fell the night, upsprung the breeze,
  And all the darkling hours they plied,
Nor dreamt but each the self-same seas
  By each was cleaving, side by side:

E'en so—but why the tale reveal
  Of those, whom, year by year unchanged,   10
Brief absence joined anew, to feel
  Astounded, soul from soul estranged?

At dead of night their sails were filled,
  And onward each rejoicing steered—
Ah, neither blame, for neither willed,
  Or wist, what first with dawn appeared!

To veer, how vain! On, onward strain,
  Brave barks! In light, in darkness too,
Through winds and tides one compass guides—
  To that, and your own selves, be true.   20

But O blithe breeze! and O great seas,
    Though ne'er, that earliest parting past,
On your wide plain they join again,
    Together lead them home at last.

One port, methought, alike they sought,
    One purpose hold where'er they fare,—
O bounding breeze, O rushing seas!
    At last, at last, unite them there!

ARTHUR HUGH CLOUGH

Put Off Thy Bark from Shore, Though Near the Night

Put off thy bark from shore, though near the night,
And leaving home and friends and hope behind,
Sail down the lights. Thou scarce canst fail to find,
O desolate one, the morning breaking white,
Some shore of rest beyond the laboring wave.
Ah, 'tis for this I mourn: too long I have
Wandered in tears along life's stormy way
Where day to day no haven or hope reveals.
Yet on the bound my weary sight I keep
As one who sails, a landsman on the deep,
And longing for the land, day after day
Sees the horizon rise and fall and feels
His heart die out, still riding restlessly
Between the sailing cloud and the seasick sea.

FREDERICK GODDARD TUCKERMAN

In Cabin'd Ships at Sea

In cabin'd ships at sea,
The boundless blue on every side expanding,
With whistling winds and music of the waves, the large imperious
      waves,
Or some lone bark buoy'd on the dense marine,
Where joyous full of faith, spreading white sails,
She cleaves the ether mid the sparkle and the foam of day, or under
      many a star at night,
By sailors young and old haply will I, a reminiscence of the land, be
      read,
In full rapport at last.

Here are our thoughts, voyagers' thoughts,
Here not the land, firm land, alone appears, may then by them be said,   10
The sky o'erarches here, we feel the undulating deck beneath our feet,
We feel the long pulsation, ebb and flow of endless motion,
The tones of unseen mystery, the vague and vast suggestions of the briny
      world, the liquid-flowing syllables,
The perfume, the faint creaking of the cordage, the melancholy rhythm,
The boundless vista and the horizon far and dim are all here,
And this is ocean's poem.

Then falter not O book, fulfill your destiny,
You not a reminiscence of the land alone,
You too as a lone bark cleaving the ether, purpos'd I know not whither,
      yet ever full of faith,
Consort to every ship that sails, sail you!   20
Bear forth to them folded my love, (dear mariners, for you I fold it here
      in every leaf;)
Speed on my book! spread your white sails my little bark athwart the
      imperious waves,
Chant on, sail on, bear o'er the boundless blue from me to every sea,
This song for mariners and all their ships.

WALT WHITMAN

Joy, Shipmate, Joy!

Joy, shipmate, joy!
(Pleas'd to my soul at death I cry,)
Our life is closed, our life begins,
The long, long anchorage we leave,
The ship is clear at last, she leaps!
She swiftly courses from the shore,
Joy, shipmate, joy!

WALT WHITMAN

O Captain! My Captain!³

O Captain! my Captain! our fearful trip is done,
The ship has weather'd every rack, the prize we sought is won,
The port is near, the bells I hear, the people all exulting,
While follow eyes the steady keel, the vessel grim and daring;
      But O heart! heart! heart!
       O the bleeding drops of red,
         Where on the deck my Captain lies,
         Fallen cold and dead.

O Captain! my Captain! rise up and hear the bells;
Rise up—for you the flag is flung—for you the bugle trills,   10
For you bouquets and ribbon'd wreaths—for you the shores a-crowding,
For you they call, the swaying mass, their eager faces turning;
      Here Captain! dear father!
       This arm beneath your head!
        It is some dream that on the deck,
         You've fallen cold and dead.

My Captain does not answer, his lips are pale and still,
My father does not feel my arm, he has no pulse nor will,
The ship is anchor'd safe and sound, its voyage closed and done,
From fearful trip the victor ship comes in with object won;   20
      Exult O shores, and ring O bells!
       But I with mournful tread,
        Walk the deck my Captain lies,
         Fallen cold and dead.

WALT WHITMAN

From The Building of the Ship
Lines 377–398

Thou, too, sail on, O Ship of State!
Sail on, O UNION, strong and great!
Humanity with all its fears,
With all the hopes of future years,   380
Is hanging breathless on thy fate!
We know what Master laid thy keel,
What Workmen wrought thy ribs of steel,
Who made each mast, and sail, and rope,
What anvils rang, what hammers beat,
In what a forge and what a heat
Were shaped the anchors of thy hope!
Fear not each sudden sound and shock,
'Tis of the wave and not the rock;
'Tis but the flapping of the sail,   390
And not a rent made by the gale!
In spite of rock and tempest's roar,
In spite of false lights on the shore,
Sail on, nor fear to breast the sea!
Our hearts, our hopes, are all with thee,
Our hearts, our hopes, our prayers, our tears,
Our faith triumphant o'er our fears,
Are all with thee,—are all with thee!

HENRY WADSWORTH LONGFELLOW

Seaweed

When descends on the Atlantic
    The gigantic
Storm-wind of the equinox,
Landward in his wrath he scourges
    The toiling surges,
Laden with seaweed from the rocks:

From Bermuda's reefs; from edges
    Of sunken ledges,
In some far-off, bright Azore;
From Bahama, and the dashing,   10
    Silver-flashing
Surges of San Salvador;

From the tumbling surf, that buries
    The Orkneyan skerries,
Answering the hoarse Hebrides;
And from wrecks of ships, and drifting
    Spars, uplifting
On the desolate, rainy seas;—

Ever drifting, drifting, drifting
    On the shifting   20
Currents of the restless main;
Till in sheltered coves, and reaches
    Of sandy beaches,
All have found repose again.

So when storms of wild emotion
    Strike the ocean
Of the poet's soul, erelong
From each cave and rocky fastness,
    In its vastness,
Floats some fragment of a song: 30

From the far-off isles enchanted,
    Heaven has planted
With the golden fruit of Truth;
From the flashing surf, whose vision
    Gleams Elysian[4]
In the tropic clime of Youth;

From the strong Will, and the Endeavor
    That forever
Wrestle with the tides of Fate;
From the wreck of Hopes far-scattered,   40
    Tempest-shattered,
Floating waste and desolate;—

Ever drifting, drifting, drifting
    On the shifting
Currents of the restless heart;
Till at length in books recorded,
    They, like hoarded
Household words, no more depart.

    HENRY WADSWORTH LONGFELLOW

The Tide Rises, the Tide Falls

The tide rises, the tide falls,
The twilight darkens, the curlew calls;
Along the sea-sands damp and brown
The traveller hastens toward the town,
    And the tide rises, the tide falls.

Darkness settles on roofs and walls,
But the sea, the sea in the darkness calls,
The little waves, with their soft, white hands,
Efface the footprints in the sands,
    And the tide rises, the tide falls.

The morning breaks; the steeds in their stalls
Stamp and neigh, as the hostler calls;
The day returns, but nevermore
Returns the traveller to the shore,
    And the tide rises, the tide falls.

HENRY WADSWORTH LONGFELLOW

Ultima Thule

Dedication: To G. W. G.[5]

With favoring winds, o'er sunlit seas,
We sailed for the Hesperides,[6]
The land where golden apples grow;
But that, ah! that was long ago.

How far since then the ocean streams
Have swept us from the land of dreams,
That land of fiction and of truth,
The lost Atlantis of our youth!

Whither, ah, whither? are not these
The tempest-haunted Orcades,[7]
Where sea-gulls scream, and breakers roar,
And wreck and sea-weed line the shore?

Ultima Thule! Utmost Isle!
Here in thy harbors for awhile
We lower our sails, awhile we rest
From the unending endless quest.

HENRY WADSWORTH LONGFELLOW

Ships That Pass in the Night

Ships that pass in the night, and speak each other in passing,
Only a signal shown and a distant voice in the darkness;
So on the ocean of life we pass and speak one another,
Only a look and a voice, then darkness again and a silence.

HENRY WADSWORTH LONGFELLOW

Ships That Pass in the Night

Out in the sky the great dark clouds are massing;
   I look far out into the pregnant night,
Where I can hear a solemn booming gun
   And catch the gleaming of a random light,
That tells me that the ship I seek is passing, passing.

My tearful eyes my soul's deep hurt are glassing;
   For I would hail and check that ship of ships.
I stretch my hands imploring, cry aloud,
   My voice falls dead a foot from mine own lips,
And but its ghost doth reach that vessel, passing, passing.

O Earth, O Sky, O Ocean, both surpassing,
   O heart of mine, O soul that dreads the dark!
Is there no hope for me? Is there no way
   That I may sight and check that speeding bark
Which out of sight and sound is passing, passing?

PAUL LAURENCE DUNBAR

The Chambered Nautilus

This is the ship of pearl, which, poets feign,
   Sails the unshadowed main,—
   The venturous bark that flings
On the sweet summer wind its purpled wings
In gulfs enchanted, where the Siren sings,
   And coral reefs lie bare,
Where the cold sea-maids rise to sun their streaming hair.

Its webs of living gauze no more unfurl!
  Wrecked is the ship of pearl!
  And every chambered cell,   10
Where its dim dreaming life was wont to dwell,
As the frail tenant shaped his growing shell,
  Before thee lies revealed,—
Its irised ceiling rent, its sunless crypt unsealed!

Year after year beheld the silent toil
  That spread his lustrous coil;
  Still, as the spiral grew,
He left the past year's dwelling for the new,
Stole with soft step its shining archway through,
  Built up its idle door,   20
Stretched in his last-found home, and knew the old no more.

Thanks for the heavenly message brought by thee,
  Child of the wandering sea,
  Cast from her lap forlorn!
From thy dead lips a clearer note is born
Than ever Triton blew from wreathèd horn!
  While on mine ear it rings,
Through the deep caves of thought I hear a voice that sings:—

Build thee more stately mansions, O my soul,
  As the swift seasons roll!   30
  Leave thy low-vaulted past!
Let each new temple, nobler than the last,
Shut thee from heaven with a dome more vast,
  Till thou at length art free,
Leaving thine outgrown shell by life's unresting sea!

OLIVER WENDELL HOLMES

Sea-Shore

I heard, or seemed to hear, the chiding Sea
Say: Pilgrim, why so late and slow to come?
Am I not always here?—thy summer home.
Is not my voice thy music, morn and eve?—
My breath thy healthful climate in the heats,
My touch thy antidote, my bay thy bath?
Was ever building like my terraces?
Was ever couch magnificent as mine?
Lie on the warm rock-ledges, and there learn
A little hut suffices like a town.   10

I make your sculptured architecture vain—
Vain beside mine. I drive my wedges home,
And carve the coastwise mountain into caves.
Lo! here is Rome and Nineveh and Thebes,
Karnak and Pyramid and Giant's Stairs[8]
Half-piled or prostrate,—and my newest slab
Older than all thy race.

Behold the Sea,
The opaline, the plentiful and strong,
Yet beautiful as is the rose in June,   20
Fresh as the trickling rainbow of July;
Sea full of food, the nourisher of kinds,
Purger of earth, and medicine of men;
Creating a sweet climate by my breath,
Washing out harms and griefs from memory,
And, in my mathematic ebb and flow,
Giving a hint of that which changes not.
Rich are the sea-gods:—who give gifts but they?
They grope the sea for pearls, but more than pearls:
They pluck Force thence, and give it to the wise.   30
For every wave is wealth to Dædalus,[9]
Wealth to the cunning artist who can work
This matchless strength. Where shall he find, O waves!
A load your Atlas[10] shoulders cannot lift?

I with my hammer pounding evermore
The rocky coast, smite Andes into dust,
Strewing my bed, and, in another age,
Rebuild a continent of better men.
Then I unbar the doors: my paths lead out
The exodus of nations: I disperse   40
Men to all shores that front the hoary main.
I, too, have arts and sorceries;
Illusion dwells forever with the wave.
I know what spells are laid. Leave me to deal
With credulous and imaginative man;
For, though he scoop my water in his palm,
A few rods off he deems it gems and clouds.
Planting strange fruits and sunshine on the shore,
I make some coasts alluring, some lone isle,
To distant men, who must go there, or die.

RALPH WALDO EMERSON

The Fisher's Boy

My life is like a stroll upon the beach,
    As near the ocean's edge as I can go;
My tardy steps its waves sometimes o'erreach,
    Sometimes I stay to let them overflow.

My sole employment is, and scrupulous care,
    To place my gains beyond the reach of tides,—
Each smoother pebble, and each shell more rare,
    Which Ocean kindly to my hand confides.

I have but few companions on the shore:
    They scorn the strand who sail upon the sea;
Yet oft I think the ocean they've sailed o'er
    Is deeper known upon the strand to me.

The middle sea contains no crimson dulse,
    Its deeper waves cast up no pearls to view;
Along the shore my hand is on its pulse,
    And I converse with many a shipwrecked crew.

                    HENRY DAVID THOREAU

Man Sails the Deep a While

Man sails the deep a while;
        Loud runs the roaring tide;
        The seas are wild and wide;
O'er many a salt, o'er many a desert mile,
        The unchained breakers ride,
        The quivering stars beguile.

Hope bears the sole command;
        Hope, with unshaken eyes,
        Sees flaw and storm arise;
Hope, the good steersman, with unwearying hand,
        Steers, under changing skies,
        Unchanged toward the land.

O wind that bravely blows!
        O hope that sails with all
        Where stars and voices call!
O ship undaunted that for ever goes
        Where God, her admiral,
        His battle signal shows!

10

251

What though the seas and wind
　　Far on the deep should whelm   20
　　Colours and sails and helm?
There, too, you touch that port that you designed—
　　There, in the mid-seas' realm,
　　Shall you that haven find.

Well hast thou sailed: now die,
　　To die is not to sleep.
　　Still your true course you keep,
O sailor soul, still sailing for the sky;
　　And fifty fathom deep
　　Your colours still shall fly.

ROBERT LOUIS STEVENSON

The Ship of Earth

Thou Ship of Earth, with Death, and Birth, and Life, and Sex aboard,
　　And fires of Desires burning hotly in the hold,
I fear thee, O! I fear thee, for I hear the tongue and sword
　　At battle on the deck, and the wild mutineers are bold!

The dewdrop morn may fall from off the petal of the sky,
　　But all the deck is wet with blood and stains the crystal red.
A pilot, GOD, a pilot! for the helm is left awry,
　　And the best sailors in the ship lie there among the dead!

SIDNEY LANIER

God Fashioned
the Ship of the World Carefully

God fashioned the ship of the world carefully.
With the infinite skill of an all-master
Made He the hull and the sails,
Held He the rudder
Ready for adjustment.
Erect stood He, scanning His work proudly.
Then—at fateful time—a wrong called,
And God turned, heeding.
Lo, the ship, at this opportunity, slipped slyly,
Making cunning noiseless travel down the ways.
So that, forever rudderless, it went upon the seas
Going ridiculous voyages,
Making quaint progress,
Turning as with serious purpose
Before stupid winds.
And there were many in the sky
Who laughed at this thing.

STEPHEN CRANE

At Sea

Yea, we go down to sea in ships—
    But Hope remains behind,
And Love, with laughter on his lips,
    And Peace, of passive mind;
While out across the deeps of night,
    With lifted sails of prayer,
We voyage off in quest of light,
    Nor find it anywhere.

O Thou who wroughtest earth and sea,
    Yet keepest from our eyes
The shores of an eternity
    In calms of Paradise,
Blow back upon our foolish quest
    With all the driving rain
Of blinding tears and wild unrest,
    And waft us home again!

JAMES WHITCOMB RILEY

253

Burning Drift-Wood

Before my drift-wood fire I sit,
  And see, with every waif I burn,
Old dreams and fancies coloring it,
  And folly's unlaid ghosts return.

O ships of mine, whose swift keels cleft
  The enchanted sea on which they sailed,
Are these poor fragments only left
  Of vain desires and hopes that failed?

Did I not watch from them the light
  Of sunset on my towers in Spain,   10
And see, far off, uploom in sight
  The Fortunate Isles I might not gain?

Did sudden lift of fog reveal
  Arcadia's vales of song and spring,
And did I pass, with grazing keel,
  The rocks whereon the sirens sing?

Have I not drifted hard upon
  The unmapped regions lost to man,
The cloud-pitched tents of Prester John,[11]
  The palace domes of Kubla Kahn?[12]   20

Did land winds blow from jasmine flowers,
  Where Youth the ageless Fountain fills?
Did Love make sign from rose blown bowers,
  And gold from Eldorado's[13] hills?

Alas! the gallant ships that sailed
  On blind Adventure's errand sent,
Howe'er they laid their courses, failed
  To reach the haven of Content.

And of my ventures, those alone
  Which Love had freighted, safely sped,   30
Seeking a good beyond my own,
  By clear-eyed Duty piloted.

O mariners, hoping still to meet
  The luck Arabian voyagers met,
And find in Bagdad's moonlit street,
  Haroun al Raschid[14] walking yet,

Take with you, on your Sea of Dreams,
　　The fair, fond fancies dear to youth.
I turn from all that only seems,
　　And seek the sober grounds of truth.　　　　　　　40

What matter that it is not May,
　　That birds have flown, and trees are bare,
That darker grows the shortening day,
　　And colder blows the wintry air!

The wrecks of passion and desire,
　　The castles I no more rebuild,
May fitly feed my drift-wood fire,
　　And warm the hands that age has chilled.

Whatever perished with my ships,
　　I only know the best remains;　　　　　　　　　50
A song of praise is on my lips
　　For losses which are now my gains.

Heap high my hearth! No worth is lost;
　　No wisdom with the folly dies.
Burn on, poor shreds, your holocaust
　　Shall be my evening sacrifice!

Far more than all I dared to dream,
　　Unsought before my door I see;
On wings of fire and steeds of steam
　　The world's great wonders come to me,　　　　60

And holier signs, unmarked before,
　　Of Love to seek and Power to save,—
The righting of the wronged and poor,
　　The man evolving from the slave;

And life, no longer chance or fate,
　　Safe in the gracious Fatherhood.
I fold o'er-wearied hands and wait,
　　In full assurance of the good.

And well the waiting time must be,
　　Though brief or long its granted days,　　　　70
If Faith and Hope and Charity
　　Sit by my evening hearth-fire's blaze.

And with them, friends whom Heaven has spared,
　　Whose love my heart has comforted,
And, sharing all my joys, has shared
　　My tender memories of the dead,—

Dear souls who left us lonely here,
    Bound on their last, long voyage, to whom
We, day by day, are drawing near,
    Where every bark has sailing room.   80

I know the solemn monotone
    Of waters calling unto me;
I know from whence the airs have blown
    That whisper of the Eternal Sea.

As low my fires of drift-wood burn,
    I hear that sea's deep sounds increase,
And, fair in sunset light, discern
    Its mirage-lifted Isles of Peace.

JOHN GREENLEAF WHITTIER

Hope

We sailed and sailed upon the desert sea
Where for whole days we alone seemed to be.
At last we saw a dim, vague line arise
Between the empty billows and the skies,
That grew and grew until it wore the shape
Of cove and inlet, promontory and cape;
Then hills and valleys, rivers, fields, and woods,
Steeples and roofs, and village neighborhoods.
And then I thought, "Sometime I shall embark
Upon a sea more desert and more dark
Than ever this was, and between the skies
And empty billows I shall see arise
Another world out of that waste and lapse,
Like yonder land. Perhaps—perhaps—perhaps!"

WILLIAM DEAN HOWELLS

Heaven-Haven

A Nun Takes the Veil

I have desired to go
   Where springs not fail,
To fields where flies no sharp and sided hail,
   And a few lilies blow.

And I have asked to be
   Where no storms come,
Where the green swell is in the havens dumb
   And out of the swing of the sea.

GERARD MANLEY HOPKINS

Sleep at Sea

Sound the deep waters:—
Who shall sound that deep?—
Too short the plummet,
And the watchmen sleep.
Some dream of effort
Up a toilsome steep;
Some dream of pasture grounds
For harmless sheep.

White shapes flit to and fro
From mast to mast;   10
They feel the distant tempest
That nears them fast:
Great rocks are straight ahead,
Great shoals not past;
They shout to one another
Upon the blast.

    . . . .

Driving and driving,
The ship drives amain:
While swift from mast to mast
Shapes flit again,   20
Flit silent as the silence
Where men lie slain;
Their shadow cast upon the sails
Is like a stain.

No voice to call the sleepers,
No hand to raise:
They sleep to death in dreaming
Of length of days.
Vanity of vanities,
The Preacher says: 30
Vanity is the end
Of all their ways.

CHRISTINA ROSSETTI

I Started Early—Took My Dog—

I started Early—Took my Dog—
And visited the Sea—
The Mermaids in the Basement
Came out to look at me—

And Frigates—in the Upper Floor
Extended Hempen Hands—
Presuming Me to be a Mouse—
Aground—upon the Sands—

But no Man moved Me—till the Tide
Went past my simple Shoe— 10
And past my Apron—and my Belt
And past my Bodice—too—

And made as He would eat me up—
As wholly as a Dew
Upon a Dandelion's Sleeve—
And then—I started—too—

And He—He followed—close behind—
I felt His Silver Heel
Upon my Ankle—Then my Shoes
Would overflow with Pearl— 20

Until We met the Solid Town—
No One He seemed to know—
And bowing—with a Mighty look—
At me—The Sea withdrew—

EMILY DICKINSON

Sea-Distances

His native sea-washed isle
  Was bleak and bare.
Far off, there seemed to smile
  An isle more fair.

Blue as the smoke of Spring
  Its far hills rose,
A delicate azure ring
  Crowned with faint snows,

At dusk, a rose-red star
  Set free from wrong,   10
It beaconed him afar,
  His whole life long.

Not till old age drew nigh
  He voyaged there.
He saw the colours die
  As he drew near.

It towered above him, bleak
  And cold, death-cold.
From peak to phantom peak
  A grey mist rolled.   20

Then, under his arched hand,
  From that bare shore,
Back, at his own dear land,
  He gazed, once more.

Clothed with the tints he knew,
  He saw it smile,—
Opal, and rose and blue,
  His native isle.

Alfred Noyes

Port of Many Ships

'It's a sunny pleasant anchorage, is Kingdom Come,
Where crews is always layin' aft for double-tots o'rum,
'N' there's dancin' 'n' fiddlin' of ev'ry kind o'sort,
It's a fine place for sailor-men is that there port.
    'N' I wish—
    I wish as I was there.

'The winds is never nothin' more than jest light airs,
'N' no-one gets belayin'-pinned, 'n' no-one never swears,
Yer free to loaf an' laze around, yer pipe atween yer lips,
Lollin' on the fo'c's'le, sonny, lookin' at the ships.   10
    'N' I wish—
    I wish as I was there.

'For ridin' in the anchorage the ships of all the world
Have got one anchor down 'n' all sails furled.
All the sunken hookers 'n' the crews as took 'n' died.
They lays there merry, sonny, swingin' to the tide.
    'N' I wish—
    I wish as I was there.

'Drowned old wooden hookers green wi' drippin' wrack,   20
Ships as never fetched to port, as never came back,
Swingin' to the blushin' tide, dippin' to the swell,
'N' the crews all singin', sonny, beatin' on the bell.
    'N' I wish—
    I wish I was there.'

JOHN MASEFIELD

Crossing the Bar

Sunset and evening star,
    And one clear call for me!
And may there be no moaning of the bar,
    When I put out to sea,

But such a tide as moving seems asleep,
    Too full for sound and foam,
When that which drew from out the boundless deep
    Turns again home.

Twilight and evening bell,
    And after that the dark!
And may there be no sadness of farewell,
    When I embark;

For tho' from out our bourne of Time and Place
    The flood may bear me far,
I hope to see my Pilot face to face
    When I have crost the bar.

ALFRED, LORD TENNYSON

To Marguerite—Continued

Yes! in the sea of life enisled,
With echoing straits between us thrown,
Dotting the shoreless watery wild,
We mortal millions live *alone*.
The islands feel the enclasping flow,
And then their endless bounds they know.

But when the moon their hollows lights,
And they are swept by balms of spring,
And in their glens, on starry nights,
The nightingales divinely sing;   10
And lovely notes, from shore to shore,
Across the sounds and channels pour—

Oh! then a longing like despair
Is to their farthest caverns sent;
For surely once, they feel, we were
Parts of a single continent!
Now round us spreads the watery plain—
Oh might our marges meet again!

Who order'd, that their longing's fire
Should be, as soon as kindled, cool'd?   20
Who renders vain their deep desire?—
A God, a God their severance ruled!
And bade betwixt their shores to be
The unplumb'd, salt, estranging sea.

MATTHEW ARNOLD

Sail and Oar

Woman sails, man must row:
Each, disdainful of a tow,
Cuts across the other's bows
Shame or fury to arouse—
And evermore it shall be so,
Lest man sail, or woman row.

ROBERT GRAVES

The Narrow Sea

With you for mast and sail and flag,
And anchor never known to drag,
Death's narrow but oppressive sea
Looks not unnavigable to me.

ROBERT GRAVES

The Ship of Death

I

Now it is autumn and the falling fruit
and the long journey towards oblivion.

The apples falling like great drops of dew
to bruise themselves an exit from themselves.

And it is time to go, to bid farewell
to one's own self, and find an exit
from the fallen self.

II

Have you built your ship of death, O have you?
O build your ship of death, for you will need it.

The grim frost is at hand, when the apples will fall
thick, almost thundrous, on the hardened earth.

And death is on the air like a smell of ashes!
Ah! can't you smell it?

And in the bruised body, the frightened soul
finds itself shrinking, wincing from the cold
that blows upon it through the orifices.

III

And can a man his own quietus make with a bare bodkin?[15]

With daggers, bodkins, bullets, man can make
a bruise or break of exit for his life;
but is that a quietus, O tell me, is it quietus?

Surely not so! for how could murder, even self-murder
ever a quietus make?

262

IV

O let us talk of quiet that we know,
that we can know, the deep and lovely quiet
of a strong heart at peace!

How can we this, our own quietus, make?

V

Build then the ship of death, for you must take
the longest journey, to oblivion.

And die the death, the long and painful death
that lies between the old self and the new.

Already our bodies are fallen, bruised, badly bruised,
already our souls are oozing through the exit
of the cruel bruise.

Already the dark and endless ocean of the end
is washing in through the breaches of our wounds,
already the flood is upon us.

Oh build your ship of death, your little ark
and furnish it with food, with little cakes, and wine
for the dark flight down oblivion.

VI

Piecemeal the body dies, and the timid soul
has her footing washed away, as the dark flood rises.

We are dying, we are dying, we are all of us dying
and nothing will stay the death-flood rising within us
and soon it will rise on the world, on the outside world.

We are dying, we are dying, piecemeal our bodies are dying
and our strength leaves us,
and our soul cowers naked in the dark rain over the flood,
cowering in the last branches of the tree of our life.

VII

We are dying, we are dying, so all we can do
is now to be willing to die, and to build the ship
of death to carry the soul on the longest journey.

A little ship, with oars and food
and little dishes, and all accoutrements
fitting and ready for the departing soul.

Now launch the small ship, now as the body dies
and life departs, launch out, the fragile soul
in the fragile ship of courage, the ark of faith
with its store of food and little cooking pans
and change of clothes,
upon the flood's black waste
upon the waters of the end
upon the sea of death, where still we sail
darkly, for we cannot steer, and have no port.

There is no port, there is nowhere to go
only the deepening blackness darkening still
blacker upon the soundless, ungurgling flood
darkness at one with darkness, up and down
and sideways utterly dark, so there is no direction any more
and the little ship is there; yet she is gone.
She is not seen, for there is nothing to see her by.
She is gone! gone! and yet
somewhere she is there.
Nowhere!

VIII

And everything is gone, the body is gone
completely under, gone, entirely gone.
The upper darkness is heavy as the lower,
between them the little ship
is gone
she is gone.

It is the end, it is oblivion.

IX

And yet out of eternity, a thread
separates itself on the blackness,
a horizontal thread
that fumes a little with pallor upon the dark.

Is it illusion? or does the pallor fume
a little higher?
Ah wait, wait, for there's the dawn,
the cruel dawn of coming back to life
out of oblivion.

Wait, wait, the little ship
drifting, beneath the deathly ashy grey
of a flood-dawn.

Wait, wait! even so, a flush of yellow
and strangely, O chilled wan soul, a flush of rose.

A flush of rose, and the whole thing starts again.

X

The flood subsides, and the body, like a worn sea-shell
emerges strange and lovely.
And the little ship wings home, faltering and lapsing
on the pink flood,
and the frail soul steps out, into her house again
filling the heart with peace.

Swings the heart renewed with peace
even of oblivion.

Oh build your ship of death, oh build it!
for you will need it.
For the voyage of oblivion awaits you.

D. H. Lawrence

as is the sea marvelous

as is the sea marvelous
from god's
hands which sent her forth
to sleep upon the world

and the earth withers
the moon crumbles
one by one
stars flutter into dust

but the sea
does not change
and she goes forth out of hands and
she returns into hands

and is with sleep . . . .

love,
      the breaking

of your
      soul
      upon
my lips

                    e. e. cummings

At Melville's Tomb

Often beneath the wave, wide from this ledge
The dice of drowned men's bones he saw bequeath
An embassy. Their numbers as he watched,
Beat on the dusty shore and were obscured.

And wrecks passed without sound of bells,
The calyx of death's bounty giving back
A scattered chapter, livid hieroglyph,
The portent wound in corridors of shells.

Then in the circuit calm of one vast coil,
Its lashings charmed and malice reconciled,
Frosted eyes there were that lifted altars;
And silent answers crept across the stars.

Compass, quadrant and sextant contrive
No farther tides. . .High in the azure steeps
Monody shall not wake the mariner.
This fabulous shadow only the sea keeps.

                    HART CRANE

Sea-Ruck

Washback of the waters, swirl of time,
Flashback of time, swirl of the waters,

Loll and stroke, loll and stroke,

The world remade, the world broken,
Knocked rhythm, make of the slime,

The surge and control, stroke of the time,
Heartbreak healing in the grime, and groaner

Holding its power, holding the hurl,
Loll and hurl, power to gain and destroy,

The tall destruction not to undo

A saffron inevitable sun, far and near,
Some vast control, beyond tear and fear,

Where the blood flows, and nights go,
Man in his makeshift, there is home,

And the dark swells, the everlasting toll,
And being like this sea, the unrolling scroll,

Stroke and loll, loll and stroke, stroke, loll

Richard Eberhart

Sailors' Harbour

My thoughts, like sailors becalmed in Cape Town harbor,
Await your return, like a favorable wind, or like
New tackle for the voyage, without which it is useless starting.
We watch the sea daily, finish our daily tasks
By ten in the morning, and with the day to waste,
Wander through the suburbs, with quiet thoughts of the brothels,
And sometimes thoughts of the churches.

In the eating-houses we always contrive to get near to
The window, where we can keep an eye on the life-
Bearing sea. Suddenly a wind might blow, and we must not miss   10
First sight of the waves as they darken with promise for us.
We have been here too long. We know the quays,
And the streets near the quays, more than should ever be necessary.
When can we go on our way?

Certain we are of this, that when the wind comes,
It may be deceptive and sweet and finally blow
To shipwreck and ruin between here and the next port of call.
At all times we think of this. At last we have come to know
The marine charts can safely assure us of less and less
As we go farther south. So we cannot go out on the boulevards   20
Or climb Table Mountain,[16]

Though if we had certainty, here there might be delight.
But all that is world in itself, the mountain, the streets,
The sand-dunes outside the town, we shyly and sadly return from.
They are too much to bear. And our curiosity
Lies alone in the over-scrubbed decks and the polished brasses
(For we have to look trim in the port) and in
The high-piled ambiguous cargo.

HENRY REED

To the Harbormaster

I wanted to be sure to reach you;
though my ship was on the way it got caught
in some moorings. I am always tying up
and then deciding to depart. In storms and
at sunset, with the metallic coils of the tide
around my fathomless arms, I am unable
to understand the forms of my vanity
or I am hard alee with my Polish rudder
in my hand and the sun sinking. To
you I offer my hull and the tattered cordage
of my will. The terrible channels where
the wind drives me against the brown lips
of the reeds are not all behind me. Yet
I trust the sanity of my vessel; and
if it sinks, it may well be in answer
to the reasoning of the eternal voices,
the waves which have kept me from reaching you.

FRANK O'HARA

Marina[17]

Quis hic locus, quae regio, quae mundi plaga?

What seas what shores what grey rocks and what islands
What water lapping the bow
And scent of pine and the woodthrush singing through the fog
What images return
O my daughter.

   Those who sharpen the tooth of the dog, meaning
Death
Those who glitter with the glory of the humming-bird, meaning
Death
Those who sit in the stye of contentment, meaning   10
Death
Those who suffer the ecstasy of the animals, meaning
Death

   Are become unsubstantial, reduced by a wind,
A breath of pine, and the woodsong fog
By this grace dissolved in place

   What is this face, less clear and clearer
The pulse in the arm, less strong and stronger—
Given or lent? more distant than stars and nearer than the eye

   Whispers and small laughter between leaves and hurrying feet   20
Under sleep, where all the waters meet.

   Bowsprit cracked with ice and paint cracked with heat.
I made this, I have forgotten
And remember.
The rigging weak and the canvas rotten
Between one June and another September.
Made this unknowing, half conscious, unknown, my own.
The garboard strake leaks, the seams need caulking.

This form, this face, this life
Living to live in a world of time beyond me; let me   30
Resign my life for this life, my speech for that unspoken,
The awakened, lips parted, the hope, the new ships.

   What seas what shores what granite islands towards my timbers
And woodthrush calling through the fog
My daughter.

T. S. ELIOT

Once by the Pacific

The shattered water made a misty din.
Great waves looked over others coming in,
And thought of doing something to the shore
That water never did to land before.
The clouds were low and hairy in the skies,
Like locks blown forward in the gleam of eyes.
You could not tell, and yet it looked as if
The shore was lucky in being backed by cliff,
The cliff in being backed by continent;
It looked as if a night of dark intent
Was coming, and not only a night, an age.
Someone had better be prepared for rage.
There would be more than ocean-water broken
Before God's last *Put out the Light* was spoken.

ROBERT FROST

Boats in a Fog

Sports and gallantries, the stage, the arts, the antics of dancers,
The exuberant voices of music,
Have charm for children but lack nobility; it is bitter earnestness
That makes beauty; the mind
Knows, grown adult.
        A sudden fog-drift muffled the ocean,
A throbbing of engines moved in it,
At length, a stone's throw out, between the rocks and the vapor,
One by one moved shadows
Out of the mystery, shadows, fishing-boats, trailing each other,   10
Following the cliff for guidance,
Holding a difficult path between the peril of the sea-fog
And the foam on the shore granite.
One by one, trailing their leader, six crept by me,
Out of the vapor and into it,
The throb of their engines subdued by the fog, patient and cautious,
Coasting all round the peninsula
Back to the buoys in Monterey harbor. A flight of pelicans
Is nothing lovelier to look at;
The flight of the planets is nothing nobler; all the arts lose virtue   20
Against the essential reality
Of creatures going about their business among the equally
Earnest elements of nature.

ROBINSON JEFFERS

The Yachts

contend in a sea which the land partly encloses
shielding them from the too heavy blows
of an ungoverned ocean which when it chooses

tortures the biggest hulls, the best man knows
to pit against its beating, and sinks them pitilessly.
Mothlike in mists, scintillant in the minute

brilliance of cloudless days, with broad bellying sails
they glide to the wind tossing green water
from their sharp prows while over them the crew crawls

ant-like, solicitously grooming them, releasing,   10
making fast as they turn, lean far over and having
caught the wind again, side by side, head for the mark.

In a well guarded arena of open water surrounded by
lesser and greater craft which, sycophant, lumbering
and flittering follow them, they appear youthful, rare

as the light of a happy eye, live with the grace
of all that in the mind is feckless, free and
naturally to be desired. Now the sea which holds them

is moody, lapping their glossy sides, as if feeling
for some slightest flaw but fails completely.   20
Today no race. Then the wind comes again. The yachts

move, jockeying for a start, the signal is set and they
are off. Now the waves strike at them but they are too
well made, they slip through, though they take in canvas.

Arms with hands grasping seek to clutch at the prows.
Bodies thrown recklessly in the way are cut aside.
It is a sea of faces about them in agony, in despair

until the horror of the race dawns staggering the mind,
the whole sea become an entanglement of watery bodies
lost to the world bearing what they cannot hold. Broken,   30

beaten, desolate, reaching from the dead to be taken up
they cry out, failing, failing! their cries rising
in waves still as the skillful yachts pass over.

WILLIAM CARLOS WILLIAMS

The Idea of Order at Key West

She sang beyond the genius of the sea.
The water never formed to mind or voice,
Like a body wholly body, fluttering
Its empty sleeves; and yet its mimic motion
Made constant cry, caused constantly a cry,
That was not ours although we understood,
Inhuman, of the veritable ocean.

The sea was not a mask. No more was she.
The song and water were not medleyed sound
Even if what she sang was what she heard,   10
Since what she sang was uttered word by word.
It may be that in all her phrases stirred
The grinding water and the gasping wind;
But it was she and not the sea we heard.

For she was the maker of the song she sang.
The ever-hooded, tragic-gestured sea
Was merely a place by which she walked to sing.
Whose spirit is this? we said, because we knew
It was the spirit that we sought and knew
That we should ask this often as she sang.   20

If it was only the dark voice of the sea
That rose, or even colored by many waves;
If it was only the outer voice of sky
And cloud, of the sunken coral water-walled,
However clear, it would have been deep air,
The heaving speech of air, a summer sound
Repeated in a summer without end
And sound alone. But it was more than that,
More even than her voice, and ours, among
The meaningless plungings of water and the wind,   30
Theatrical distances, bronze shadows heaped
On high horizons, mountainous atmospheres
Of sky and sea.

           It was her voice that made
The sky acutest at its vanishing.
She measured to the hour its solitude.
She was the single artificer of the world
In which she sang. And when she sang, the sea,
Whatever self it had, became the self

That was her song, for she was the maker. Then we,   40
As we beheld her striding there alone,
Knew that there never was a world for her
Except the one she sang and, singing, made.

Ramon Fernandez, tell me, if you know,
Why, when the singing ended and we turned
Toward the town, tell why the glassy lights,
The lights in the fishing boats at anchor there,
As the night descended, tilting in the air,
Mastered the night and portioned out the sea,
Fixing emblazoned zones and fiery poles,   50
Arranging, deepening, enchanting night.

Oh! Blessed rage for order, pale Ramon,
The maker's rage to order words of the sea,
Words of the fragrant portals, dimly-starred,
And of ourselves and of our origins,
In ghostlier demarcations, keener sounds.

WALLACE STEVENS

Sea Surface Full of Clouds

I

In that November off Tehuantepec,[18]
The slopping of the sea grew still one night
And in the morning summer hued the deck

And made one think of rosy chocolate
And gilt umbrellas. Paradisal green
Gave suavity to the perplexed machine

Of ocean, which like limpid water lay.
Who, then, in that ambrosial latitude
Out of the light evolved the moving blooms,

Who, then, evolved the sea-blooms from the clouds   10
Diffusing balm in that Pacific calm?
C'était mon enfant, mon bijou, mon âme,[19]

The sea-clouds whitened far below the calm
And moved, as blooms move, in the swimming green
And in its watery radiance, while the hue

Of heaven in an antique reflection rolled
Round those flotillas. And sometimes the sea
Poured brilliant iris on the glistening blue.

II

In that November off Tehuantepec
The slopping of the sea grew still one night.
At breakfast jelly yellow streaked the deck

And made one think of chop-house chocolate
And sham umbrellas. And a sham-like green
Capped summer-seeming on the tense machine

Of ocean, which in sinister flatness lay.
Who, then, beheld the rising of the clouds
That strode submerged in that malevolent sheen,

Who saw the mortal massives of the blooms
Of water moving on the water-floor?
C'était mon frère du ciel, ma vie, mon or.[20]

The gongs rang loudly as the windy booms
Hoo-hooed it in the darkened ocean-blooms.
The gongs grew still. And then blue heaven spread

Its crystalline pendentives on the sea
And the macabre of the water-glooms
In an enormous undulation fled.

III

In that November off Tehuantepec,
The slopping of the sea grew still one night
And a pale silver patterned on the deck

And made one think of porcelain chocolate
And pied umbrellas. An uncertain green,
Piano-polished, held the tranced machine

Of ocean, as a prelude holds and holds.
Who, seeing silver petals of white blooms
Unfolding in the water, feeling sure

Of the milk within the saltiest spurge, heard, then,
The sea unfolding in the sunken clouds?
Oh! C'était mon extase et mon amour.[21]

So deeply sunken were they that the shrouds,
The shrouding shadows, made the petals black
Until the rolling heaven made them blue,

A blue beyond the rainy hyacinth,
And smiting the crevasses of the leaves
Deluged the ocean with a sapphire blue.

20

30

40

50

IV

In that November off Tehuantepec
The night-long slopping of the sea grew still.
A mallow morning dozed upon the deck

And made one think of musky chocolate
And frail umbrellas. A too-fluent green
Suggested malice in the dry machine   60

Of ocean, pondering dank stratagem.
Who then beheld the figures of the clouds
Like blooms secluded in the thick marine?

Like blooms? Like damasks that were shaken off
From the loosed girdles in the spangling must.
C'était ma foi, la nonchalance divine.²²

The nakedness would rise and suddenly turn
Salt masks of beard and mouths of bellowing,
Would—But more suddenly the heaven rolled

Its bluest sea-clouds in the thinking green,   70
And the nakedness became the broadest blooms,
Mile-mallows that a mallow sun cajoled.

V

In that November off Tehuantepec
Night stilled the slopping of the sea. The day
Came, bowing and voluble, upon the deck.

Good clown. . . . One thought of Chinese chocolate
And large umbrellas. And a motley green
Followed the drift of the obese machine.

Of ocean, perfected in indolence.
What pistache one, ingenious and droll,   80
Beheld the sovereign clouds as jugglery

And the sea as turquoise-turbaned Sambo, neat
At tossing saucers—cloudy-conjuring sea?
C'était mon esprit bâtard, l'ignominie.²³

The sovereign clouds came clustering. The conch
Of loyal conjuration trumped. The wind
Of green blooms turning crisped the motley hue

To clearing opalescence. Then the sea
And heaven rolled as one and from the two
Came fresh transfigurings of freshest blue.   90

WALLACE STEVENS

275

At the Slackening of the Tide

Today I saw a woman wrapped in rags
Leaping along the beach to curse the sea.
Her child lay floating in the oil, away
From oarlock, gunwale, and the blades of oars.
The skinny lifeguard, raging at the sky,
Vomited sea, and fainted on the sand.

The cold simplicity of evening falls
Dead on my mind.
And underneath the piles the water
Leaps up, leaps up, and sags down slowly, farther   10
Than seagulls disembodied in the drag
Of oil and foam.

Plucking among the oyster shells a man
Stares at the sea, that stretches on its side.
Now far along the beach, a hungry dog
Announces everything I knew before:
Obliterate naiads weeping underground,
Where Homer's tongue thickens with human howls.[24]
I would do anything to drag myself
Out of this place: 20
Root up a seaweed from the water,
To stuff it in my mouth, or deafen me,
Free me from all the force of human speech;
Go drown, almost.

Warm in the pleasure of the dawn I came
To sing my song
And look for mollusks in the shallows,
The whorl and coil that pretty up the earth,
While far below us, flaring in the dark,
The stars go out.   30

What did I do to kill my time today,
After the woman ranted in the cold,
The mellow sea, the sound blown dark as wine?
After the lifeguard rose up from the waves
Like a sea-lizard with the scales washed off?
Sit there, admiring sunlight on a shell?

Abstract with terror of the shell, I stared
Over the waters where
God brooded for the living all one day.
Lonely for weeping, starved for a sound of mourning,   40
I bowed my head, and heard the sea far off
Washing its hands.

JAMES WRIGHT

NOTES

Sounds of the Sea

1. Sea deities who are half-men, half-fish.
2. Sea nymphs whose singing lured sailors to destruction; see *Odyssey,* Book XII, lines 265–326.
3. A large rock in the Firth of Clyde, off the western coast of Scotland.
4. The equator.
5. Trade winds: easterly winds that blow almost constantly in the tropics.
6. The more than 2,000 Maldive Islands are in the Indian Ocean, southwest of Ceylon.
7. In Greek mythology, the Gorgons were monsters with serpents for hair, sharp claws, and eyes whose stare turned men to stone.
8. Daughters of Night, who spun, measured, and cut the threads of men's lives.
9. A low order of angels.
10. The Greek god of wine and fertility.
11. John Masefield (?). See *Sea-Fever,* page 65.
12. A Danish king of England (995?–1035).
13. A Hindu book of erotic love.
14. In Greek mythology, Pandora was created out of clay by Hephaestus and given life by Athena. She carried a box which, when opened, released all the disease, evil, and pestilence that have since afflicted the human race—but also released hope.
15. In Zen, a nonsensical question to a student for which an answer is demanded, the idea being that the stress of meditation itself is illuminating.

Man and the Sea

1. This is a translation by Charles W. Kennedy of the first sixty-four lines of an Old English poem written in the tenth century or earlier; lines 65–124 were probably added later by a monk or scribe to give religious meaning to the poem.
2. A jewel-trading center in the Persian Gulf.
3. A female worshipper of the Roman god of wine, Bacchus; Dionysus in Greek mythology.
4. An area west of Naples where many of the Roman emperors had villas.
5. A Greek poet of the second century B.C.

6. The Navy Hymn.
7. Richard Tobias Green, Herman Melville's companion at sea and the "Toby" of his novel *Typee*.
8. From *Paul Pry*, a farcical play by John Poole.
9. The Roman god Saturn, who was the father of Jupiter and reigned over the golden age of man.
10. In classical mythology, the soul, personified as a beautiful girl hated by Venus and loved by Cupid, the goddess and god of love.
11. An ancient seaport of Phoenicia, in what is now southern Lebanon.
12. A seaport on the east coast of Cyprus, near the site of Odysseus's legendary long captivity with Calypso.
13. The land of Colchis, in the story of Jason and the Argonauts.
14. Mull, Rum, and Egg are small islands to the south of Skye, a large island of the Inner Hebrides, off the western coast of Scotland.
15. The life of a farmer; Shem was the farmer son of Noah.
16. A Spanish coastal cargo vessel; Bilbao is a seaport in northern Spain, near the Bay of Biscay.
17. Lower Hope, Gunfleet Sands, Mouse, and Gull Light are navigational points on the Channel coast of England.
18. *See* Note 17 above.
19. A Greek writer of tragedies (496–406 B.C.). Arnold said of Sophocles that he "saw life steadily, and saw it whole."
20. Christianity.
21. A dancing girl.
22. A quinquireme is an ancient vessel using five banks of oars for propulsion; Nineveh, on the Tigris River, is the ancient capital of Assyria; Ophir was a country, probably in southern Arabia, from which gems and lumber were brought to King Solomon.
23. Panama.
24. The Rock of Gibraltar and Jebel Musa, situated on either side of the Strait of Gibraltar, were known as the Pillars of Hercules.
25. A sea herb, such as sea holly.
26. The Caribbean.
27. In music, slow, graceful movements.
28. Hart Crane, who committed suicide by leaping from the deck of a steamer.
29. Margaret A. Spender, sister-in-law of the poet.
30. An Italian Renaissance painter; his patron, Pope Julius III, commissioned him to prepare sketches for Vatican tapestries.
31. "Venite"—the 95th Psalm, sung as a canticle in the morning prayer service; "Kyrie"—from the "Kyrie Eleison," a series of responses in Roman Catholic and Anglican services.
32. A hymn or chant that culminates preparation for Communion.
33. A cape in northern Washington State.
34. "To whom is given the end of pain, great king?"
35. A Trojan prince and hero of Virgil's *Aeneid*, who sailed to Italy and founded the dynasty whence came the Roman Empire.
36. *See* Note 24 above.
37. A village and bay on Nantucket Island, off the coast of Massachusetts.

38. The captain of the whaler *Pequod* in Herman Melville's *Moby Dick*.
39. In Greek mythology, Orpheus was a marvelous musician who went down to Hades and with his music charmed Persephone, goddess of the underworld, into releasing his dead wife, Eurydice.
40. Siasconset, on Nantucket Island.
41. "We have cried out."
42. Seaports in Massachusetts.
43. A king in Judah in the ninth century B.C., in whose pit God will judge the heathen.
44. "Jonah the Risen"; Jonah was released after having been entombed for three days in the belly of a whale (*see* Jonah 1:17).
45. A shrine in Norfolk, England.
46. A stream flowing past the temple on Mount Sion (*see* Isaiah 51:2).
47. Zion, the heavenly city, gathering place of the faithful, from the hill in Jerusalem where King David erected the temple.
48. "There is no ostentation or elegance."

Tales of the Sea

1. Dartmouth, a seaport in southwest England.
2. From Bordeaux.
3. From Hull, in northern England, to Cartagena, in Spain.
4. From Gotland, an island in the Baltic, to Cape Finisterre, the westernmost point in Spain.
5. Phoebus Apollo.
6. A port on the Channel coast of France, near the mouth of the River Seine.
7. *See* Man and the Sea, Note 9. "Tyber" refers to the Roman Empire.
8. Nicholas Hilliard (1537–1619), an English painter of miniatures.
9. Sarah, wife of Abraham, became pregnant after many years of barrenness (*see* Genesis 17).
10. Jonah, who slept during a storm at sea and was awakened and thrown overboard by his shipmates (*see* Jonah 1:5–16).
11. Unused cargo space below decks.
12. "Let it be done," referring to God's creation of light (*see* Genesis 1:3).
13. Aesop's fable of the frogs.
14. A secondhand clothing store.
15. Shadrach, Meshach, and Abednego (*see* Daniel 3:13–30).
16. Bajazet was an emperor of the Turks who was imprisoned by the Mongol chieftain Tamerlane.
17. Sampson lost his strength when Delilah cut off his hair (*see* Judges 16).
18. The Roman Emperor Tiberius's snakes were eaten by ants, according to an account by Suetonius.
19. Light, maneuverable vessels.
20. England.
21. God sent manna from heaven to feed the starving Israelites in the wilderness (*see* Exodus 16).
22. The poem was not completed.
23. In December 1839, the schooner *Hesperus* struck Norman's Woe, a rock off Gloucester, Massachusetts, and sank.

24. The largest liner of her day, the *Titanic,* crossing the Atlantic on her maiden voyage, sank on 15 April 1912, with great loss of life.

25. Admiral Nelson's victory over the combined French and Spanish fleets on 21 October 1805, off Cadiz, Spain. Nelson was killed in the battle.

26. With a storm at high tide, the waves from the English Channel (Front-sea) swept over the barriers into the harbor at Weymouth (Back-sea); Dead-men's Bay is West Bay, west of Weymouth.

27. A promontory that forms one side of Weymouth Harbor.

28. An anchorage off the southeast coast of England.

29. William Howard, Lord Effingham (1510?–1573), Sir Richard Grenville (1542–1591), Sir Walter Raleigh (1552?–1618), Sir Francis Drake (1540?–1596), John Benbow (1653–1702), Cuthbert Collingwood (1750–1810), John Byron (1723–1786), Robert Blake (1599–1657), and Horatio, Lord Nelson (1758–1805) were all English admirals of great reputation.

30. Robert Devereux, Earl of Essex (1566–1601) and Charles Howard, Earl of Nottingham, were English seamen during the time of Queen Elizabeth I. Essex shared command of the expedition that captured Cadiz in 1596, and Howard was the commander against the Spanish Armada in 1588.

31. Drake was second-in-command of the English fleet that intercepted the Spanish Armada, a fleet of around 130 ships and 30,000 men sent by Philip II of Spain to invade England.

32. Viscount Duncan of Camperdown, who defeated the Dutch fleet under Admiral De Winter, off Camperdown in 1797.

33. Admiral Nelson, disobeying the orders of his commanding officer, attacked and defeated the Danes in 1801 in the Oresund, the sound between Denmark and Sweden, on which Copenhagen is situated.

34. George Rodney (1719–1792), English admiral who defeated the French under Admiral de Grasse in the West Indies in 1782.

35. The U.S. frigate *Constitution,* which was scheduled to be scrapped in 1830. Holmes's poem was distributed throughout the United States and resulted in her reprieve.

36. The sea battle off the coast of Britain on 23 September 1779.

37. A small harbor in northwest France, where the French Admiral de Tourville was defeated by an Anglo-Dutch fleet in 1692.

38. St. Malo is a small seaport at the mouth of the Rance River in Brittany.

39. The sands between St. Malo and Mont St. Michel.

40. A fortified town at the mouth of the Rance River.

41. Cape St. Vincent is the site of the English naval victory over the French in 1797; Nelson's victory of the Cape of Trafalgar took place in 1805 (*see* Note 25 above).

42. In 1571, naval forces under Don John of Austria (1547–1578), brother of Philip II of Spain, defeated the Moslem Turks off Lepanto, in western Greece, stemming the tide of Moslem conquest.

43. Selim II (1524?–1574), sultan of the Ottoman Empire.

44. Charles IX, king of France (1550–1574).

45. Philip II, king of Spain (1527–1598).

46. Mohammed.

47. Azrael and Ariel are angels of death and destruction in the Koran; Ammon

is an Egyptian god; giants and genii are supernatural creatures in Arabian mythology.

48. A derogatory term used by the Turks to describe non-Moslems.
49. Destiny or fate in Islam.
50. Alcalá, a city near Madrid.
51. St. Michael's Mount, a rocky islet off the coast of Cornwall.
52. "Glory to God!"
53. "Long live Spain!"
54. Miguel de Cervantes, author of *Don Quixote,* lost an arm in the battle.

The Laughter of the Waves

1. Batavia is Holland, Caledonia is Scotland, and Hibernia is Ireland.
2. Calliope, muse of epic poetry; Homer wrote the *Iliad* and *Odyssey*; Milton wrote *Paradise Lost*; Virgil wrote the *Aeneid*; and Horace was a Roman poet whose major work is *Satires.*
3. A god of medicine and son of Apollo.
4. A warrior follower of Achilles in the Trojan War.
5. Galen was a Greek physician (129–199), whose writing influenced medicine for centuries; William Cullen was an eighteenth-century English physician and writer of medical works.
6. Lord Chesterfield (1694–1773), whose *Letters to His Son* were full of practical advice for the young man of the day; *Seaman's Guide* was an eighteenth-century guidebook of nautical information; William Congreve (1670–1729) was an English comic dramatist whose *Mourning Bride* was published in 1697.
7. A beautiful youth in Greek mythology.
8. Shipboard stew.
9. David Garrick (1717–1779) was an English Shakespearian actor; Cato (95–46 B.C.) was a Roman politician known for his character and integrity; Lothario was a libertine and seducer in Nicholas Rowe's *The Fair Penitent* (1703); Cleone was the daughter of Asopus, a river god in Greek mythology; Richard III was an English king whose story is told in Shakespeare's play of the same name; the orlop is the lowest of four or more decks.
10. Edward Hawke (1705–1781) was an English admiral who defeated the French at Quiberon Bay in 1759; Richard Howe (1726–1799) was an English admiral during the American Revolution.
11. Thomas Paine (1737–1809), American political philosopher and author of *Common Sense* and *The Rights of Man.*
12. Frederick the Great (1712–1786).
13. In Greek mythology, Leander, a youth of Abydos, was in love with Hero, who lived in Sestos on the other side of the Hellespont; when he drowned as he tried to swim to the other side, Hero threw herself in the water and was drowned also.
14. *See* Note 13 above. Byron swam the Hellespont in 1810 with Lieutenant Ekenhead, a British naval officer.
15. The ship in which Jason and his men sailed to Colchis to recover the Golden Fleece.

16. In punishment for rebellion against the gods, Prometheus was pinioned to a rock in Hades, where a vulture continually gnawed at his liver.
17. In Dante's *Inferno,* Ugolino ceases his punishment of gnawing on the skull of his enemy long enough to tell his story.
18. Charon is the ferryman who transports souls across the River Styx in Hades.
19. A river in northern Spain.
20. *See* Note 14 above.
21. The Suez Canal.
22. Regular Army soldiers.
23. On 26 February 1852, off the coast of South Africa, the British troopship *Birkenhead* struck a rock and sank, with the loss of 454 officers and men. "*Birkenhead* drill" refers to the disciplined calm of the 74th Highlanders, who stood fast in ranks on the sinking ship so that women and children could gain the safety of the ship's boats.
24. Ports of call frequently visited by English merchant vessels.
25. Types of tobacco.
26. From Aeolus, Greek god of the winds.
27. See *The Tempest,* page 151.
28. See *Sea-Fever,* page 65.

Legends of the Sea

1. Composed by the poet Homer around the ninth century B.C. and translated by George Chapman about 1614, this is the story of the wanderings of Odysseus (Ulysses) as he returned from the Trojan War.
2. A goddess, daughter of Atlas, who held Odysseus captive for seven years on the island of Ogygia.
3. The North, South, East, and West winds, respectively.
4. The goddess of dawn.
5. A nereid, wife of Neptune.
6. Athena, goddess of wisdom and patroness of Odysseus.
7. *See* Sounds of the Sea, Note 2.
8. Polyphemus, the one-eyed giant son of Poseidon whom Odysseus blinded in his escape, according to the *Odyssey,* Book IX.
9. A dangerous whirlpool off the coast of Sicily, in the Strait of Messina, opposite Scylla.
10. A rock on the Italian side of the Strait of Messina, personified as a female monster that seized and devoured sailors who passed too close.
11. A headland in southern Rhode Island, between Narragansett Bay and Block Island Sound.
12. Montauk Point, on the eastern tip of Long Island.
13. Block Island, off the coast of Rhode Island.
14. Elysium, the place in the hereafter where those blessed by the gods dwell.
15. Bound tightly with ropes or chains.
16. Stripping the blubber and skin from a whale.

The Sea as Metaphor

1. This poem and the one that follows are translations by Charles W. Kennedy of Old English religious poems.
2. "Whither blows the wind."
3. Abraham Lincoln.
4. Elysium was the place in the hereafter where those blessed by the gods dwelt.
5. George Washington Greene, a longtime friend of Longfellow.
6. Daughters of the evening who, in Greek mythology, guard a tree of golden apples west of the Pillars of Hercules (*see* Man and the Sea, Note 24).
7. The Orkney Islands, off the coast of Scotland, identified with the edge of the world.
8. Rome ruled the western world for centuries; Nineveh was the capital of the Assyrian Empire; Thebes was a city in Egypt; Karnak, at the site of Thebes, has great ruins.
9. Designer of the labyrinth in Crete for Minos; imprisoned by Minos, Daedalus fashioned wings of wax and feathers so that he and his son, Icarus, could escape.
10. The father of Calypso; he was forced by the gods to support heaven on his head and shoulders.
11. A legendary priest in the Middle Ages who was supposed to be the ruler of a kingdom somewhere in eastern Africa.
12. The line echoes Samuel Taylor Coleridge's poem *Kubla Kahn*, which deals with the founder of the Mogul dynasty in western China in the thirteenth century.
13. A legendary city of gold in South America.
14. The caliph of Baghdad in *Arabian Nights*.
15. A quietus is a finishing stroke or period of inactivity; a bodkin is a long, slender instrument for making holes in cloth or leather.
16. A mountain near Capetown, South Africa.
17. Marina was the daughter of Pericles in Shakespeare's play *Pericles*. She was lost by her father for many years, then found. The epigram reads, "What place is this, what country, what region of the world?"
18. A town in southern Mexico.
19. "It was my child, my darling, my heart."
20. "It was my heavenly brother, my life, my wealth."
21. "Oh! It was my ecstasy and my love."
22. "It was my faith, divine indifference."
23. "It was my bastard spirit, ignominy."
24. Homer's epic poems, the *Iliad* and *Odyssey*, were sung by him, not written.

Acknowledgments

W. H. AUDEN: "Master and Boatswain," copyright 1944 by W. H. Auden. Reprinted from W. H. AUDEN: COLLECTED POEMS, by W. H. Auden, edited by Edward Mendelson, by permission of Random House, Inc.

GEORGE BARKER: "Pacific Sonnets" vii, viii, and ix reprinted by permission of Faber and Faber Ltd. from EROS IN DOGMA by George Barker.

LAURENCE BINYON: "John Winter" by Laurence Binyon reprinted by permission of Mrs. Nicolete Gray and The Society of Authors on behalf of the Laurence Binyon Estate.

ELIZABETH BISHOP: "The Fish" and "Seascape" from THE COMPLETE POEMS by Elizabeth Bishop. Copyright © 1933, 1940, 1941, 1947, 1969 by Elizabeth Bishop. Reprinted by permission of Farrar, Straus and Giroux, Inc.

R. P. BLACKMUR: "Half-Tide Ledge," from *Poems of R. P. Blackmur*, with Introduction by Denis Donoghue (copyright © 1977 by Princeton University Press), p. 149. Reprinted by permission of Princeton University Press.

RUPERT BROOKE: "The Fish" and "A Channel Passage" reprinted by permission of DODD, MEAD & COMPANY, INC. from THE COLLECTED POEMS OF RUPERT BROOKE. Copyright 1915 by Dodd, Mead & Company. Copyright renewed 1943 by Edward Marsh.

G. K. CHESTERTON: "Lepanto" reprinted by permission of DODD, MEAD & COMPANY, INC. from THE COLLECTED POEMS OF G. K. CHESTERTON. Copyright 1932 by Dodd, Mead & Company, Inc. Copyright renewed 1959 by Oliver Chesterton.

ALEX COMFORT: "Epitaph" from THE SONG OF LAZARUS by Alex Comfort. Copyright 1945, © renewed 1973 by Alex Comfort. Reprinted by permission of Viking Penguin Inc.

HART CRANE: Selections are reprinted from THE COMPLETE POEMS AND SELECTED LETTERS AND PROSE OF HART CRANE, with the permission of Liveright Publishing Corporation. Copyright 1933, © 1958, 1966 by Liveright Publishing Corporation.

STEPHEN CRANE: "A Man Adrift on a Slim Spar" from THE POEMS OF STEPHEN CRANE reprinted by permission of Cooper Square Publishers.

E. E. CUMMINGS: "as is the sea marvelous" is reprinted from TULIPS & CHIMNEYS by E. E. Cummings by permission of Liveright Publishing Corporation. Copyright 1923, 1925 and renewed 1951, 1953 by E. E. Cummings. Copyright

Index to Authors, Poems, and First Lines